HITCHCOCKIAN THRILLERS

HITCHCOCKIAN THRILLERS

Must-See Films in the Style of the Suspense Master

Stephen Rebello

BLOOMSBURY ACADEMIC
NEW YORK • LONDON • OXFORD • NEW DELHI • SYDNEY

BLOOMSBURY ACADEMIC

Bloomsbury Publishing Inc, 1359 Broadway, 12th Floor, New York, NY 10018, USA
Bloomsbury Publishing Plc, 50 Bedford Square, London, WC1B 3DP, UK
Bloomsbury Publishing Ireland, 29 Earlsfort Terrace, Dublin 2, D02 AY28, Ireland

BLOOMSBURY, BLOOMSBURY ACADEMIC and the Diana logo are
trademarks of Bloomsbury Publishing Plc

First published in the United States of America 2026

Copyright © Stephen Rebello, 2026

Cover design: Sally Rinehart
Cover images (left to right): © Columbia Pictures; © IFC Film/Photofest;
© Columbia Pictures; © Paramount Pictures/Photofest; © Paramount Pictures

All rights reserved. No part of this publication may be: i) reproduced or transmitted in any form, electronic or mechanical, including photocopying, recording or by means of any information storage or retrieval system without prior permission in writing from the publishers; or ii) used or reproduced in any way for the training, development or operation of artificial intelligence (AI) technologies, including generative AI technologies. The rights holders expressly reserve this publication from the text and data mining exception as per Article 4(3) of the Digital Single Market Directive (EU) 2019/790.

Bloomsbury Publishing Inc does not have any control over, or responsibility for, any third-party websites referred to or in this book. All internet addresses given in this book were correct at the time of going to press. The author and publisher regret any inconvenience caused if addresses have changed or sites have ceased to exist, but can accept no responsibility for any such changes.

Library of Congress Cataloging-in-Publication Data

Names: Rebello, Stephen author
Title: Hitchcockian thrillers : must-see films in the style of the suspense master / Stephen Rebello.
Description: New York : Bloomsbury Academic, 2026.
Identifiers: LCCN 2025031880 (print) | LCCN 2025031881 (ebook) | ISBN 9781493079599 hardback | ISBN 9798765160749 pdf | ISBN 9781493079605 epub
Subjects: LCSH: Thrillers (Motion pictures)–History and criticism | Hitchcock, Alfred, 1899-1980–Influence | LCGFT: Film criticism
Classification: LCC PN1995.9.S87 R43 2026 (print) | LCC PN1995.9.S87 (ebook)
LC record available at https://lccn.loc.gov/2025031880
LC ebook record available at https://lccn.loc.gov/2025031881

ISBN: HB: 978-1-4930-7959-9
ePDF: 979-8-7651-6074-9
eBook: 978-1-4930-7960-5

Typeset by Integra Software Services Pvt. Ltd.
Printed and bound in the United States of America

For product safety related questions contact productsafety@bloomsbury.com.

To find out more about our authors and books visit www.bloomsbury.com
and sign up for our newsletters.

Contents

List of Referenced Films	vi
Foreword: What's Hitchcockian Anyway?	ix
1 Will He Kiss Me or Kill Me?	1
2 Cloak and Dagger	27
3 But I Can't Remember Where or When	60
4 Las Hijas de Carlotta Valdez	84
5 Tight Spot	101
6 Psychos	134
7 Gone	184
8 A Race of Peeping Toms	201
9 Lady Beware	207
10 Woman Trouble	221
11 On the Run	252
12 Foreign Correspondents	277
Index	292

List of Referenced Films

12 Monkeys
23 Paces to Baker Street
36 Hours
The 4th Man
Angel Face
Apartment Zero
Arabesque
Basic Instinct
The Bedroom Window
Black Bag
Blow Out
Blow-Up
Body Double
The Bride Wore Black
Bunny Lake Is Missing
Buried
Cape Fear
Carrie
Charade
The Chase
Chase a Crooked Shadow
The Collector
The Counterfeit Traitor
Dangerous Crossing
The Dark Mirror
Dark Passage
Dark Purpose
The Day of the Jackal

Dead Again
Dead Heat on a Merry-Go-Round
Decision to Leave
Déjà Vu
Diabolique
Disturbia
Double Door
Dressed to Kill
Duel
Enemies
Entrapment
Experiment in Terror
Eye of the Needle
The Fallen Idol
The Fan (1981)
The Fan (1996)
Final Analysis
Five Fingers
Flightplan
Fly-by-Night
Foul Play
Frantic
From Russia, with Love
Gaslight
The Gazebo
The Girl on the Train
Gone Girl
Halloween

Hangover Square
Homicidal
Honeymoon with a Stranger (Piège pour un homme seul)
In a Lonely Place
Insomnia
Jane Eyre
Jewel Thief
Journey into Fear
Julie
A Kiss Before Dying
La Femme Infidèle
Laura
Le Boucher
Leave Her to Heaven
Locked
The Locket
M
Man Hunt
Marathon Man
Memento
Midnight Lace
The Midnight Warning
Mirage
Misery
Mission: Impossible 2
Mississippi Mermaid
Moment to Moment
Mother
Mulholland Drive
The Naked Edge
The Nanny
Niagara
Nightmare (1956)
Nightmare (1964)
Night Must Fall
The Night of the Hunter
Night Train to Munich
Obsession
Odd Man Out
Panic Room
Paranoiac
Parasite
Peeping Tom
Perfect Blue
Phantom Thread
Phone Booth
Picnic at Hanging Rock
Play Misty for Me
Plein Soleil (*Purple Noon*)
The Prize
Repulsion
Road Games
Rosemary's Baby
Rough Cut
The Running Man
Scarlet Street
Scream of Fear
Se7en
Seconds
Secret Beyond the Door
The Servant
Shattered
Shutter Island
Side Effects
The Silence of the Lambs
The Silent Partner
Sisters
So Long at the Fair
Sorry, Wrong Number
The Spiral Staircase
Still of the Night

Stoker
Strait-Jacket
Straitjacket
Sudden Fear
Ten Days' Wonder
That Man from Rio
The Third Man
The Third Secret
Three Days of the Condor
The Tourist
Transsiberian
Twisted Nerve
The Uninvited

Unknown
The Vanishing
Wait until Dark
What Ever Happened to Baby Jane?
What Lies Beneath
The Window
Witness for the Prosecution
The Woman in the Window
Woman of Straw
Woman on the Run
A Woman's Face
A Woman's Vengeance

Foreword: What's Hitchcockian Anyway?

In a career that spanned six decades, Alfred Hitchcock created fifty-three films, many of which remain the platinum standard for movie thrillers. It's no wonder that although Hitchcock died forty-five years ago, every season, every year, critics label some new movie or TV show, book or play, as "Hitchcockian."

The term "Hitchcockian" has become as misused and misunderstood as other catchall, grab-bag genre categories, such as "film noir." First appearing in print in 1930, the word "Hitchcockian" is defined by the 2016 *Oxford English Dictionary* thus:

Hitchcockian (adjective) *Relating to or resembling the films of Alfred Hitchcock.*

That's okay, so far as it goes, but for purposes of this book, I would expand that definition to the following:

Hitchcockian (adjective) *Relating to or pertaining to Alfred Hitchcock or resembling the films of Alfred Hitchcock, regarding the themes, plots, or film techniques of his suspense, spy, and psychological thrillers.*

For this book, I chose from hundreds of films and deliberately narrowed them down to exclude:

- Whodunits, such as the *Knives Out* franchise, for instance. Why? Because, as Rian Johnson, the director of those three movies put it, "Hitchcock famously hated whodunits because it's a genre where one of its pitfalls is it can be a lot of big buildup to one big surprise at the end. Hitchcock was all about empathy-based suspense. [Hitchcock] gets the audience caring about someone and then you make the audience sweat how they can get out of it." Or, as

Hitchcock himself put it, "A whodunit is an intellectual process, like a mystery. But suspense is essentially an emotional process. Therefore, you can only get the suspense element by giving the audience information, not withholding." Got that?

- Teen-oriented slasher and supernatural movies built around "found footage," the devil, killer clowns, evil dolls, dead kids, creepy kids. and other genre clichés.

- Comedy spoofs and pastiches, such as *Dead Men Don't Wear Plaid* (1982), *Throw Mama from the Train* (1987), and *High Anxiety* (1977).

- Remakes (official or unofficial) of Hitchcock movies. (Yes, I know that in 1956 Hitchcock remade his own 1934 kidnap thriller *The Man Who Knew Too Much*.)

So what are some of the hallmarks of the fifty-three movies Hitchcock made in his lifetime and what makes other directors' movies Hitchcockian?

- The use of a MacGuffin (state secrets, stolen money, a missing latchkey the characters want, chase, kill for) to drive the plot. Hitchcock once explained the MacGuffin thusly: "In most films about spies, it is the thing that the spies are after. In the days of Rudyard Kipling, it would be the plans of the fort in the Khyber Pass. [In a spy film], it could be the plans of an airplane engine. And the plans of an atom bomb or anything you like." In the director's *The 39 Steps* (1935), it is *literally* the British military's top secret airplane plans locked for safekeeping in the mind of music hall entertainer "Mr. Memory." In his famous *The Lady Vanishes* (1938), it is a secret wartime message hidden in an innocent-sounding folk song. The weirdly interconnected hero and villain in *Strangers on a Train* (1951) are in hot pursuit of the hero's incriminating missing cigarette lighter. The spies in *North by Northwest* (1959) are on the hunt for a CIA agent (who doesn't actually exist) and the government secrets embedded on microfilm hidden in a pre-Columbian statue. Forty thousand dollars in stolen cash sets the plot in motion in *Psycho* (1960), but it is the whereabouts/existence of a homicidal geriatric madwoman that keeps viewers guessing.

In other directors' famous movies, the MacGuffin can be anything from the statue of a bird (*The Maltese Falcon*, 1941) to whatever's in that briefcase (*Pulp Fiction*, 1994). In other words, a MacGuffin is a pretext, an invention, a red herring created to motivate the action, fun, suspense, and intrigue without requiring too much scrutiny. As Hitchcock endlessly explained the nonsensical aspects of the term to interviewers: "I'll put it to you this way. Two men are sharing a railway compartment. One man says, *What's that package up there in the baggage rack?* The other answers, *Oh, that's a MacGuffin.* The first one asks, *What's a MacGuffin?* The other man says, *Well, it's an apparatus for trapping lions in the Scottish Highlands.* The first man says, *But there are no lions in the Scottish Highlands.* And the other one answers, *Well, then, that's no MacGuffin.* So you see that a MacGuffin is nothing at all."

Or, when the older Hitchcock grew weary of the longer explanation: "The MacGuffin is the thing that the spies are after, but the audience doesn't care."

- Favoring suspense over surprise by giving the audience information the characters don't possess. (In *The Man Who Knew Too Much*, we are told that a gunman will shoot a foreign dignity at the exact moment when the cymbals clash during a concert piece; in *Rear Window*, the heroine risks her life to invade the apartment of a suspected wife killer in search of incriminating evidence while the murderer climbs the stairs toward his apartment; in *The Birds*, the heroine sits waiting unsuspectingly on a bench outside a schoolhouse while birds amass silently behind her on a jungle gym awaiting the schoolchildren about to exit the school.)
- Suspense sequences and violent events staged in everyday settings (a shooting during a dance at a hotel, a murder during a classical concert in the Royal Albert Hall, gunfire breaking out in the cafeteria at Mount Rushmore, an attack by a crop-dusting plane

in the middle of a sunny cornfield, birds swooping down on children and adults during an outdoor birthday party.)

- Glamorous, beautifully dressed, often duplicitous characters in elegant surroundings; characters who hide their deepest selves and motivations behind masks of normalcy and polished, socially acceptable behaviors.

- Using subjective camera techniques that put the viewer in the place of the character to encourage empathy; in other films, to comment on morality and the voyeuristic tendencies common to audiences.

You will note that I've given each film discussed in the book a highly subjective rating ranging from one to four Alfreds, with four denoting as near to the heights of Hitchcock as mere mortals are likely to get and one reserved for films banished to the far side of Hitchcock. By all means, take these ratings as seriously as you would any MacGuffin from a Hitchcock thriller.

The rating system is as follows:

♟♟♟♟ The master himself might have been proud of having made this one.

♟♟♟ Close but still on the far side of Mount Hitchcock.

♟♟ It's never as easy as Hitchcock makes it look.

♟ Hitchcock Imitator Participation Trophy.

1 Will He Kiss Me or Kill Me?

Some of Hitchcock's greatest and most resonant films gain great dramatic tension from the conflicts between the heroine and hero (or hero and hero)—sometimes even more than they do from the suspense machinations of the narrative. From the outset to the finale of his career, Hitchcock and his screenwriters powered their films by investigating themes of doubt, suspicion, and lack of trust between the central characters, especially in marital and romantic situations. Consider the stale, prickly relationships of the long-married couples in *Rich and Strange* (1931) and *The Man Who Knew Too Much* (1934, 1956); in those films, reestablishing closeness and trust between partners requires everything from extramarital affairs and international espionage to disorienting foreign travel and harrowing near-death experiences.

But, in Hitchcock's most dramatic films, the relationship between the heroes and heroines can turn lethal. In *Rebecca* and *Suspicion*, Hitchcock cast Joan Fontaine as lovestruck young women who spend much of the films' running time fearful and wondering not only whether they've married moody, devious murderers but also whether they themselves are destined to become victims. Throughout the action in *Spellbound*, *Notorious*, and *Under Capricorn*, Ingrid Bergman is in constant danger from the men in her life—possibly psychotic amnesiac Gregory Peck, callous, hard-bitten spy Cary Grant, and volatile ex-convict Joseph Cotten. In *Rope*, the bickering and falling-out between the homicidal male couple constantly threatens to turn murderous. In *Marnie*, the hostility between the titular troubled serial embezzler and the equally complicated book publisher who traps her into marrying him overwhelms the director's attempts at portraying a love story in the grand manner; Mark and Marnie are like loaded guns aimed at each other for nearly the entire running time.

Hanging over these Hitchcockian movies is that age-old question that fuels melodramas: *Will he kiss me or kill me?* But we know today that the question is not just the stuff of entertainment. By statistics last compiled by the United States Bureau of Justice in 2021, 34 percent of the estimated 4,970 female murder victims were killed by an intimate partner; 6 percent of the 17,970 males murdered were victims of intimate partner homicide.

In the world of Hitchcock, love can be transformational, lethal, or both.

JANE EYRE (1943)

An orphaned survivor of a harsh childhood gets hired as a governess to the neglected young daughter of a mysterious, troubled wealthy man.

THE MACGUFFIN: Mrs. Rochester

It's understandable that some people think Alfred Hitchcock directed *Jane Eyre*. He was offered it by the film's original producer, David O. Selznick. Both thought it was too close to *Rebecca*, and both let it go to other moviemakers. Film fans may easily confuse author Charlotte Brontë's suspenseful, romantic, horror-tinged gothic novel published in 1847 with Daphne du Maurier's suspenseful, romantic, horror-tinged 1938 gothic romance *Rebecca*; even du Maurier herself admitted she'd been influenced by *Jane Eyre.* 20th Century Fox certainly hoped to foster that confusion. Even in the *Jane Eyre* trailer, a stylish 1940s woman strides to her bookshelf, runs her fingers along the spines of her books and lingers on *Rebecca* before picking *Eyre*. Both films cast Joan Fontaine similarly as mousy, vulnerable, lovestruck young women who marry bullying, moody, abusively dismissive, considerably older rich men who keep them virtually captive in their grand, spooky manors haunted by ghostly presences.

Both Brontë's and du Maurier's narratives feature volatile ex-wives, mysterious locked rooms, raging fires, madwomen, secrets, deceit, betrayals, and dark revelations. The screen version of *Jane Eyre* is even graced with a rumbling, moody, and melodramatic wall-to-wall musical score by Bernard Herrmann, who went on to become Hitchcock's and Orson Welles's frequent and preferred composer. But *Jane Eyre* has romantic, atmospheric, and scary pleasures—some Hitchcockian, some not—of its own. As shot by cameraman George S. Barnes (Oscar winner for *Rebecca*), scripted by Aldous Huxley, John Houseman, Henry Koster, Robert Stevenson, and an uncredited Val Lewton, the Robert Stevenson–directed movie casts a spell right from its long opening section featuring Peggy Ann Garner as the unwanted, unloved orphaned but assertive young Jane being grudgingly raised by a cruel aunt, Mrs. Reed (Orson Welles stalwart Agnes Moorehead). Garner is so good and the scenes so effective and Dickensian that much of the work of Fontaine (who won the *Jane Eyre* role over Vivien Leigh and Jennifer Jones, among others) is done for her before she takes over where Garner leaves off. Welles as "Mr. Rochester" (Ronald Colman was announced but moved on) comes on so blustery and bigger than life that he almost obliterates Fontaine, who is often reduced to bland, schoolgirl mooning and simpering in her reaction shots. (Why is grown-up Jane duller and so much less steely than the kiddie version?) In fact, Welles is so memorable (though much of his dialogue was obviously rerecorded in postproduction) that he creates an imbalance in a movie titled for the heroine, not him. (Welles joked that his reviews were the worst for any actor since the days of John Wilkes Booth.)

The exceptionally strong, mostly British supporting cast includes Henry Daniell, the young Elizabeth Taylor and Margaret O'Brien, Sara Allgood (also seen in Hitchcock's *Juno and the Paycock*), John Sutton, and Ethel Griffies (also in *The Birds*). Although *Jane Eyre* is not as rich, entertaining, and emotionally rewarding as *Rebecca*, it is a fine movie for a rainy night and remains many people's pick of the dozen or so filmed versions of Brontë's timelessly popular novel. ♟♟♟

GASLIGHT (1944)

An avaricious husband sadistically tortures and manipulates his wealthy wife into thinking she is going mad.

THE MACGUFFIN: Priceless heirloom jewels

Decades before days when erotic movie thrillers sizzled more overtly, courtesy of the spontaneous combustion of, say, Catherine Deneuve and Jean-Paul Belmondo in *Mississippi Mermaid*, Sharon Stone and Michael Douglas in *Basic Instinct*, and Kathleen Turner and William Hurt in *Body Heat*, the less showy but palpable chemistry between Ingrid Bergman and Charles Boyer in *Gaslight*—that great-great-grandaddy of sadomasochistic sexual thrillers—helped blaze the trail. Patrick Hamilton's play debuted on the London stage in 1938 and inspired a noted 1940 British film before director George Cukor and MGM created such an effective American version four years later that it earned seven Oscar nominations and two wins.

Both versions tell the same tale—an insecure, newly married Victorian heiress is persuaded to question her sanity when her new husband isolates and psychologically torments her into thinking that she is imagining the bizarre things she sees and hears. Phantom footsteps pad around an empty attic, and gaslights dim in the bedroom of the townhouse willed to Paula Alquist by her opera singer aunt, whose murderer remains undetected. Her husband, Gregory Anton, scolds Paula for losing objects when he deliberately hides them from her. Meanwhile, he openly flirts with the tarty young Cockney maid Nancy.

Among the expert touches Cukor brought to this Gothic classic is his casting brilliance in sandwiching the magnificently febrile, emotionally accessible Bergman (the screen's reigning icon of noble masochistic suffering in *Intermezzo*, *Casablanca*, *Notorious*, *Joan of Arc*, and more) between two attractive extremes—the suave, sensual, and cruel Continental roué and social parasite (Boyer) and the upstanding, handsome Scotland Yard good guy Brian Cameron (Joseph Cotten of Hitchcock's *Shadow of a Doubt* and *Under Capricorn*). Even better,

Cukor and Bergman make certain that we feel the potent, deadly undertow of the heroine's enslaved addiction to Anton.

Modern sensibilities obsessed with presentism would perhaps prefer a heroine who'd wise up more quickly to being gaslit so that she might spend the last third of the film in an orgy of bloodthirsty revenge against her vile abuser. But that likely would be the heroine of a pandering, quickly forgotten movie. Instead, *Gaslight* endures. Often miscredited as a Hitchcock, not only because it stars Bergman, his quintessential leading lady in three films of the 1940s, but also because its stars a favorite Hitchcock leading man, Cotten, and then there's also the redoubtable character actress Dame May Whitty from *The Lady Vanishes*. Even more Hitchcockian, though, is the fact that

Continental roué Charles Boyer plays toxic abuser to his wealthy wife Ingrid Bergman in *Gaslight*.
Film Publicity Archive/United Archives via Getty Images

Gaslight is not a mere whodunit but more precisely a why-he-dunit—a troubling, still relevant portrayal of diabolical manipulation, subjugation, and sadistic control.

Eighty-one years after *Gaslight* packed movie theaters, one in three women in the United States has experienced rape, physical violence, or emotional abuse or stalking by an intimate partner. Millions more of us have experienced years of unending pernicious political gaslighting or so-called "flooding the zone"—deliberately contaminating information networks with misinformation designed to paralyze response. So *Gaslight*, the stage play and film that coined the term, seems only more troubling and contemporary with the passage of time. ♟♟♟♟

SECRET BEYOND THE DOOR (1947)

A bored, highly independent heiress, who impulsively marries a mysterious magazine publisher, finds her new husband's East Coast mansion featuring rooms that replicate famed murder sites—with room for one more.

THE MACGUFFIN: The key to the locked room that reveals a husband's dark obsession

What do you get when you cross *Rebecca* with *Spellbound* and throw in a little bit of *Bluebeard* for kinky kicks? The answer can be found in the enjoyably preposterous, florid *Secret Beyond the Door*, directed by the towering and tyrannical Fritz Lang (*M*, *Metropolis*, *Spies*) from an overheated but undernourished screenplay concocted by the director and Silvia Richards (*Possessed*, *Rancho Notorious*) from a story by Rufus King (*The Hidden Hand*). The fun and lunacy begin in Mexico with Joan Bennett (muttering fascinatingly strange, self-revelatory narration in her New Jersey accent almost throughout the movie) as shrewd, wealthy, relationship-averse Manhattanite beauty Celia Lamphere, who takes one look at dashing but obviously ill-at-ease on camera Michael Redgrave (*The Lady Vanishes*) and gets about as tingly and turned on as a celluloid leading lady was allowed to do in the 1940s. "There was a tingling at the nape of my neck as though the air had turned cool," she confesses. "I felt eyes touching me like fingers. There was a current flowing between us… warm and sweet… and frightening, too, because he saw behind my makeup what no one had ever seen, something I didn't know was there."

But how could she possibly resist leaping headfirst into a quicky marriage with this moody, erudite, well-tailored Mark Lamphere when he makes cow eyes at her and woos her with frilly poetic drivel comparing her face to a phenomenon he once experienced in South Dakota wheat country before a cyclone hit? He says, "You have it in your face—the same hush before the storm and when you smile it's like the first breath of wind bending down the wheat. I know that behind that smile is a turbulence." Although wised-up viewers will instantly peg Lamphere as a BSing manipulator of the first order, as Bennett listens to Mark's romantic mumbo jumbo the camera of the great Stanley Cortez (*The Magnificent Ambersons*) worships Bennett's utterly blank, dispassionate stare as she says, "I heard his voice and then I didn't hear it anymore because the beating of my blood was louder." *Whew.*

We suppose Lang himself might have seen in his leading lady the "hush-before-the-storm" quality the script describes. But those of us less smitten by Bennett (gowned, made up, and coiffed at her most Hedy Lamarr–like but still strictly Fort Lee, Jersey) will just have to take the filmmaker's word for it. No sooner does Celia ignore her premarital terrors as she's dragging herself down the wedding chapel aisle (*I don't even know him! This is no time to think of danger. This is my wedding day*, she muses) than her Mr. Wrong begins revealing himself to be a full-on nutter. He storms away from their honeymoon suite because Celia coquettishly locks her boudoir door, and when she questions him about his frequent fits of moodiness, he yammers on about the failing architecture magazine he publishes. But that's nothing compared to what happens once Lamphere rushes his new bride off to his East Coast love nest in Levender Falls, stranding her in his musty, gothic, marked-down Manderley monstrosity with tribal masks lining the staircase walls and filled to the brim with such cryptic types as Lamphere's maniacally organized unmarried sister (Anne Revere) who rules the roost with an iron hand, and a wannabe Mrs. Danvers secretary (Barbara O'Neill) secretly in love with Mark who drapes one side of her face with a scarf, purportedly to hide burns she suffered saving Mark's son David in a summer house fire.

Also lurking about the house is his son (fourteen-year-old Mark Dennis, whose waxiness and dubbed[?] disembodied voice anticipates the bizarre "Warren" of William Castle's *Psycho* imitation, *Homicidal*). David is the product of Mark's disastrous earlier marriage to the now-dead Eleanor, who is remembered for her "aloofness" and "enamel quality." Lang saves the movie's weirdest moments for Mark and Celia's rained-out wedding party when the groom leads the guests (including Celia's nattering high-society pal Natalie Schafer) on a house tour displaying the results of his "hobby"—a collection of rooms fanatically replicating the locales of famous murders of women. Guess who and what he has in mind for locked Room 7? Will the twisted but lovestruck new bride—who finally catches on that Mark holds a homicidal grudge against all womankind because of his mother—save herself and her mate through her attempts at pseudo-psychology which anticipate those of the hero trying to break through the phobias and obsessions of his new wife in *Marnie*? Will the gifted actor Michael Redgrave ever manage to justify Celia's obsession for him by being convincingly charming or charismatic for even one single scene? Will the filmmakers succeed in stuffing the movie with even more callbacks to much better Hitchcock movies, including vistas of rolling fog, dangerous marital partners, and a mansion set on fire?

Fritz Lang directs and cinematographer Cortez (with whom he clashed) photographs the highly troubled production and cast (with whom he also clashed) with such high-style panache and—one suspects—self-amusement, even when few in the cast appear to be in on the joke, that it's hard to resist the good-natured creepiness, decorative chintz, and moments of high camp. Look, *Secret Beyond the Door* is nowhere near the level of such previous Lang-Bennett collaborations *Man Hunt*, *The Woman in the Window*, and *Scarlet Street*, but taken as a flawed but highly entertaining document of the end of their affiliation, it becomes even more weird and fascinating. ♚ ♚ ♙

SORRY, WRONG NUMBER (1948)

A selfish, hypochondriacal Manhattan heiress accidentally overhears a phone conversation between two men plotting a woman's murder for that night. Alone and growing frantic because no one she calls will believe or help her, she learns too late the identity of the intended victim.

THE MACGUFFIN: The heroine's money

The brilliant and usually faultless Babara Stanwyck weeps, wails, whines, and wheedles, joyously letting out all the stops and barreling her way to a fourth Best Actress Oscar nomination by portraying spoiled, bedridden Manhattan heiress Leona Stevenson spiraling into paranoid panic when a cross-wired telephone call exposes her to a conversation about a murder set to take place almost immediately that same night. The main setting of the tale is the upper-floor bedroom of the heroine's vast Manhattan abode; the work of masterful production designer Hans Dreier and Sol Polito's atmospheric lighting and cinematography entrap the main character in a prison of her own devising in director Anatole Litvak's (*All This, and Heaven Too*, *The Snake Pit*) dragged-out screen version of Lucille Fletcher's tense one-act radio play that caused such shivers in 1943 that it got rebroadcast seven more times.

Paramount hired Fletcher to expand her half hour's entertainment by another hour, mostly by adding so many complicated flashbacks involving her pharmaceuticals baron father (Ed Begley), subplots, and ancillary characters (Leif Erickson, William Conrad, John Bromfield, et al.) that even some of the flashbacks have flashbacks. Because the plot—and tension—hinge so heavily on unlikely coincidences and one highly improbable telephone technical glitch after another, overlength does the movie no favors. Still, the powerhouse Stanwyck soldiers on, emoting her way through a series of calls that expose the criminal activities and homicidal intentions of her hunky, henpecked, shadowy husband, Henry (Burt Lancaster), who's been two-timing her with her old college chum Sally (Ann Richards). We don't care much. But the movie's reputation rests on its setup and its electrifying last third when an intruder breaks into the Sutton Place townhouse with orders to finish off the heroine while her husband is on the line urging her to overcome her neuroses by getting the hell out of that sickbed and out of that damned mausoleum of a house any way she can.

If you can power past the bloated middle section, and so long as you can hang with Stanwyck overdoing the shrill histrionics, you're in for an enjoyable shiver or two. Hitchcock's *Dial M for Murder* and *Sorry, Wrong Number* share similarities—wealthy wife, scheming husband, murder during a telephone call—and both have their fans. But, if you ask us, Hitchcock chose not only the better-written telephonic thriller but also the one best suited to his prodigious gifts for manipulating claustrophobic spaces and giving visual crackle to wordy scenes. ♟♟♟

Nasty invalid heiress Barbara Stanwyck overhears her own death being plotted in *Sorry, Wrong Number*.
Film Publicity Archive/United Archives via Getty Images

IN A LONELY PLACE (1950)

When a surly Hollywood screenwriter becomes a murder suspect, his seductive, troubled actress neighbor provides his only alibi.

THE MACGUFFIN: The right man

Outside of moments in *Rear Window*, *Shadow of a Doubt*, *The Wrong Man*, *Psycho*, and *Frenzy*, Alfred Hitchcock's films would rarely be hailed for their urban grittiness. But if the director ever felt the call to take that kind of deep dive, I like to think that a bluesy, lowdown, poetic beauty like *In a Lonely Place* might have been the result. Loosely adapted by screenwriter Andrew Solt from a crime novel by Dorothy B. Hughes and directed by Nicholas Ray (*Rebel Without a Cause*, *Bigger Than Life*), *In a Lonely Place* stars Humphrey Bogart (seldom better) as gifted, cynical, fallen, combative, battle-scarred Hollywood screenwriter Dixon Steel, who is down to his last dime. His agent urges him to make a quick buck adapting a best-selling soap opera novel Dixon refuses to even read. While day drinking at the same bar, he punches out a jerk who has been cruel to an aged actor down on his luck and fights a studio head's smug, entitled son.

Overhearing hatcheck girl Mildred Atkinson (Martha Stewart) singing that soap opera book's praises at a bar, he invites her back to his apartment. Both she and the book she babbles about bore him silly; instead, his eyes roam constantly to the enigmatic blonde across the courtyard, a similarly embittered struggling actress named Laurel Gray (Gloria Grahame, in full suicide blonde mode). Dixon ships home the hatcheck girl with bus fare. The next morning, a police detective ex-army pal hauls in Dixon to the station for questioning: Mildred's corpse has been found tossed into a valley. Laurel, whom he's never met formally, is at the station, too, providing Dix with an alibi, and not just because, as she says, "I like his face."

The gloriously grown-up and doom-laden movie, enhanced by the moody cinematography of Burnett Guffey (*From Here to Eternity*, *Bonnie and Clyde*), doesn't obsess with the forensics of the murder case, nor does it trivialize or explain away Bogart's alcoholic character by trying to head-shrink him. Nor do the moviemakers turn the film into a cross-country chase for the grouchy Dix, the Hitchcockian wrong man. Instead, it locks down into the heartbreaking relationship between two broken people and into the fears of Laurel—who knows a thing or two about men's darkness—that she may have sealed her fate by hooking up with the explosive ticking time bomb that is Dix. Their pressure-cooker relationship becomes even more paranoid because they are constantly watched by the police; not only that, but they live in small Spanish-style courtyard apartments that, like the Greenwich Village courtyard apartments in *Rear Window*, are a voyeur's dream. She helps him stop drinking and he goes back to work, but he's too full of self-hatred to make the cure stick.

We won't spoil any more of the film, which leads to an almost unbearably heartbreaking portrait of two people who clearly love each other but cannot make things work. One has a raging beast inside him, and it always seems to win out in the end. *In a Lonely Place* marks

Love is a battlefield for struggling actress Gloria Grahame and volatile screenwriter Bogart in *In a Lonely Place*.
Columbia Pictures/Photofest © Columbia Pictures

some peak work for Grahame, Ray, and especially Bogart, who found the material, shepherded it, and produced it (he originally planned on casting John Derek in the leading role). A rarity in its intimacy and rawness and superbly acted, *In a Lonely Place* takes many Hitchcock elements and brilliantly stands them on their head. ♟♟♟♟

SUDDEN FEAR (1952)

A psychopathic, unscrupulous actor seduces and marries a wealthy older playwright, then plots with his lover to murder her.

THE MACGUFFIN: An incriminating audio recording

Although the emotive and fervid Joan Crawford may be the antithesis of the cool, sophisticated, subtly sexy, possibly dangerous Hitchcock blonde, *Sudden Fear* casts her in a role somewhat analogous to Joan Fontaine's Oscar-winning lovestruck heiress role in Hitchcock's *Suspicion*. Emphasis on *somewhat*. Where *Sudden Fear*, directed by David Miller (*Midnight Lace*), is gritty and nasty, *Suspicion* is silken and posh. Where Joan Fontaine gets swept off her feet by amoral rascal, sophisticate, and possible murderer Cary Grant, the mature, vulnerable Crawford falls hard for macho, ballsy working-class galoot Jack Palance. Where Fontaine's genteel heroine almost passively accepts what she fears might be her untimely end at the hands of the man she loves, Crawford packs a gun, makes a plan, and seems willing to go for blood vengeance.

Similarities and differences from *Suspicion* aside, *Sudden Fear* is not only highly entertaining but also Hitchcockian through and through in its twisted marital relationship, its probing of the theme of betrayal of trust between lovers, its strangers-on-a-train verbal seduction sequence, its plot twists, and its relentless suspense as a woman in jeopardy turns the tables on her betrayers. The script by the prolific Lenore J. Coffee (*Old Acquaintance*) and Robert Smith, based on the 1948 novel by Edna Sherry, establishes Crawford as highly successful Broadway playwright Myra Hudson (no relation to those feuding sisters Baby Jane or Blanche, apparently) getting actor Lester

Blaine (Palance) fired from the leading-man role in her newest show *Half-Way to Heaven*. Watching Lester in rehearsal, she explains her reasoning to the show's producer and director: "He has to be the kind of charm boy that makes every woman in the audience sit right up and go 'Umm!' the instant he walks on that stage.... He's not my idea of a romantic leading man!" (The real-life Crawford's idea of a romantic leading man as Lester was Marlon Brando, who wanted no part of *Sudden Fear*. Or her.)

Later, on a New York to San Francisco train, Lester turns up and turns on the juice—all sharklike smiles, flashing eyes, and Shakespearean quotations—and all too soon, poor little rich girl Myra deludes herself into believing that she's finally found someone who truly loves her for herself not her jillions. Once she and Lester get hastily hitched, that's exactly when the whole movie gets Hitched, what with Myra dictating changes to her will (leaving Lester her play royalties, fortune, houses, the works) but forgetting to switch off the dictating machine when she rushes off to greet her party guests. Enter con man Lester and his longtime lover Irene (Gloria Grahame, a perfect *femme fatale* for a *homme fatale*), who mistakenly discover Myra's original obsolete will (leaving everything to a noble foundation) and, while they discuss their plans to kill her, the Dictaphone records their every diabolical word of betrayal. Soon, the distraught Myra applies her playwriting know-how to her own predicament: she'll shoot Lester and frame Irene for murder. (Hitchcock would have made sure he and his screenwriters created reasons why Myra doesn't simply go straight to her lawyers or to the police.)

The movie's tingly last half hour includes a grippingly acted closeup scene of Crawford trying to keep silent while hiding in a closet while an unhinged Palance sends a windup toy dog toddling right to Crawford's footsteps. Later, she's running madly in high heels up and down late-night streets of San Francisco while he runs after her, first on foot, then trying to mow her down with the car she bought him. The movie is ridiculous, juicy, acted full-tilt and enthralling, precisely because it isn't afflicted with Hollywood's contemporary mania for being "realistic" and making sure that the performances are "underplayed." A big bravo for its unhinged qualities. *Sudden Fear* is evocatively photographed

Monstrous younger husband Jack Palance teaches playwright Joan Crawford the meaning of *Sudden Fear*.
Bettmann/Getty Images

by Charles Lang (*The Uninvited*, *The Big Heat*), powerfully scored by Elmer Bernstein, and acted by the always committed, always *extra* Crawford in the tour-de-force mode that earned her third and final Oscar nomination. And, though Palance is no substitute for Brando (who *would* be?), it is fun watching him sink his choppers into an evil-leading-man role. What's not to enjoy? ♟♟♟

NIAGARA (1953)

A couple on a honeymoon/business trip begin to suspect that the sexy young wife in a nearby cabin is plotting with her lover to murder her troubled, war veteran husband.

THE MACGUFFIN: A veteran's sanity

When the departure of Vera Miles and Grace Kelly forced Alfred Hitchcock to recast the plum role of the beautiful, enigmatic victim/femme fatales in *Vertigo* and *Marnie*, respectively, the most surprising candidate who asked to be considered for both roles was Marilyn Monroe, who wanted badly to work with Hitchcock. Even the director himself, who preferred to cast more reserved, subtly sexy actresses, called Monroe "an interesting idea." While Monroe's sometimes crippling insecurities might have driven the meticulously prepared Hitchcock psycho, the blonde bombshell's performance in a thriller made years earlier suggests what we may have missed. *Niagara*—an overheated, undernourished Henry Hathaway–directed suspense melodrama in which Monroe's sexpot character plots with her young lover (Richard Allan) to murder her possessive, moody war veteran husband (Joseph Cotten, replacing James Mason, the director's choice)—shares so many elements similar enough to *Vertigo* to make it almost seem like a primitive run-through.

After all, *Niagara* offers a troubled older man obsessed by a devious, alluring younger blonde, suspense sequences staged against world-famous landmarks and backdrops, a murder plot that backfires, even a stairway pursuit up to a bell tower—aspects superficially close enough to make some people mistake *Niagara* for being one of Hitchcock's own. The remarkable thing about *Niagara* is that it is so trashily entertaining and handsomely filmed in gloriously overripe "three-strip" Technicolor by cameraman Joe MacDonald (*My Darling Clementine*) that people overlook how dramatically flaccid, overly long, and lacking in suspense it is. That is a disappointment since it was helmed by the skilled but notoriously abusive Henry Hathaway (*Kiss of Death*), whom even John Wayne called "the meanest son of a bitch in the business." What's more, *Niagara* leads one to expect more because it was the brainchild of screenwriter-producer Charles Brackett, hot off his *Sunset Boulevard* triumph. Sure, in a star-making performance, Monroe scorches everything and everyone around her, and she and Niagara Falls are natural wonders without equal. But, for once, Hitchcock and Orson Welles favorite Joseph Cotten is all villainy and no shading as Monroe's dour spouse, and as the neighboring couple of Monroe and

Jealous older husband Joseph Cotten spells doom for unfaithful wife Marilyn Monroe in *Niagara*.
United/Hulton/Getty Images

Cotten at the Niagara-adjacent motel, Jean Peters and Max Showalter are reduced to broad cartoons. Sadly, these days, much like a visit to the famous falls themselves, *Niagara* works best as a distant nostalgic memory. ♟♟♟

JULIE (1956)

A widow hastily remarries a handsome, insanely jealous classical pianist who keeps her in a constant state of terror because she knows that he murdered his former wife.

THE MACGUFFIN: The identity of the wife-murderer

Few spectacles are sadder in Hollywood than that of seeing attractive and talented Hitchcock stars stranded in a thriller with the guiding hand of a Hitchcock-level creative talent nowhere in sight. Such is the unhappy and undeserved fate of the eternally underappreciated Doris Day (*The Man Who Knew Too Much*) and the criminally charming and handsome Louis Jourdan (*The Paradine Case*) in *Julie*, written, directed, and produced by Andrew L. Stone (*Cry Terror!*). The insanity and ineptitude begin with Day (as Julie Benton) warbling over the credits the godawful, Oscar-nominated (!) theme song ("Must I go where he leads me? Though it be through eternity, Oh I know I will never be free, Free from the voice that calls 'Julie'…") while her demented estranged classical pianist husband Lyle Benton (Jourdan) chases her through a park. And not in a romantic way. Seconds later, he leaps into Day's car when she's supposed to be escaping him—although we see her frantically turning and turning the steering wheel while the rearview mirror clearly shows a straight road. Suddenly, the two are arguing at their country club and soon after they're in full road rage mode as she struggles to keep her car under control around the curvy Monterey, California, coast roads while the explosive Lyle jams down her foot on the gas pedal. What sparked all this furor? Lyle spotted Julie speaking to another man at their country club.

And that's just the beginning of the madness of this highly amusing but abysmally stupid mélange—the screenplay, packed with terrible dialogue, was *also* Oscar nominated—cobbled together from scraps of *Suspicion*, *Gaslight*, and a dozen other "You in danger, girl" epics about heroines determined to ignore every warning sign that they have saddled themselves with a controlling and abusive psychotic mate. How dense can stewardess Julie be that she does not catch on until she prods Lyle's outright confession that her previous husband did not die by suicide but was murdered by Lyle so that he could make her his? When she runs away and hides in her beach cottage, she gets no help from the local police when she reports Lyle's behavior. Finally, she flees more dramatically, thanks to an old airline pal (Barry Sullivan), who arranges for her to secretly spirit herself away from Lyle on a cross-country flight. Except Lyle slips himself onto the flight too, shoots the pilot and copilot, and for plot reasons too silly to be explained with a straight face, forces the already stressed-out Julie to land the plane herself guided by instructions from the control tower.

Doris Day did not want to make this movie because of her painful firsthand experiences with violent spouses, but she was forced to by her then equally abusive husband, agent and producer Marty Melcher, who with his handpicked attorney was quietly defrauding Day of her career earnings to the tune of an estimated sixty-six million dollars. Forcing his wife into doing the painful, ludicrous, unintentionally funny *Julie* may be one of Melcher's—and Hollywood's—most flagrant examples of partner abuse. 👥

A KISS BEFORE DYING (1956)

A handsome young psychopathic fortune hunter targets a wealthy pair of sisters.

THE MACGUFFIN: The heiress's millions

Talk about Hitchcock-style casting. 20th Century Fox cast the smooth-talking, handsome Leonardo De Caprio of the 1950s—twenty-six-year-old contract player Robert Wagner—as a sociopathic gold-digger mama's boy college student who murders his naïve, socially prominent secret girlfriend (Joanne Woodward) after she tells him she's pregnant and that her copper tycoon father will probably deny her inheritance. The police rule the death a suicide, leaving our ghoulish antihero free to then pursue the dead girl's sister (Virginia Leith), who begins to suspect that he has murder in mind for her, too. And that's when things finally get scary.

Ira Levin's widely praised Edgar Award–winning 1953 debut novel won a lot of attention from Hollywood, but Hitchcock wasn't interested, though the book is well written, cleverly plotted, quietly creepy in the Hitchcock style, and certainly could have offered Grace Kelly a good role. The novel also features a bizarre mother-son relationship (the great Mary Astor does the honors in the film) that in some ways

CHAPTER 1 WILL HE KISS ME OR KILL ME?

prefigures that of Norman and "Norma" Bates. And, as with most of Hitchcock's movies, the suspense stems from giving the audience information, not withholding it. We know from the start exactly what young monster "Bud" Corliss is up to. But will he be stopped in time?

It's tempting to speculate whether Hitchcock could have made a better movie out of the odd, disturbing but ultimately unsatisfying *A Kiss Before Dying* than did screenwriter Lawrence Roman and director Gerd Oswald, for whom it marked his directorial debut. It certainly would have been cast better. Woodward said she thought it the worst movie she'd ever made, let alone the worst movie *ever* made. But Wagner is quite convincing as a bland, icy, amoral louse; I mean, talk about the banality of evil. Still, unless you've suffered through the 1991 remake starring Matt Dillon and Sean Young, you don't know the true meaning of pain. ♟♟♟

MIDNIGHT LACE (1960)

The sanity of a newly wedded heiress comes into question as she warns her husband and friends that an unseen stranger threatens her every move and near-fatal accidents begin happening all around her.

THE MACGUFFIN: An heiress's millions; a lacy black dress that figures in the finale

By delivering two powerful dramatic performances back-to-back, Doris Day wiped the smirks off the faces of many of those who mocked her perpetually sunny screen persona and doubted her dramatic chops. Her work in *Love Me or Leave Me* (1955) as the domestically abused singer Ruth Etting and, the following year, as the restlessly retired entertainer wife of James Stewart and the distraught mother of a kidnapped little boy in Hitchcock's American remake of his *The Man Who Knew Too Much* proved that the dramatic potential of the former big band singer and queen of lightweight Hollywood musicals had been underutilized. But the box-office darling went clear off the rails in *Midnight Lace*, "women's picture" producer Ross Hunter's glossy, preposterous woman-in-jeopardy thriller in which Day spends much of the 110-minutes running shrieking, gasping, and teetering on the brink of hysteria before toppling way, way over the deep end.

Dressed in a succession of creations by five-time Oscar-winning fashion designer Irene, Day plays a recently married American heiress in London who, while strolling through an obvious studio soundstage meant to replicate fogbound Grosvenor Square, suddenly hears death threats made in the whiny, insinuating male voice of an unseen phantom. Soon after she's being bombarded by vile anonymous phone calls in the same voice; then she's nearly pulverized by a falling girder at a building site, gets trapped in an elevator, and is continually stalked by a tall shadowy phantom presence. Meanwhile, the rest of the cast members are stuck playing suspects and red herrings, and they're clearly handpicked from the unofficial Alfred Hitchcock Stock Company. There's a hunky, stolid construction foreman (John Gavin, the poor man's Rock Hudson, from *Psycho*), let alone John Williams (rehashing his wry inspector role from *Dial M for Murder*), Anthony Dawson (Grace Kelly's strangler-for-hire from *Dial M for Murder*), and

Wealthy Doris Day has a madman stalking her through London in *Midnight Lace*.
United/Hulton/Getty Images

Herbert Marshall (*Murder*, *Foreign Correspondent*), the debt-ridden treasurer in the firm run by Day's husband. As usual in Ross Hunter pictures, the supporting cast also numbers old friends and stalwarts, including Myrna Loy, Roddy McDowall, and Hermione Badley, whose characters lead the plot down pointless dead ends.

The starry, Hitchcock-adjacent casting is only fitting, though, because *Midnight Lace*, scripted by Ben Roberts and Ivan Goff from a middling Janet Green play, *Matilda Shouted Fire*, is jerry-built from bits of *Dial M for Murder* and *Suspicion*. The ever-surly Rex Harrison—hot again after his Broadway and West End success in *My Fair Lady*—plays Day's neglectful husband as though he's perturbed and embarrassed to be seen in such silly circumstances. Considering that *Midnight Lace* is nothing more than a glossed-up retread of *Gaslight*, who are we to blame him?

THE NAKED EDGE (1961)

Goaded by a blackmailer's letter, a wife becomes suspicious that her husband might have murdered his business partner five years earlier.

THE MACGUFFIN: An incriminating letter

"Only the man who wrote *Psycho* could jolt you like this!" shouted the posters at movie houses, which were (purportedly) equipped with flashing red lights warning ticket buyers: "No one—absolutely no one—will be seated during the last 13 minutes." But this staid, jolt-free little British-American thriller needed all the *Psycho*-style promotional razzmatazz it could get. Let's break down the hype. The unnamed man referred to in the ads—the one who wrote *Psycho*—was not Alfred Hitchcock, as the people behind *The Naked Edge* probably hoped some might think, but Joseph Stefano, who had skillfully adapted for Hitchcock the 1959 Robert Bloch novel about a boy, an embezzling secretary, a seedy motel, a knife, an old dark house, and a knife-wielding mother. But with *The Naked Edge*, Stefano didn't have the benefit of a perennially underestimated Bloch book from which to work but Max Erlich's novel *First Train to Babylon*. He also did not have Hitchcock as his director and collaborator but the workmanlike

Michael Anderson, who made *Around the World in 80 Days*. In a highly emotional performance playing a role somewhat similar to Joan Fontaine's in Hitchcock's 1941 psychological romantic suspense thriller *Suspicion*, Deborah Kerr (whom Hitchcock had momentarily considered to play frustrated secretary Marion Crane in *Psycho*) stars as Martha, the noble, loving wife of London-based American businessman George Radcliffe (Gary Cooper) who grows suspicious of her husband when a missing mailbag and a long-lost blackmail letter resurface accusing George of having years ago stabbed to death his businesses partner and stolen that mailbag loaded with cash.

Meanwhile, as the crime's chief witness, George's court testimony years earlier condemned a "wrong man" called Donald Heath (Ray McAnally) to life imprisonment for the murder and robbery of George's ex-partner Jason Roote (Martin Boddey).

The erosion of trust between two lovers central to *The Naked Edge* is a classic Hitchcock theme. But the chatty, lackadaisical script squanders whatever potential for frissons and thrills the film might have had; meanwhile, Anderson's mopey direction occasionally resorts to pointlessly showy camera stunts and desperate attempts at generating suspense (watch the heroine lose her icy cool while shoving her way through rows of laundry drying on clotheslines!). For his part, Cooper (who was clearly ill during the film's production) can do little more than appear reassuring, unreadable, impatient, seductive, and menacing as Kerr unearths ever more damning evidence against him.

The supporting cast members—Michael Wilding (Hitchcock's *Stage Fright*, *Under Capricorn*), Diane Cilento (excellent), Hermione Gingold, Eric Portman, and Peter Cushing—do what they can with very little, but the gaping plot holes, obvious red herrings, and general foolishness of it all challenge them (and us) to keep straight faces.

As in Hitchcock's *Spellbound*, there's some scary, if forced, tension involving an old-fashioned straight razor (hence the movie's title), and the movie's only tense moments erupt, as *Psycho*, in and around a bathtub. But these fleeting shudders come way too late in the action to count for more than a mild heart flutter or two. The whole affair ends with an offscreen announcer asking the audience not to reveal to friends the identity of who killed Jason Roote. More power to you if you're still awake by the finale, let alone remember who Jason Roote was or why anyone should have bothered to do him in. How unfortunate that Cooper dodged Hitchcock's attempts to cast him as the leading man of such 1940s films as *Saboteur* and *Foreign Correspondent* but waited decades too late to instead tackle this half-hearted imitation as his "Hitchcock picture." Even sadder, though, that something as anemic as *The Naked Edge* went on to become the final, posthumously released film of the giant who starred in *High Noon*, *Sergeant York*, *Meet John Doe*, *The Pride of the Yankees*, *Ball of Fire*, and *Friendly Persuasion*. ♟♟

CHARADE (1963)

A newly widowed beauty gets menaced by three violent friends of her husband who will do anything to keep her from finding the missing fortune they stole together. Meanwhile, the terrified widow wonders if she can trust a mysterious charmer who may not be the good guy he says he is.

THE MACGUFFIN: A stolen cache of dirty money

"The best Hitchcock movie Hitchcock never made." It's been said and written so many times about *Charade* that it's practically obligatory to mention it. But why it's said is no mystery. *Charade* plays like its makers ran it through a Hitchcock movie checklist before making it. One-word title, à la *Spellbound*, *Suspicion*, *Saboteur*, or *Notorious*? Check. Insanely charming and gorgeous movie stars, bespoke-tailored and adoringly photographed? Double-check because *Charade* stars that world-class smoothie Cary Grant—star of four *actual* Hitchcock movies—shooting sparks with the enchanting Audrey Hepburn, whom Hitchcock tried to cast in several films. How about a mood-setting title sequence with a seductive musical theme? *Charade* delivers these, too, courtesy of Maurice Binder's vertiginous psychedelic arrows and whirling spirals backed by a percussive version of Henry Mancini's now famous theme song—they're a nod to those iconic Saul Bass *Vertigo* and *North by Northwest* title sequences full of spirals and arrows set to the undertow of Bernard Herrmann's hypnotic music. Toss in Peter

Stone's twisty, darkly comic romantic soufflé of a screenplay and Stanley Donen's silken direction loaded with Hitchcock-style signature touches—Grant dangling from perilous heights (*To Catch a Thief*, *North by Northwest*), scary/funny shock jump cuts (*The 39 Steps*, *To Catch a Thief*), and Hepburn's chic, thoroughly 1960s woman-in-jeopardy role, updating the beleaguered heroines of such Hitchcock movies as *The Lady Vanishes*, *Sabotage*, and *Suspicion*.

Plus, *Charade* features so many witty double entendres and so much of that now extinct late-stage Hollywood dazzle that it would pair nicely with either of Hitchcock's glossier Technicolor confections of the 1950s (still looking at you *To Catch a Thief* and *North by Northwest*). *Charade* delivers the Hitchcock-style goods on so many counts—international intrigue, high-style glamour in swank locales, Old Hollywood star power (the rogue's gallery supporting cast alone features Walter Matthau, James Coburn, and George Kennedy)—that it almost seems churlish to carp. As beguiling as it is, *Charade* is too surface, show-offy, and pleased with itself to be up there in the Hitchcock pantheon. Does it pack the emotional resonance or thematic complexity of even the most flimsy and gossamer efforts of the master of suspense? Not even close. It's too much of a pastiche, ersatz version of Hitchcock for that. But when it clicks, it's delightfully diverting.

The things that stick with us—Grant's aplomb during his comic, fully dressed "shower scene"; Hepburn vulnerable and doe-eyed in Givenchy cooing to Grant, "You know what's wrong with you? Nothing!," or her staring adorably into his cavernous cleft chin and musing, "How do you shave in there?"; those chases through a movie-lover's idealized vision of Paris; the children's puppet show; and theater scenes—are glorious, evanescent, impossible-to-duplicate moments in the lost art of old-style Hollywood moviemaking. Case in point: director Jonathan Demme remade *Charade* in 2002's *The Truth about Charlie* starring in the Cary Grant role Mark Wahlberg (replacing intended star Will Smith) and Thandiwe Newton, the latter of whom proved to be the only reason to see it. If anything, the film cruelly exposed that the Hollywood Dream Factory had lost its lease on magic and that the wider world had changed irrevocably.

Revisiting *Charade* today makes one nostalgic for the promise of America before the horror of the assassination of President Kennedy, when romance, flirting, and verbal foreplay between potential lovers wasn't automatically considered problematic, when movie stars as peerless as Cary Grant and Audrey Hepburn existed, and when some of us naively thought Hollywood could go on forever bottling champagne entertainments as effervescent as *Charade*—fake Hitchcock (with a touch of Lubitsch) or not. Hitchcock himself heard the death knell and stopped trying. Besides, his heart was no longer in it. With *Psycho* and *The Birds* (the latter in theaters six months before *Charade*), he showed us that he knew the mold had been broken and the world had turned colder and crueler. ♟♟♟♟

When they played their charade, the impeccable Audrey Hepburn and Cary Grant charmed audiences worldwide.
Screen Archives/Moviepix /Getty Images

2 Cloak and Dagger

In twelve movies, from 1934 to 1969, Alfred Hitchcock and such invaluable screenwriters as Charles Bennett, Ben Hecht, and Ernest Lehman virtually invented the espionage thriller for the cinema the way James Fenimore Cooper, John Buchan, Joseph Conrad, Somerset Maugham, Graham Greene, and Eric Ambler did in literature. And, in fact, the trail was first blazed in cinemas by Louis Feuillade with *Fantômas* (1913) and Fritz Lang with *Spione* (1928).

Each of Hitchcock's spy efforts of the 1930s, from *The Man Who Knew Too Much* (1934) and *The 39 Steps* (1935) to *Secret Agent* (1936), *Sabotage* (1936), and *The Lady Vanishes* (1938), deals contemporaneously with the specific concerns, fears, anxieties, conflicting emotions, and moral concerns of the English during the run-up to the Second World War. Similarly, with each of the director's 1940s WWII espionage adventures made in the United States, his preoccupations are not with disseminating propaganda, nor with promoting specific ideals or "causes," let alone any specific political viewpoint. So such films as *Foreign Correspondent* (1940), *Saboteur* (1942), and *Notorious* (1946) gain in emotional resonance and entertainment value because they focus on the impact of war and spying on human morality and interpersonal relationships.

In his spy thrillers of the post–WWII era of the Cold War '50s and '60s, Hitchcock's cynicism, disdain, and despair deepen considerably— as witnessed in the flippant approach to espionage as a capricious, potentially lethal game in *North by Northwest* (1959), followed by the especially dour *Torn Curtain* (1966) and *Topaz* (1969), in which callous double agents pose as international diplomats and thwarted nuclear scientists blunder into espionage and unleash chaos out of a need for revenge. In the latter films, Hitchcock makes it clear that he sides with the little people—the indigent but idealistic mothers and sons who give their lives for "the cause," the betrayed mistresses of dangerous and powerful men, the families who become collateral damage in the power moves of uncaring spymasters.

It is interesting to note that, even to the end of his career in the late 1970s, when jokey James Bond movies and their imitators had saturated the market, after Hitchcock himself showed with *Torn Curtain* and *Topaz* that even he had lost his footing in the espionage genre, he spent years persisting in repeated attempts to film another big-scale spy thriller with three major movie stars, a romantic/action affair set in London, Finland, and finally aboard a pair of trains racing frantically toward the Finnish-Russian border. Hitchcock, standing primarily on the shoulders of Fritz Lang, became the most noted innovator in the spy film genre. But, in his late seventies, it was, sadly, too late for him to reinvent the form.

NIGHT TRAIN TO MUNICH (1940)

In 1939, after the Nazis seize Prague, German and British intelligence agents stop at nothing to capture a prominent Czech scientist-inventor and his daughter before the pair can reach freedom over the Swiss border.

THE MACGUFFIN: An invaluable new type of armor plating

For those who have seen the romantic and comedic 1938 espionage classic *The Lady Vanishes*, it's impossible to watch *Night Train to Munich* without recalling Hitchcock's earlier thriller. This is, of course, intentional. Both films are front-loaded with international intrigue and romance courtesy of the same screenwriters, Sidney Gilliat and Frank Launder. Both films deliver action, romance, and danger aboard a train. Both star Margaret Lockwood and feature the comedic team of Basil Radford and Naunton Wayne as the cricket-obsessed British twits Charters and Caldicott. The big difference is that this one is directed by Carol Reed, nine years before he made film history with *The Third Man*.

The first half hour or so is full of unexpectedly powerful dramatic touches that one wonders when or *if* the fun will ever begin. Reed makes stark use of actual newsreel footage of German troops invading Poland and occupying Czechoslovakia; he also stages scenes of Lockwood and dashing Paul Henreid meeting and romancing as fellow prisoners in a concentration camp. But look, no one remembers *Night to Munich* for its realism or, for that matter, its plot. Its pleasures exist in the margins, at least until Reed brings them to the forefront. The movie gets its most unexpected lift from the cheeky performance of young, flippant, vain Rex Harrison as Dickie Randall; he plays an apparently footloose character who is not only a singer who is not only multilingual but also a smooth double agent. The less conventionally attractive Harrison plays a trickier, more complex variation of handsome Michael Redgrave's character in *The Lady Vanishes*, and his caustic sarcasm and vanity bounce delightfully off Lockwood's more serious and

Love and treachery bloom between concentration camp prisoners Margaret Lockwood and Paul Henreid in *Night Train to Munich*.
Hulton Archive/Moviepix/Getty Images

sweetly sexy role. Even if their wisecracks aren't on the level of those in Hitchcock's movie, it's still fun to hear Lockwood zing Harrison with a line like, "If a woman ever loved you the way you love yourself, it would be one of the great romances of history."

The movie also bristles with pointed political satire and precisely targeted Nazi bashing. Says a character clad in a German uniform: "Freedom in Germany is far superior to other countries. It's carefully controlled and regulated by the state." And there are such other wry touches as a bookstore displaying copies of *Mein Kampf* right alongside *Gone with the Wind*. It also leads up to a rattlingly satisfying and suspenseful finale at the Swiss border that even Hitchcock might have admired. If droll, low-key British humor is not your thing, give this one a miss. For others, it's a delight. ♟♟♟♙

FLY-BY-NIGHT (1941)

A doctor accused of murdering a scientist must break up a Nazi spy ring to clear his name while also being pursued by the police.

THE MACGUFFIN: The top-secret formula for a wartime weapon

Zippy, unpretentious, and, at times, peppered with risqué, almost pre-Code-style naughtiness, this enjoyable B movie, directed by Robert Siodmak (*Phantom Lady* and *Criss-Cross*) and photographed by John Seitz (*Double Indemnity*), starts with a bang. During a raging thunderstorm, mysterious European scientist Tieler (Martin Koslek) kills a guard while escaping a mental hospital where Nazis have been torturing him to spill the secrets of a MacGuffin called G-32, a powerful secret military weapon concocted by a prominent scientist (Miles Mander). Meanwhile, the police question young medical intern Geoff Burton (Richard Carlson), whose car has run out of gas near the sanatorium; they suspect him of being the escaped murderer. Burton convinces the cops that he's not their guy (momentarily, anyway) only to get carjacked at gunpoint by Tieler. Seeking refuge at the intern's apartment, Tieler pleads for his help in preventing the Germans from learning the formula for G-32; not long later, Tieler is found stabbed to death.

Officially accused of murder, Burton—now framed as the classic, Hitchcock-style "wrong man"—leaps out his window and almost immediately encounters smart, attractive, lingerie-clad illustrator Pat Lindsey (Nancy Kelly), who becomes his highly reluctant accomplice in the manner of Hitchcock heroines in *The 39 Steps* and *The Girl Was Young* (1937). And with that, the chase is on. Clearly, *Fly-by-Night* is a shameless, impudent steal of *The 39 Steps* in which the hero must clear his name by tracking down the inventor of G-32 *and* save America from the Nazis before the bumbling cops mess up everything by arresting him. The amusing script's complications include a sequence forcing the hero and heroine to get married and spend their wedding night in a marriage chapel/boarding house. For plot reasons too featherweight to detail, Geoff needs to mend a rip in his pants. He interrupts the wedding night activities to go downstairs to ask his baffled elderly hosts (Mary Gordon, Oscar O'Shea) for a needle and thread. When Geoff appears for a second time in search of a pair of scissors, the couple look (understandably) hopelessly perplexed. When he returns requesting, of all things, a shoehorn, it's a laugh-out-loud moment. Carlson's comic timing and the straitlaced older couple's bewildered expressions sell the wedding eve dirty joke with stylish audacity.

There's also a delightful car chase requiring the leading man and lady to switch vehicles. They leap from their moving vehicle onto a car transporter truck and hide out in the back seat of a sedan and, while the truck is speeding along, eventually back the sedan off the truck and onto the highway, going on their merry way. Although the screenplay by Jay Dratler (two years pre-*Laura*) doesn't consistently provide the cast with Hitchcock-level dialogue, Carlson (the same year as he appeared in *The Little Foxes*) and Kelly (fifteen years before *The Bad Seed*) play off each other nicely. Producer Joan Harrison, who collaborated with Hitchcock on nine seminal movies and his television series, liked *Fly-By-Night* enough to hire Siodmak to direct her production of *Phantom Lady*. Although by no means a must-see, *Fly-By-Night* is not just one of the very earliest Hitchcockian movies, it's also a cheeky, enjoyable, sweetly naughty homage cleverly made on a shoestring budget. ♟♟♟

MAN HUNT (1941)

A famed British big-game hunter becomes the hunted when a Nazi guard catches him outside the private residence of Adolf Hitler with his telescopic-lens-assisted rifle aimed at the maniacal dictator.

THE MACGUFFIN: A signed letter of confession

Alfred Hitchcock's Hollywood success in the 1940s was a massive thorn in the side of that undisputed titan of the German film industry Fritz Lang. Lang, maker of such thematically rich and visually dazzling Expressionist masterworks as *Metropolis*, *Dr. Mabuse the Gambler*, and *Die Nibelungen*, fled Nazi Germany in 1936 and had every right to expect he would continue his meteoric ascendency in the American film industry. But he found little of the fame, fortune, or creative agency afforded fellow émigré Hitchcock, who was almost a decade his junior. Instead, the dictatorial and often abusive Lang, the virtual progenitor of the espionage and thriller film genres in which Hitchcock triumphed, often found himself saddled with skimpy budgets, so-so material, and lesser stars. Lang, as the story goes, inherited *Man Hunt* when director John Ford exited the project at the very last minute; scripted by Dudley Nichols from the popular and still highly enjoyable 1939 Geoffrey Household novel *Rogue Male*, the movie, although a rush job, nevertheless turned out to be one of Lang's better Hitchcockian efforts.

Redolent of *The 39 Steps*, the film opens with a grabby, largely silent sequence featuring those long tracking shots Lang and Hitchcock favored; we follow famed British marksman Captain Alan Thorndike (Walter Pidgeon) as he stalks prey through an impressive 20th Century Fox soundstage forest identified on screen as "Somewhere in Germany." (Lang devotees describe the evocative forest set as "Wagnerian"; of course, had Hitchcock shot on the identical set, his detractors might have ridiculed it as "obviously fake.") Thorndike reaches a precipice, coolly aims his high-powered rifle, and trains his telescopic sights on an unsuspecting Adolf Hitler stepping outside of his mountain hideaway home in Berchtesgaden. Thorndike is about to squeeze the trigger when a Nazi sentry jumps him from behind and hauls him in for questioning by icily insidious fellow big-game hunter and aristocrat Major Quive-Smith (George Sanders, *Rebecca*, *Foreign Correspondent*). Our hero undergoes torture that leaves him facially scarred, pursuit by bloodhounds, and a staged, meant-to-be-fatal "accident" for refusing to sign a phony confession stating that the British government sent him to assassinate Hitler.

Commandeering a dingy, he barely manages to escape his captors and then, with the help of a plucky British cabin boy (a charming Roddy McDowall, already a pro at thirteen), boards a London-bound Danish freighter. Once back in not-so-merry-old England, he is pursued high and low by villains (notably, the menacing secret agent known only as "Mr. Jones," played by John Carradine) down foggy, shadowy cobblestone London streets and, in a standout sequence recalling some the oppressive paranoia and claustrophobia of *M*, the Underground. Along the way, he earns the love and loyalty of Cockney streetwalker Jerry (Joan Bennett, charmingly gauche and appealing in the first of her four Lang-directed movies), on whose character Lang so dotes that he all but lets the air out of the suspense he's been building. But Jerry also changes the course of the narrative and deepens the hero's emotional journey; to powerful unnecessay repetition of the word effect, musical composers Alfred Newman and David Buttolph lace throughout this romantic stretch of the film a sentimental theme song for Jerry, "A Nightingale Sang in Berkeley Square" (lyrics by Eric Maschwitz and music by Manning Sherwin).

As anti-Nazi espionage thrillers go—*Man Hunt* was shot when the United States had not yet entered World War II and the nation was supposed to be on the side of neutrality—although no masterpiece, is effective anti-Nazi propaganda and rousing entertainment. So rousing, in fact, that the famously contrarian movie critic Otis Ferguson of the *New Republic* opined that even Hitchcock himself could learn a thing or two from it—without bothering to explain what, exactly. (Peter O'Toole starred in a 1976 BBC TV adaptation; no updates since, but in 2016 it was announced that Benedict Cumberbatch would produce and star in a remake. We're still waiting.) ♟♟♟♟

JOURNEY INTO FEAR (1943)

Nazis mark for death an American engineer and arms expert for aiding the Turkish navy, but the head of the secret police smuggles him onto a tramp steamer full of seductive and dangerous characters—including his would-be assassins.

THE MACGUFFIN: A munitions plan to stop the Nazis

Journey into Fear was originally earmarked as a project for director Robert Stevenson (*Jane Eyre*) from a screenplay by Ben Hecht (*His Girl Friday*, *Notorious*) based on Eric Ambler's 1940 novel; Michèle Morgan was to star, perhaps opposite either the lithe Fred Astaire (!) or the hulking Dennis O'Keefe (did two less similar actors ever exist?). By the time the film made it to the screen as a timely world war espionage thriller, Orson Welles had been in, then out, as director, replaced at Welles's own suggestion by Norman Foster (director of several Charlie Chan and Mr. Moto movies and *Woman on the Run*). Hecht's script was thrown out and Welles cowrote a new one with Joseph Cotten (yes, *that* Joseph Cotten). *Journey into Fear* became a comic thriller packed with so many Hitchcockian elements that one might suspect producer Welles and the many cast members he plucked from his Mercury Players stock company were either trying to beat the British suspense master at his own game or to simply spoof him. If Welles was attempting the former, he failed and knew it.

Journey into Fear plays like a fancy dinner party to which the right guests turned up but the party fizzled anyway. Joseph Cotten (*Shadow of a Doubt*, *The Third Man*) stars as Howard Graham, a munitions engineer on business in Turkey who becomes a target for assassination by Nazi gestapo agents. Graham learns this while at a nightclub with a Turkish business colleague. He gets volunteered to be part of a magician's stage act, the place goes black, shots ring out, and when the lights switch back on the magician's been shot but Graham's safe in the magician's box; clearly, Graham was the true target. The head of the secret police (hokey, delightful Welles) gets Graham smuggled onto a Black Sea–bound Greek tramp steamer to hide him from his would-be assassins (Graham's resourceful, not so patient wife, played by Ruth Warrick, awaits him).

Aboard the claustrophobic, overcrowded boat Graham encounters such assorted figures as an unhappily married couple (Agnes Moorehead, Frank Readick) and a professional adagio dance team (Jack Durant and Dolores del Rio in much-reduced versions of the roles apparently originally intended for Fred Astaire and Michèle Morgan) before realizing that he's also surrounded by his potential murderers.

Director Foster ratchets up the tension by utilizing the tight confines of the boat but with none of the flair, instinct, nor mastery of Hitchcock. What the film has, though, is a memorably relentless bespectacled killer (played by nonactor Jack Moss, an associate producer on *The Magnificent Ambersons* whom Welles pursued and cast). He gets the film's highly atmospheric precredit scene, a beauty, in which he prepares his gun while the needle on a gramophone gets stuck in the record's groove. (Shades of a moment in *The Man Who Knew Too Much* when the assassin listens repeatedly to a phonograph record of the precise moment in a cantata when he must shoot and kill a dignitary.) Without uttering a word of dialogue, Moss scares the bejesus out of the audience, and he, along with Cotten as the Hitchcockian average man swept up in extraordinary circumstances, are the best things in the movie. Unfortunately, the film's nervous and unsupportive studio, RKO, recut *Journey into Fear* and trimmed it down to sixty-nine minutes—with Welles quipping that the editing looked as if it had been performed with a "lawnmower"—before it was tossed away to the public as if it were a B movie. A slightly longer European cut—a funnier, spry, slightly more coherent B+ version—turns up occasionally at film retrospectives. ♟♟♙

THE THIRD MAN (1949)

A broken-down American pulp novelist gets summoned to post-WWII Vienna to work for an old friend, only to find himself attending his friend's funeral and investigating the mysterious circumstances of his death.

THE MACGUFFIN: The phantom "third man" who witnessed the death of Harry Lime

A great film that stands the test of time—especially one made up of parts that perhaps should not necessarily fit together—is a miracle. This one is a baroque, atmospheric hall of mirrors reflecting thousands of brilliant choices and happy accidents, mysterious even to those involved in making those choices. Why is *The Third Man* such an all-timer? Let's start with that zither music. Legend has it that once masterly British director Carol Reed (*Odd Man Out*, *The Fallen Idol*) heard Anton Karas playing the zither in a smoky basement beer hall he completely abandoned the idea of a more traditional musical score and hired Karas to play and write the haunting theme that threads throughout the film. Karas's jaunty, melancholic, dissolute, even macabre tune—which became a bestselling hit record in the 1950s—sinks us instantly into the mood of despair, desperation, cynicism, corruption, and moral decay that shroud post-WWII Allied-occupied Vienna, where anything and everything is for sale. Then, there's the spare, stinging screenplay by novelist Graham Greene, who after being hired by producer Alexander Korda immersed himself in the vice-laden city, where he learned of the city's thriving black-market trade in precious ten-thousand-dollar-a-bottle penicillin, stolen from hospitals and diluted, often with lethal substances. Greene scribbled onto an envelope the key to the entire film: "I had paid my last farewell to Harry a week ago when his coffin was lowered into the frozen February ground, so that it was with incredulity that I saw him pass by without a sign of recognition, among the host of strangers on the Strand."

Greene built his scenario around a naïve, down-on-his-luck American pulp writer Holly Martins (Joseph Cotten), who leaps at the chance to stay with and write publicity for his longtime pal in Vienna, Harry Lime (Orson Welles, unforgettable despite limited screen time), only to be told Lime was recently mysteriously struck and killed by a taxi. A bristly British policeman, Major Calloway (Trevor Howard), stuns Holly by telling him that Lime reigned as one of the city's most wicked and shameless racketeers. Out to restore his good friend's reputation—and to find the elusive "third man" who was present at the time of

Lime's death—Holly dives deep into the city's underbelly, which gets him chased down any number of menacing, moodily photogenic nighttime cobblestone streets lined with bombed-out rubble.

In a film deeply influenced by Italian neorealism, Holly falls hard for Lime's sorrowful former lover (the mournfully beautiful Alida Valli, who had starred in 1947 for Hitchcock in *The Paradine Case*), who actively wishes for her own death. The film also presents a gallery of astonishing faces of handpicked nonprofessional and professional cast members, filmed by director Reed and cinematographer Robert Krasker Martin against the backdrop of spectral, war-pocked ruins. Reed and the cameraman spent production downtime experimenting with the tilted Dutch angles that underscore the unease and disorder of the time and place. It's for good reason that viewers remember so many moments from the film, such as our glimpse of Lime in a doorway illuminated by the light of an upstairs window. (Of course, if cofinancier David O. Selznick had his way, Noël Coward would have played Lime; had Orson Welles proven too difficult, Reed was ready to rush Trevor Howard into the role.)

The Third Man also offers indelible set pieces, including the showdown between Holly and Harry looking down on humanity from high atop a Ferris wheel and Welles's chilling delivery of his self-written cuckoo clock speech about the power of good and evil. "Look down there," says Lime. "Tell me. Would you really feel any pity if one of those dots stopped moving forever? If I offered you twenty thousand pounds for every dot that stopped, would you really tell me to keep my money? Or would you calculate how many dots you could afford to spare?" Then there's the spectacular way Reed and Krasker stage and film the underground sewer chase. Cotten is so exactly right for his role (coproducer Selznick chased Cary Grant, who wanted too much money), and Welles's Lime is justifiably legendary. He's a charming, baby-faced monster.

But it is Valli who grabs the heart as the woman who learns every despicable thing about her ex yet cannot stop loving him. The fatalistic, world-weary final moment between Valli and Cotten is a thing of beauty—even if it might be deeply unsatisfying to those thirsty for a

Orson Welles as the opportunistic Harry Lime hides from his pursuers, appropriately, in a Vienna sewer.
Donaldson Coll/Moviepix/Getty Images

cheap, romantic Hollywood ending. It's intriguing to speculate what Hitchcock would have done with *The Third Man*, especially considering the low regard in which he was held by Greene ("a silly, harmless clown," he called the director) and by Welles ("Egotism and laziness," which sounds suspiciously like projection, with a side of envy.). ♟♟♟♟

FIVE FINGERS (1952)

In 1944, an ambitious valet to the British ambassador in Turkey becomes wealthy by selling top-secret British war documents to the Germans, who mistrust him. He gives some of the money for safekeeping to a destitute Polish countess, and they plan their escape to South America. Can they trust each other?

THE MACGUFFIN: The photocopies of Britain's war plans

If your taste in spy thrillers runs toward the brainy, witty, ironic, sophisticated, and delightfully cynical, here's a gem for you, directed with silken finesse by Joseph L. Mankiewicz (*The Ghost and Mrs. Muir*, *All About Eve*) and scripted by the first-class Michael Wilson (*A Place in the Sun*), both of whose work was Oscar-nominated. Based on factual events documented in the book *Operation Cicero* by L. C. Moyzisch (who objected to being portrayed in the film as clumsy and jittery by the scene-stealing Walter Hampden), *Five Fingers* stars James Mason (Hitchcock's suave villain in *North by Northwest*) as Ulysses Diello (Elyesa Bazna in real life), the discreet, impeccable, implicitly trusted valet to the British Ambassador in Ankara during WWII. Hungry to reinvent himself as a monied gentleman and to get himself far away from Turkey, he risks everything by clandestinely photographing top-secret British military documents; for outrageous sums, he cooly hands them over to Moyzisch and the Nazis, who give him a code name, "Cicero"; obsessed to learn his actual identity, the Germans insist that Diello must be a British double agent feeding them disinformation. Happily, they don't act on the explosive and deadly accurate information given them by the cynically opportunistic Diello, who only cares that he continued getting paid.

The movie hits its stride with the introduction of the sublimely chic Danielle Darrieux as a Frenchwoman—widowed, down on her luck ex-Countess Anna Staviska—whom the irredeemable rascal Diello invites to partner in his espionage games and more. Their seductive banter is worthy of Hitchcock (one can imagine him casting Cary Grant and Ingrid Bergman in the roles) or of a continental spies-and-sex comedy by director Ernst Lubitsch (who might have cast his version with, say, Gary Cooper opposite Claudette Colbert or Marlene Dietrich). Although the Diello–Countess Staviska liaison is a complete invention by Mankiewicz and Wilson in a film scrupulously shot on actual locations, their byplay is so delicious that only a churl would complain.

Yes, at 108 minutes, the movie hangs around for too long and perhaps could have used a breakneck chase sequence or two, but Mankiewicz was all about dialogue and characters, not melodrama. As critics noted at the time of the film's release, *Five Fingers* stands proudly aside the work of such suspense maestros as Hitchcock and novelist Graham Greene. Although entirely unlike either film (and far less romantic or emotional), we see it as an interesting companion piece to *Notorious* or *Casablanca*. ♟♟♟♟

THE COUNTERFEIT TRAITOR (1962)

An apolitical American expatriate businessman living in Sweden, blacklisted by the Allies for selling oil to the Nazis, agrees to clear his name by spying on the Germans, putting him and his lover in deep jeopardy.

THE MACGUFFIN: The secret locales of the Nazis' oil refineries

If people today talk at all about this fact-inspired espionage thriller, it's often to call it "old-fashioned," as in not a breezy, gimmicky, irreverent 007 movie from the 1960s. Fair enough. Instead, *The Counterfeit Traitor* is a serious, solidly made, well-acted, overly talky but quite touching movie—for those of us who can still appreciate that sort of thing. William Holden plays an American expatriate oil executive who, blacklisted during World War II, has become a Swedish citizen who routinely (and perfectly legally if not morally defensibly) sells his wares to the Nazis. A mercenary British agent (Hugh Griffith) in Stockholm blackmails our tarnished hero Erickson into spying on the Germans—informing the Allies of the locales of the Germans' newest refineries—in exchange for wiping him off their blacklist. That's when the adventures, treacheries, and double-crosses begin. In no time at all, Erickson is blatantly strongarming his friends to join the cause, being forced to publicly disrespect a Jewish friend (Ernst Schröder), and being dumped by his wife (Ingmar Bergman regular Eva Dahlbeck from *Smiles of a Summer Night*, wasted here), paving the way for a tender romance with his spy contact, beautiful, wealthy, married German dissident Marianne Möllendorf (Lilli Palmer, giving the film a heartbeat). The suspense, which is considerable, hinges on when and how Erickson will be unmasked.

The performances are uniformly strong, subtle, and unshowy, with Holden (Hitchcock's most sought-after holdout as a leading man) effectively tamping down his movie star charisma to create a complicated central spy figure, whose actions and survival rely on forethought, planning, and great personal sacrifice, not on hyped-up movie derring-do. And, contrary to the red-meat macho action heroes many now expect from spy movies, he can do absolutely nothing when he sees from a window the victim of a Nazi hanging at a factory, after which the fellow workers can only return to their jobs, not tear the place down in rage. *The Counterfeit Traitor*, indifferently directed by George Seaton and easily forty-five minutes too long, suggests something akin to what Hitchcock attempted six years later with *Torn Curtain* and, still later, with *Topaz*—to reclaim from 007 the spy thriller as a genre in which espionage is portrayed as the grimy, inhumane, often futile business it is. ♟♟♟

THE PRIZE (1963)

Fallen on hard times, an alcoholic, womanizing novelist plunges himself and his beautiful chaperone into international intrigue when he comes to believe that a Nobel Prize–winning physics expert has been replaced by a lookalike imposter.

THE MACGUFFIN: A kidnapped physics genius

MGM and director Mark Robson (*From the Terrace*) hotly pursued *North by Northwest* screenwriter Ernest Lehman to adapt for the big screen Irving Wallace's bestselling novel *The Prize*—about a guilt-ridden alcoholic widower hoping to regain his will to live by flying to Sweden to accept the Nobel Prize in literature for his anticommunist novel. Lehman instead saw Wallace's novel as the chance to write a spritely suspense chase espionage comedy that turned out to be what he later dismissed as a "road company, not first-rate *North by Northwest*-type film." His assessment wasn't far off. Anything thrilling and amusing that happened to the blithe, debonair Madison Avenue ad man played effortlessly by Cary Grant in Hitchcock's movie happens less thrillingly or amusingly to the boozy novelist played by handsome, out-of-his-league Paul Newman in Robson's pale imitation. One example: the tense, elegantly comic auction scene in Hitchcock's movie gets depressingly dumbed down as a nudist colony lecture scene in Robson's. Or how about how both Grant and Newman play escape scenes clad only in a towel? Or how master cinematographer William H. Daniels (Garbo's first-choice cameraman) films a love scene between the amiably bemused Newman and the purring, pleasant blonde beauty Elke Sommer as Newman's Swedish guide as Grant and Eva Marie Saint were in the grand Hitchcock manner, glamourous soft focus and all?

The similarities go on and on, and comparisons being, as they say, odious, let's just say that those similarities overwhelmingly favor *North by Northwest* over *The Prize*. Which is not to say that the latter, though silly, convoluted, and dragged-out at 134 minutes, is without its Hitchcockian pleasures. We get Hitchcock movie stalwart Leo G. Carroll (*Rebecca*, *Strangers on a Train*, *North by Northwest*, etc.) as a

Spies, nudists, a sexy blonde, a towel-clad Paul Newman, a kidnapping—*The Prize* must have sounded good on paper.
Silver Screen Collection/Moviepix/Getty Images

delightful Swedish steward attending to all the demanding, fussy Nobel winners. Enjoyable, too, is Micheline Presle as a stylish French scientist attracted by Newman, Edward G. Robinson in dual roles (a patriotic, Nobel-winning scientist and his communist brother, though sadly wasted in both), along with Diane Baker (*Marnie*) playing Robinson's apparently placid but duplicitous niece. *The Prize* looks pretty, is a modestly entertaining Hitchcock pastiche that benefits from its cast and lively score by Jerry Goldsmith, but is almost instantly forgettable. ♟♟♟

FROM RUSSIA, WITH LOVE (1963)

To recapture a Soviet encryption gizmo, James Bond entangles himself in an assassination plot with a Russian beauty.

THE MACGUFFIN: A decoding machine

In 1959, Alfred Hitchcock and Cary Grant gave movie audiences the brilliant spy thriller *North by Northwest*. It had nothing to do with 007, nor was it based on an Ian Fleming novel, but many call it *the* first great James Bond movie. So it makes sense that, in 1959, Bond novelist Fleming telegrammed Hitchcock asking if he would be interested in directing the novelist's script for what was meant to be the first official Bond feature film, *Thunderball*. Richard Burton's name was floated for the Bond role, but the actor was wary of an "untested concept" and asked for too much money. And as I dramatized in my (ultimately, uncredited) script drafts for the 2012 movie *Hitchcock*, the master of suspense himself dismissed the idea of tackling another spy thriller like *Thunderball*, observing, "I've already made that movie—I called it *North by Northwest*." He wasn't wrong. And then Hitchcock instead made the radically different, career-altering *Psycho*.

Meanwhile, the fifty-five-year-old Cary Grant thought himself too old to play 007, but he provisionally accepted the job when he was the number one choice of producer Cubby Broccoli, a friend and best man at his wedding. But the elusive Grant would only commit to doing one 007 film, not the five Harry Saltzman and Broccoli wanted him to do, so they went to other candidates, including fifty-year-old James

Mason (*North by Northwest*), as well as the decades younger Patrick McGoohan, Roger Moore, and James Fox before hitting the jackpot with the rough-edged, flinty, charismatic, but then-unknown twenty-nine-year-old Scotsman named Sean Connery. And in *From Russia with Love* he comes into his own: brooding, macho, sex on a stick. The plot that surrounds Connery may sometimes be wobbly, but the stylish, sexy, entertaining thriller (second only to *Goldfinger* in the 007 cannon) *is* rife with Hitchcockian elements.

For one thing, as in Hitchcock's espionage thrillers, it is not especially political, nor does it come down too hard on any one nation or ideology. For another, it features a beautiful blonde—this one in the person of Tatania Romanova (played by Daniela Bianchi, an Italian model whose entire performance, like Ursula Andress's in *Dr. No*, was dubbed), a Soviet consulate clerk pretending to be a defector. Then there's a nod to Hitchcock's career-long predilection for mannish, sexually ambiguous female characters (in *Rebecca*, *Suspicion*, *Notorious*, more) epitomized by the great Lotte Lenya as Rosa Klebb. Watch her vamp Romanova when she's ordering her to bed Bond; watch how Klebb can go toe to toe with any man, especially if she's wearing her special boot fitted with a poison dagger. And, in a tense sequence staged in a cabin aboard the *Orient Express*, Bond goes mano a mano against one of *the* great villains in the canon, Robert Shaw's mercilessly sadistic Donald "Red" Grant, the godlike blond alpha male to Connery's dark brute alpha. Hitchcock often filmed violence at close range, and director Terence Fisher and hero editor Peter Hunt knew how to jazz up the fight footage for maximum impact. A last note about "Red" Grant, who reveals himself by ordering red wine with fish, a gustatory offense that would have instantly marked any Hitchcock villain as déclassé—on such touches legends are built. ♟♟♟♟

THAT MAN FROM RIO (1964)

A French serviceman on a week's furlough must rescue his kidnapped girlfriend, hunt for irreplaceable stolen idols, and somehow stay alive while being pursued by globe-hopping international thugs.

THE MACGUFFIN(S): A priceless Amazon idol swiped from a Paris museum; a kidnapped girlfriend

This breathless, impish, propulsive comedy thriller from French director Philippe de Broca (*King of Hearts*) takes inspiration from Hitchcock's *North by Northwest*, James Bond adventures, Stanley Donen's *Charade*, and chase adventures dating back to the presound era. Even Steven Spielberg name-checked *That Man from Rio* as an influence for him and George Lucas in creating *Raiders of the Lost Ark*; de Broca and his cowriters Jean-Paul-Rappeneau, Ariane Mnouchkine, and Daniel Boulanger themselves took inspiration from illustrator Hergé's phenomenally popular and influential series of comic strip albums celebrating the adventures of *Tintin* and Spielberg directed the animated *The Adventures of Tintin* in 2011.

Revisiting *That Man from Rio* for the first time since I first saw it with my dad when it was reissued in the 1970s alongside de Broca and Belmondo's earlier blockbuster swashbuckler *Cartouche*, de Broca's nervy lark starring the irrepressible young Jean-Paul Belmondo proves a delight (although its patronizing procolonial attitudes toward those "exotic foreigners," the Portuguese, irked the hell out of my father and me since we *are* Portuguese; deservedly, this aspect of the film has aged badly).

Other than that, this is a caper movie for people in love with caper movies. Belmondo plays Adrien Dufourquet, a rascally, slightly dimwitted soldier on an eight-day furlough who arrives in Paris to visit his posh and lovely fiancée Agnes (*The Young Girls of Rochefort* star and older sister of Catherine Deneuve, Françoise Dorléac, who perished in a tragic 1967 car crash). He finds Agnes under questioning because a museum curator, Professor Catalan (Jean Servais, peerless), a colleague of her late archaeologist father, has just been snatched by Amazon tribesmen, who've also made off with a priceless statue. (And what did Catalan and Agnes's late father take during their "artifact-hunting" trips to the Brazilian rainforests but three ancient statues?) Before Adrien and Agnes can head to Brazil in pursuit of the kidnappers and the statue that holds the secret to a hidden fortune, the bad guys drug and kidnap Agnes, who knows where her dad buried another of those statues on their former estate in Rio.

Though Adrien has no passport or ticket, he charms his way onto a flight to Rio, and we're off to the races. Belmondo arrives in Brazil and starts showing off his charisma and action star chops in doing his own stunts—such foolish and heart-stopping feats as dangling from a plane. Dorléac and Belmondo generate real chemistry, and she delights as a truly nimble comic. As goofy, self-effacing, and slapstick a take on Hitchcock as it is, *That Man from Rio* earned a Best Screenplay Oscar nomination and was an international box-office success that spawned a bigger, more stunt-heavy Belmondo–de Broca successor, *Up to His Ears*. Both are witty, sexy 1960s artifacts, but be warned: their pleasures will be utterly wasted on the humorless or the chronic virtue signalers. ♟♟♟

THE DAY OF THE JACKAL (1973)

A militant underground group hires a cold, chameleonic British assassin to kill French President Charles de Gaulle.

THE MACGUFFIN: The identity of the master assassin

Expect mastery from director Fred Zinnemann's movie version of Frederick Forsythe's novel—after all, the man's dossier included sixty-five Oscar nominations and twenty-four wins during a career that encompassed *High Noon*, *The Men*, *From Here to Eternity*, *The Nun's Story*, *The Search*, and more. The based-on-fact assassination thriller *The Day of the Jackal*, one of Zinneman's greatest, displays his hallmarks—a superb screenplay (by Kenneth Ross), meticulous, almost documentary-like realism, and a fascination with the psychology of loners facing crises of conscience or faith.

One of *the* great suspense films not directed by Hitchcock, it stars the perfectly cast low-key Edward Fox (who won the role for his talent and ability to blend into the woodwork when Zinnemann rejected as "too memorable" Jack Nicholson, Roger Moore, and Michael Caine) as a cool, enigmatic British assassin and master of disguises offered $250,000 by the OAS to assassinate French President Charles de Gaulle. Assigned to find and stop the handsome blond cypher nicknamed "The Jackal" is a deputy police commissioner, played with hangdog charm by the wonderful French character actor Michel Lonsdale. Their pairing is superb; in the characters' perfectionistic professionalism, lack of ego, and utter ruthlessness, this cat and mouse are inextricably linked.

Even though 1973 audiences knew that De Gaulle resigned the presidency in 1969 and died of a heart attack in 1970, the movie's narrative is so tight and persuasive, the characters presented with such low-key quirkiness, and Zinneman's work so brutally efficient that *Day of the Jackal* wrecked nerves and often won audience cheers at the finale. The only flaw when one encounters the movie again today is its quaint premise that our governments have any real handle on terrorism. Still, it's a brilliant, taut, witty thriller with many standout moments and sequences. The hotel suite scene alone, featuring Fox seducing and coolly murdering an aristocratic beauty (Delphine Seyrig, perfect), is such a great Hitchcockian vignette that one wishes *Day of the Jackal* could be counted on Hitchcock's own résumé instead of the suspense master's far less entertaining and vital 1969 movie *Topaz*. (Strictly for the record: 1997 brought *The Jackal* a wholly pointless remake starring Bruce Willis and Richard Gere, no less, while 2024 delivered the distinctive looking Eddie Redmayne in a TV redo that cast him as a supposedly forgettable, anonymous master assassin who somehow keeps making rookie mistakes. Not at all bad but wildly overstretched; stick with the Zinnemann.) The more we see it, the more we think *The Day of the Jackal* is not only the last of its kind but also a bit of a masterpiece. ♟♟♟♟

THREE DAYS OF THE CONDOR (1975)

When a brainy, bookish CIA worker returns to his office and finds all his coworkers dead, he must outwit and outrun the culprits until he finds anyone he can trust.

THE MACGUFFIN: A spy novel translated into Arabic, Dutch, and Spanish

Director Sydney Pollack, working from Lorenzo Semple Jr. and David Rayfiel's screenplay adaptation of James Grady's novel *Six Days of*

MARATHON MAN (1976)

A young grad student and long-distance runner, whose government-agent brother is murdered in pursuit of a Nazi war criminal, finds himself being pursued by Nazi and shadowy American agents.

THE MACGUFFIN: Smuggled diamonds

Explaining to the press his formulae for creating suspense thrillers, Hitchcock often told reporters how he loved putting ordinary men in extraordinary circumstances. Odd how few to none of those reporters ever dared to ask whether one could call Hitchcock's ideal leading man, the suave, impeccable, impossibly charming and handsome Cary Grant (who starred in four films for Hitchcock) ordinary. We bring this up because *Marathon Man* is an almost textbook example of a film that adheres to so many classic tenets of the Hitchcockian rulebook. Fortunately, director John Schlesinger (*Midnight Cowboy*, *Sunday Bloody Sunday*) and his collaborators also know which ones to bend. Sure, the young Hitchcock could have cast the young Cary Grant as Babe, the Columbia University grad student and fanatical runner who—when his government agent brother gets murdered while hunting down a notorious war criminal—gets thrown neck deep into an espionage nightmare involving stolen jewels and psychopaths out to get him. But in tackling the William Goldman/Robert Towne screenplay version of William Goldman's bestselling paranoid thriller novel, director Schlesinger slathered a gritty, dirtied-up 1970s patina onto Hitchcock's *The 39 Steps* and *North by Northwest*.

To further make the film feel more modern, he chose Al Pacino (whom Hitchcock wanted for *Family Plot*) and Julie Christie (whom Hitchcock had considered casting in a 1960s shocker Universal squelched) for the two starring roles; Paramount's boss, Robert Evans, strong-armed Schlesinger and brushed aside Pacino (whom Evans didn't want for *The Godfather* either). Marthe Keller replaced the ever-elusive Christie. Schlesinger and his screenwriters retained the MacGuffin (a fortune in smuggled diamonds) and streamlined Goldman's overly complicated plot machinations and stripped things down, a la Hitchcock, to what mattered: Babe being relentlessly pursued by both a murderous Nazi named Szell (Laurence Olivier, decades past *Rebecca* and suffering from cancer) and by killers from a shadowy US agency. It's a movie of memorable scenes so well acted and staged that they often camouflage some gaping plot holes.

The most famous of these scenes—borrowed from Hitchcock's 1934 version of *The Man Who Knew Too Much*—helplessly paralyzes Babe in the dentist's chair while former dentist Szell terrorizes him with a drill. Certainly, the scenes dramatizing the tense love affair between Babe and Marthe Keller (can either of these two be trusted?) are pure Hitchcock. A stroll through Manhattan's diamond district becomes an emotional minefield as concentration camp victims begin recognizing the monster who tortured them. There's also the fun and games of the creeps trying to drown Babe in his bathtub. Even minus the many prerelease deletions of violent scenes that apparently repelled preview audiences (Szell disemboweling Babe's brother, played

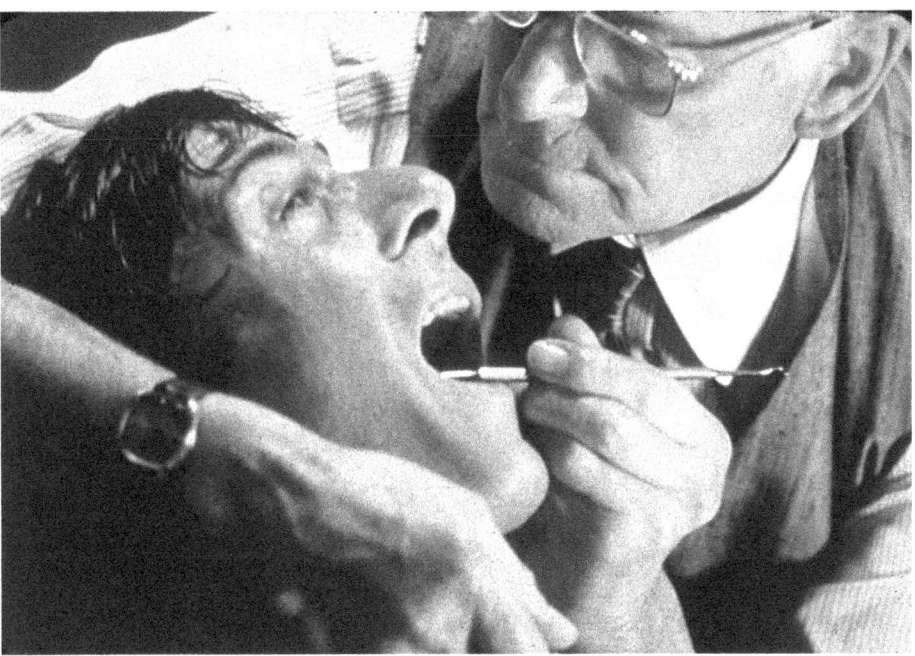

In *Marathon Man*, Laurence Olivier plays the sadistic Nazi war criminal and Dustin Hoffman the nosy grad student whom he tortures in his dentist's chair.
Fotos International/Archive Photos/Getty Images

by Roy Scheider; a nearly ten-minute fight scene involving Scheider and two assassins; close-ups of Szell drilling directly into Babe's tooth, etc.), *Marathon Man* packed a punch. Well acted by Hoffman, Olivier, Keller, Scheider, and William Devane (*Family Plot*), it is the kind of first-class, edge-of-the-seat popcorn thriller they keep trying to make but no longer seem to know how. *Is it safe?* ♟♟♟♙

FOUL PLAY (1978)

A recently divorced San Francisco librarian accidentally lands herself in the middle of a deadly papal assassination conspiracy. A bumbling cop helps her out of danger while foiling the murder plot.

THE MACGUFFIN: Film stuffed into a pack of cigarettes

For some, this assassination thriller is a lightly romantic, quirky comedic riff on Hitchcock's *The Man Who Knew Too Much*, 116 minutes of laughs, slapstick, and suspense. For others, it's a loud, strained, unnecessarily crude, overly long, wearying game of "Quick, spot the obvious Hitchcock reference!" *Harold and Maude* writer Colin Higgins (director of *Silver Streak*) stuffed this one with so many Hitchcock nods that, minus them, the movie might run only a lean forty-five minutes. So the action is set in San Francisco (*Vertigo*, *The Birds*). The heroine is not only blonde but also a female variation of the director's famed "the wrong man" theme (*The Lodger*, *The 39 Steps*, *Confess*, *The Wrong Man*, *North by Northwest*, *Frenzy*, et al.). This movie's update of the classic Hitchcock blonde is charming, ditzy Goldie Hawn (considered for a hot minute to play the bogus medium in *Family Plot*), who was born decades too late for the heyday of screwball comedies. Although director Higgins meant the role for Farrah Fawcett, Hawn is delightful as Gloria Monday (yep!) a forlorn, shy, newly divorced librarian warned by some of here female friends to avoid date rape by carrying mace and brass knuckles (she does), while others urge her to dive headfirst back into the dating pool. So what does she do but pick up stranded hitcher Scotty (Bruce Solomon, *Mary Hartman, Mary Hartman*), who seems less interested in Gloria than worried about the car tailing them.

Scotty also slips into her purse the movie's MacGuffin: a crucial bit of film tucked inside a pack of cigarettes. Gloria waits for him to arrive for their date in a revival movie theater, but when Scotty does he gushes blood all over the popcorn and keels over, warning, "Beware of the dwarf." When Gloria alerts the manager and the house lights go up, faster than you can say *The Lady Vanishes*, there's no Scotty, no blood, zero. Come on, not even a sign of the goons who spirited his body out the theater's side door? Now Gloria gets beset by creeps who are after the MacGuffin. Or something. That dwarf Scotty warned her about? She's told he came to the library looking for her, but in his place comes an albino man who tries to kill her. Wouldn't this be a good moment for Gloria to hit the nearest police station? But, no, Higgins stops the movie stone cold dead. Instead, Gloria rushes to the nearest singles bar, where nerdy Stanley Tibbetts (Tim Conway disliked the role Higgins wrote for him, so Dudley Moore got to make his US movie debut instead) takes her to his place and thoroughly embarrasses himself by stripping to his skivvies with a pair of (*Rear Window*) binoculars dangling around his neck while he projects porn on the wall behind him. Where's that mace and those brass knuckles when our heroine needs them? Happily, Moore's movie career survived.

Soon, Detective Tony Carlson (*Saturday Night Live* breakout Chevy Chase, snagging his first starring role in a major film when first choice Harrison Ford wasn't available and alt choice Steve Martin didn't say yes) arrives on the scene to protect and defend the heroine. Handed the suave Cary Grant role (from Grant to Chevy Chase—how's that for summing up in a nutshell how drastically movie stardom standards tumbled in the '70s?), Chase does his *Saturday Night Live* schtick and comes off as an annoying, leering, self-enchanted jerk; of course, the script requires Hawn to pretend to find him as irresistible as Chase finds himself. Higgins attempts some big swings at Hitchcockian set pieces—chases, woman-in-jeopardy scenes, and the pope's assassination during a San Francisco Opera House performance of Gilbert and Sullivan's *The Mikado*—but they're so ineffectually timed and staged that they just lie there. The movie was one of the biggest hits of its year, spawned a short-lived TV series, and brought abortive plans for a 2009 remake attempt that would have starred Hawn's daughter Kate Hudson and Matthew McConaughey. We like to think of that dodged bullet as *How to Lose a Hitchcock Fan in 10 Minutes.* 👤👤

EYE OF THE NEEDLE (1981)

A psychopathic German spy and assassin, assigned to rendezvous with a Nazi submarine, gets shipwrecked on an isolated island with a lonely young wife, her disabled husband, and their young son.

THE MACGUFFIN: The Allies' D-Day invasion plans

From the mid-1960s to the end of his life, Alfred Hitchcock busied himself with plans for a romantic spy thriller set in England and Finland. The director and Universal bought the screen rights to a Ronald Kirkbride espionage novel and a riveting Sean Bourke nonfiction book about the same events. Hitchcock worked on a series of screenplays with James Costigan (*Eleanor and Franklin*), Ernest Lehman (*North by Northwest*), and David Freeman (*First Love*). The plot involved a man lying in wait to kill a dangerous double agent newly escaped from a London prison and headed to reunite with his beautiful young wife and their two sons on a remote island off the coast of Finland. The would-be assassin falls in love with the spy's abused, terrified wife, and the whole things ends with the hero rescuing the kidnapped heroine and her two sons from a train speeding toward the Finnish-Russian border. Hitchcock several times scouted European locations and discussed casting Sean Connery (or Clint Eastwood), Liv Ullmann (or Catherine Deneuve), and Walter Matthau (or Ed Lauter) in the three key roles.

Despite all the time and money spent, Hitchcock's film never got made, for many complicated reasons. Was one of them its similarity to *Eye of the Needle*, the bestselling 1978 spy novel by Ken Follett, a movie version of which was being planned around the same time? In any event, the screen version of Follett's book is about as classy, elegant, and Hitchcockian as spy movies came back in the 1980s.

Directed by Richard Marquand (*Return of the Jedi*), the film merits its rousing, lush, unabashedly romantic score by the great Miklós Rósza (his love theme revives those good old *Spellbound* vibes), and it stars Donald Sutherland as ice-blooded Henry Faber ("the Needle" for his deadly aim in plunging a stiletto into his victims), who is secretly spying on Brits during WWII and under direct orders from *der Führer* to report every detail of the do-or-die Allied invasion. Attempting a rendezvous with a Nazi sub, Faber gets shipwrecked on a remote island off the coast of Scotland populated only by an elderly alcoholic lighthouse tender, a lovely, lonely British wife Lucy (Kate Nelligan), her embittered, hard-drinking disabled former RAF husband David (Christopher Cazenove), and their young son Jo (Jonathan Nicholas Haley). When the spy passes himself off as a stranded writer and intrudes on the tense family dynamic, Hitchcock aficionados should spot the situation's parallels to the suspicious-crofter-and-kindly-wife sequence in *The 39 Steps*.

Of course, Lucy develops passionate romantic feelings for Faber, and before she learns what a fiend he is, their impossible relationship results in several brutal murders, she and her son face extreme peril, and they reach a fatefully romantic ending that even has enormous consequences for the outcome of WWII. As Faber puts it, in the words of screenwriter Stanley Mann (*Woman of Straw*, *The Collector*): "The war has come down to the two of us." *Eye of the Needle* is written, acted, scored, and directed as an old-fashioned, grown-up romantic spy movie, closer in aspiration (though not achievement) to Hitchcock's *Notorious* than to a James Bond movie—so it was probably out of touch with the tastes of audiences of its day and even more so now. Bad for the box office but, in retrospect, all the better for savoring the film's suspense and intelligence for those who still value those qualities.

Nelligan, whose expressive face often recalls the young Barbara Stanwyck's, is fascinating to watch, and she and the unusually cast Sutherland generate palpable chemistry. That said, we'd be willing to wager that had Hitchcock made it, he might have cast a more immediately appealing actor than Sutherland to play the seductive, brutal, fatally broken Faber. Imagine as "The Needle, say, Oskar

Werner in his swoony prime? And considering Hitchcock's delightfully perverse view of erotic obsession, might he have chosen to play David a roughly similar-looking actor such as Jeff Bridges or Kurt Russell? Still, with Nelligan, the stunning locations, and several strong suspense sequences, this a good enough effort, worthy of rediscovery. ♟♟♟

MISSION: IMPOSSIBLE 2 (2000)

Agent Ethan Hunt's secret espionage bosses dispatch him to Australia to find and eradicate the deadly genetically modified "Chimera" virus.

THE MACGUFFIN: A deadly virus

People love to pile on *Mission: Impossible 2*, but at least there is something comforting and reassuring about the plot as directed by stunts-bullets-and-balletic-violence-obsessed stylist John Woo. No one needs to pay much attention to the dramaturgy, especially movie fans familiar with such Hitchcock films as *To Catch a Thief* and, especially, *Notorious*. They've seen and heard this done so much more elegantly and effectively before. But the resemblance to Hitchcock's work is hardly accidental. The makers of the *Mission: Impossible* movies reached out more than once to *North by Northwest* screenwriter Ernest Lehman, the hard-to-wrangle talent who declined their invitation repeatedly. In fact, I once asked Mr. Lehman, with whom I worked on several unrealized projects, why he was so adamant about refusing that writing gig. He answered, "They don't want a screenplay; they want a few monosyllabic interludes to insert between rock climbing and rushing off to the next stunt." And that was that.

The much compromised screenplay they eventually got, though credited to Robert Towne (*Chinatown*, *The Last Detail*), presents an amoral hero who falls for the heroine, then commands her to seduce and bed an old flame (the bad guy), the better to spy on him and turn over the information to the hero (the "good" guy). In *Notorious*, that situation is erotic, complex, moving, and thrilling. In *Mission: Impossible 2* it is perfunctory and simplistic.

The villains are in possession of a deadly virus and, for humanity's sake, Ethan Hunt (Tom Cruise standing in for Cary Grant) must get it out of their hands. To do that, he needs the help of a bewitching woman (Thandiwe Newton in the Ingrid Bergman role and one of the movie's bigger assets), the former lover of lead villain (Dougray Scott in the Claude Rains role but not bringing the heat). Screenwriter Towne's best invention may be the tension he brings to the "Chimera" virus gimmick by adding a time crunch. Certain death occurs twenty-four hours after exposure. The writer pays this off in a finale bringing together the hero, his love object, the baddie, the deadly virus, and a ticking clock. The charismatic and alluring Newton tries to bring complexity, while Cruise struggles to convey any sign of passion or anguish over what he's put her character through. We don't buy their relationship, so we don't engage. All we're left with is another mind-numbing round of car and motorcycle chases, though that seems to be enough for some people. Nobody's heart seems to be in this movie. Why should ours be? ♟♟♟

BLACK BAG (2025)

The loyalties of a sexy married pair of intelligence agents get tested when one of them is suspected of being a traitor.

THE MACGUFFIN: A deadly top-secret software called Severus

The ghost of Alfred Hitchcock floats benignly over this witty, seductive, martini-dry marital comedy-drama cloaked in the trappings of an international espionage thriller. After all, in Hitchcock's greatest spy films, it isn't always big action sequences but the risks, tensions, betrayals, trust issues, and pleasures of romantic relationships that fuel the fire. Revisit *The 39 Steps*, *Foreign Correspondent*, *Notorious*, or *North by Northwest* for a reminder.

That means *Black Bag* is not for audiences who judge espionage movies as deficient, unworthy or *mid* unless their lizard brains are being prodded constantly by high-tech gadgetry, comic-book-level action sequences, chases, and ludicrous death-defying stunts. And so it is unfortunately not surprising that *Black Bag*, though it offers a chase or two, an explosion, and derring-do, mostly got ignored by ticket buyers. Yet thanks to Steven Soderberg's assured, intelligent, and snappy direction of the smart, ruthlessly spare, and efficient screenplay by David Koepp (*Mission: Impossible*, *Presence*), it is the best character-driven spy movie in ages. Those characters, and the director, attracted an ideal cast. The setup is classic. Respected Brit intelligence and master lie-detector interrogator George Woodhouse (played by Michael Fassbender with icy precision and sartorial dash worthy of Michael Caine in his three 1960s Harry Palmer spy thrillers), head of National Cyber Security Centre in London, gets given seven days to find the mole in his meticulously run organization. If he fails, tens of thousands of people will die globally. There are five suspects—one of whom may be working to sell to terrorists a secret software program, Severus; all five are romantically entangled and emotionally compromised. Like a more lethal, diabolical Benoit Blanc, George summons them all to a dinner party at his and his wife Kathryn's posh home. There's messy, volatile Freddie Smalls, whom George has rejected for a promotion (Tom Burke), and his spiky, sexy young lover (Marisa Abela, the voracious investment banker on HBO's *Industry*), not only part of the surveillance team but also weary of Freddie's indiscretions. The man who won the promotion is Colonel James Stokes (Regé-Jean Page), and his date is his current girlfriend and one of the team's therapists, Dr. Zoe Vaughan (Naomie Harris, field agent "Eve Moneypenny" in 007's *Skyfall*, *Spectre*, and *No Time to Die*). And then there's the prime suspect, Cate Blanchett as George's brilliant, edgy fellow agent and impossibly inscrutable mate, Kathryn St. Jean. Their relationship is the envy of their friends and coworkers; as wonderfully played by Fassbender and Blanchett, they suggest what *The Thin Man*'s Nick and Nora Charles might have been like had they been cowritten by Edward Albee and John Le Carré. For the two, the term "black bag" is classic spy code for "Don't ask," when any further intel about a rendezvous, plane trip, or other activity might pose security or personal concerns.

To tease out the mole, George meticulously prepares dishes of India intentionally spiced to help him pry truth and confessions from people trained (and disposed) to avoid them. A suspenseful and blistering dinner party scene—which ends with a knife plunged into the hand of one of the guests—plays like the most elegant and vicious spy interrogation scene imaginable. The film's sleek, tight ninety-four minutes are filled with classy malice and mayhem in elegant surroundings. Secrets and betrayals get aired, messed-up relationships upended, solid unions made even more solid. And, hallelujah, star power—that rarest of superpowers—is on display and celebrated. Pure pleasure, and offering a tantalizing hint of the kind of thing Hitchcock seemed to be after in *The Three Hostages*, a *Thin Man*–inspired kidnap thriller in which he planned to pair a prototypical Hitchcock blonde as the wife and co-adventurer of Sean Connery as Richard Hannay, the hero played by Robert Donat in the director's seminal 1935 screen version of *The 39 Steps*—until, that is, the Hannay estate declined to accept Hitchcock's financial terms. ♟♟♟♟

3 But I Can't Remember Where or When

Hitchcock remained a skeptic when it came to psychotherapy, and it is highly doubtful that he ever personally underwent any kind of psychological therapy. But he certainly read up on it, was fascinated by hearing personal details from colleagues who were in therapy (producer David O. Selznick, screenwriters Ernest Lehman and Joseph Stefano, among them), and on more than one occasion joked about it publicly, quipping, "Television has done much for psychiatry by spreading information about it, as well as contributing to the need for it."

In many respects, Hitchcock remained an enigma throughout his life. Yet many of his films are rife with psychological concepts, most of them Freudian and most of *those* revolving around unresolved guilt, unattended grief, and the emotional cost of repressing past traumatic events—particularly those experienced in childhood. Freud wrote that "the essence of repression lies simply in turning something away and keeping it at a distance, from the conscience." So, in Hitchcock's moody and malevolent *Shadow of a Doubt* (1943), we learn that the psychological scars of the worldly, debonair "Merry Widow Murderer" played by Joseph Cotten originated when his doting mother let his blond curls grow for too long like a little girl's and that the young boy became hysterical when he was forced to cut his hair. In the marvellously romantic and preposterous *Spellbound* (1945), those trancelike states suffered by amnesiac psychiatrist Dr. Edwardes (Gregory Peck) are triggered by his seeing parallel lines on, say, a white tablecloth, a chenille bedspread, or the strands of a brush covered in shaving cream; they stem from repressed guilt over a horrifying childhood accident involving his little brother. The psychological and metaphysical aspects of *Vertigo* are set in motion by a tragic resident of nineteenth-century San Francisco named Carlotta Valdez; after becoming the mistress of a wealthy and powerful man, she bore his child and committed suicide when that child was taken from her. Carlotta's tragic circumstances allegedly obsess and haunt the imagination of her great-granddaughter, the heroine of the film. In *Marnie* (1964) the chronically larcenous title character's terror of thunderstorms, of red, and of touch of men? She's acting out the abuse and deprivation inflicted on her during an impoverished childhood.

For these and other characters in the Hitchcock canon, the hope is, having been helped to retrieve their unbearable memories buried in the deep subconscious by, respectively, a fellow psychiatrist madly in love (Ingrid Bergman), a troubled detective (James Stewart) falling in love with the hallucinatory phantom he has been hired to follow, and a deeply flawed husband (Sean Connery), they *may* have a chance at a better future. Love can help. But a cure? Audiences can think whatever they like, but Hitchcock makes no such cozy promises.

DARK PASSAGE (1947)

An escaped convict falsely accused of murdering his wife tries avoiding capture by having his face surgically altered and, with a young woman's help, clears his name.

THE MACGUFFIN: The identity of the person who killed the hero's wife

Far-fetched, wildly melodramatic, fatalistically romantic, and beguilingly dreamlike, *Dark Passage* makes—among other things—a fascinating counterpart to Hitchcock's *Vertigo*, released eleven years later. With the hallucinatory charms of the hills of San Francisco as its backdrop, this is a tale (from a David Goodis novel) of a wrongly accused man, Vincent Parry (Humphrey Bogart), who escapes from San Quentin and gets help from a sympathetic cabbie (Tom D'Andrea) who takes him to an unlicensed back-alley surgeon (Houseley Stevenson) for a hundred-odd-dollar facial reconstruction job. He lucks into a relationship with a fascinating and enigmatic young artist (Lauren Bacall) who gives him a safe space to recuperate in her swank San Francisco hills abode and who even helps in the manhunt for the creep who murdered his wife. Why? Because the girl's father got a raw deal that jailed him on murder charges, too. Don't look for logic in *Dark Passage*; better to just go with it. The movie opens with a terrifically tense San Quentin jailbreak scene; taking a cue from several scenes in director Rouben Mamoulian's 1933 *Dr. Jekyll and Mr. Hyde* and the gimmicky 1946 crime drama *Lady in the Lake*, writer-director Delmer Daves (*The Petrified Forest*, *Love Affair*) and cinematographer Sidney Hickox (*The Big Sleep*, *White Heat*) begin *Dark Passage* with the first-person subjective camera technique that shows us the action entirely from the presurgery Bogart's point of view, withholding the star's unmistakable features until his post-surgery bandages get removed about an hour into the action. The action mostly involves Bogart trying to stay out of the clutches of the police so that he can catch the killer of both his wife and his best friend (Rory Mallinson). The weird, wonderful *Dark Passage* doesn't get the love it deserves, what with the admiration deservedly lavished on *To Have and Have Not*, *The Big Sleep*, and *Key Largo*, but Bogart and, especially, Bacall (biting into what may be her best screen opportunity opposite Bogart) spark nicely. Agnes Moorehead certainly makes her mark in her several scenes playing a shrewish busybody, and even in a movie crowded with secrets, odd angles, shadowy lighting, and visual panache, the moviemakers give her character an especially splashy and shocking farewell—a visual exclamation mark that may well have inspired a similar moment in *Vertigo*. The movie, though rarely less than intriguing and fascinatingly illogical, talks incessantly, loses tension and drive in the last stretch, and suffers from an inconclusive ending. But with Bogart, Bacall, and those hills of San Francisco, it's still worth a watch. ♟♟♟

NIGHTMARE (1956)

A jazz musician awakens from a bizarre nightmare convinced that he killed an attacker with an icepick. If it was only a nightmare, then why does he awake with blood on his arm, bruises on his neck, and in possession of an oddly shaped key and a button?

THE MACGUFFIN: A song fragment recalled in a dream

This remake of the psychological thriller *Fear in the Night* (1947) from the same writer-director Maxwell Shane (*The Glass Wall*) revolves around New Orleans jazz clarinetist and session player Stan Grayson (Kevin McCarthy) being haunted by a wild dream involving a mirrored room, a man blowtorching a safe, a sultry blonde, an attempted strangulation, a key, a button, and the ice pick that he plunges into the flesh of his attacker. It's all got to be just a bad dream, right? Sure, but then why does Stan awaken in a cold sweat with blood on his arm, bruises on his neck from his attacker's fingers, that strange key, and a button? And why does he keep hearing an elusive fragment of a bluesy song that none of his hip Bourbon Street musician friends can help him identify? Based on the novella *And So to Death* by Cornell Woolrich (his *It Had to Be Murder* inspired *Rear Window*), *Nightmare* gives us a leading character as haunted, lost, and guilt obsessed as Gregory Peck's amnesiac John Ballantyne in *Spellbound*. But poor Grayson, holed up at the Hotel New Orleans, mumbling feverish voice-over narration ("I had to get out of my room.... I had to stay out of the shadows!") and frustrated by having his innovative music charts rejected as too far out by his bandleader Billy May (the renowned trumpet man, big band conductor, composer and arranger) and even his loving girlfriend Gina (popular singer Connie Russell), shuts down. Unlike Gregory Peck in *Spellbound*, he gets no aid from a patient, maternal psychoanalyst like Ingrid Bergman in unscrambling his jumbled psyche. Instead, he gets blown off by his homicide detective brother-in-law René (Edward G. Robinson), who spends too much of the eighty-nine-minute running time barking at Stan for being an overworked, overly sensitive artiste before he's even asked him the basic investigatory questions. Meanwhile, all René and his pregnant wife, Stan's sister (Virginia Christine), want him to do is to stop acting so crazy. Like clumsy, well-meaning parental figures, they feed him, patronize him, and take him on therapeutic picnics and day trips so that he might calm the hell down and stop blacking out whenever he gets close to learning whether he's a killer. On one of those trips, to Bayou Lafourche—a truly loopy scene of which the film could have used several more—a thunderstorm reduces poor Sue to a terrified, shrieking heap of terror, like the heroine of *Marnie*. So she, René, Stan, and Gina casually break into a home Stan recognizes from his dream, lighting up the fireplace and making themselves comfy and cozy until a policeman arrives to ask them what they hell they're doing there—then drops the subject entirely because René tells him he is a detective. *What?* When it looks all but certain that Stan has killed at least one victim, René barely arrives in time to stop Stan from leaping out of his fifteenth-floor hotel room window. The whole repetitive thing winds up with the discovery of the role of that phantom song in Stan's memory (thank you, *The Lady Vanishes*), a revelatory hypnosis session (here's looking at you *Spellbound*), and a skeevy villain dispensing trippy "cough drops" and uttering posthypnotic suggestions that somehow force people to do bizarre things they would never normally do. You know, like *murder*. Hitchcock knew that the trouble with movies like these is that the third act explanations are almost invariably a snoozy letdown. Don't expect logic (never a Woolrich hallmark), but do expect performances that lurch from thoroughly professional to overwrought, a fascinatingly seedy ambience, atmospheric glimpses of vintage Bourbon Street locales, and a weird vibe that sticks around. Trivia note: Connie Russell, backed by Billy May and his orchestra, belts out a bluesy ditty titled "What's Your Sad Story?," composed by Richard M. Sherman, a long time before his and his brother Robert's Oscar-winning "Chim Chim Cher-ee" from *Mary Poppins*. ♚♚♙

THE THIRD SECRET (1964)

When a high-profile London-based psychologist is found shot dead, an apparent suicide, his teenage daughter joins forces with a volatile former patient to prove that the doctor was murdered.

THE MACGUFFIN: The psychiatrist's list of clients

When this odd little psychological mystery thriller quickly slipped in and out of movie theaters in 1964, many critics compared it (unfavorably) to the work of Hitchcock. Yes, sure, but, all these years later, *The Third Secret* is refreshingly old-school yet idiosyncratic enough to deserve a second look. The action springs from the dying words muttered by respected English psychoanalyst Dr. Leo Whitset (Peter Copley), who is found by his housekeeper with a bloody head wound and a nearby gun: "I bungled this… nobody to blame but me." The police and press treat Whitset's mysterious death as a suicide, but that makes little sense to one of his more appreciative and needy therapy clients, cynical, brutally frank, Edward R. Murrow–ish American TV commentator Alex Stedman (Stephen Boyd), whose tough-guy persona cracks after the loss of his analyst. Alex gets no help from the police or the doctor's colleagues, but his doubts about the doctor's cause of death are intensified by the doctor's keenly intelligent young daughter Catherine (Pamela Franklin, wonderful and complex), who insists her father was murdered by one of his patients. She pleads to Stedman, eyes brimming, "Will you help me, Mr. Stedman? Like my father helped you!" After Stedman lays waste to the shrink's office, he and Catherine make for an unusual pair of amateur sleuths as they share past wounds (such as the death of Stedman's young daughter) and begin to investigate the potential for violence in some of the doctor's other patients, narrowing down their suspects to a prominent judge (Jack Hawkins), an art gallery owner (Richard Attenborough) whose secretary is played by the young Judi Dench, and a lovely, anguished secretary (Diane Cilento, vivid and excellent), all battling their psychological ills minus the insightful support of their shrink. Compellingly creepy but overly garrulous and earnest, *The Third Secret* gets major boosts from the impeccable black-and-white cinematography of Douglas Slocombe (*Kind Hearts and Coronets*, *Dead of Night*), a melancholic, wistful score by Bernard Herrmann–favorite Richard Arnell, and sure-footed but unduly slow-paced direction by Charles Crichton (*Dead of Night*, *The Lavender Hill Mob*). And the finale is not only surprisingly violent but also moving. The intelligent screenplay, by Robert L Joseph (*The Hitch-Hiker*), posits there are three kinds of secrets: the kind you keep from others, the kind you keep from yourself, and the third: the truth. The truth is this: although *The Third Secret* is far from a Hitchcockian classic, it's better than its reputation suggests. ♟♟♟

36 HOURS (1964)

A US Army major gets kidnapped and thrown into an elaborate hoax designed to fool him into believing that WWII is over so that Nazi agents can pry top-secret details out of him.

THE MACGUFFIN: What happened to the hero's last six years?

One thing to be said about what ultimately becomes an overly contrived, flatly directed would-be Hitchcock-style espionage thriller is this: it starts intriguingly and stays that way until its last third. On June 1, 1944, a highly prized army intelligence officer, kidnapped and drugged in Lisbon by Nazi agents just before the invasion of Normandy, awakens in what appears to be a US Army hospital deep in Germany's Allied-occupied Black Forest. Although the chief medic looks and sounds 100 percent Yankee and the lovely, melancholic attending nurse is presented as a concentration camp survivor and the American officer's wife—why is it now 1950 instead of 1944? Why has the strapping young kidnap victim gone gray-haired, and why has his vision so deteriorated? We could also ask why a movie supposedly set in 1950 looks like 1964? The answer to that is obvious. As to other questions, as we figure out long before the movie bothers to reveal it, our hero is a captive in an elaborately staged con job, devised to trick him into thinking that the war has been over for six years and that he's slowly emerging from the fog of amnesia. The Nazis have only thirty-six hours to extract from him vital information about the specifics of the Allied invasion, you see. And once he does and realizes that he's been deceived, can he undo the damage? And can he possibly escape from the trap set for him?

The movie has drawbacks. For one, the hospital is so artificial and stagy and the playing and dialogue so stilted and detached from any sort of reality that the fun of the game gets spoiled almost instantly. (Unlike far better-made, more cleverly directed movies with similar built-in pitfalls—*The Day of the Jackal*, *The Counterfeit Traitor*, *Apollo 13*, and others—we're never entertained enough to forget that D-Day marked a turning point in WWII.) Everybody here tries, especially

Rod Taylor (*The Birds*), who stands out as the brainy German American psych and mastermind of the convoluted scheme. Eva Marie Saint (*North by Northwest*) is effective as the nurse, and James Garner (whose presence and good looks might have been interesting in an actual Hitchcock movie rather than merely a Hitchcockian one) does the best he can for an actor required to look baffled for the film's entire 115-minute running time. The scenes between Garner and Taylor (the best things in the movie) are a terrific indicator of how much better *36 Hours* might have been, given the clever premise by Roald Dahl (based on his short story "Beware of the Dog") and the screenplay by director George Seaton made in such a flat 1960s TV style that it is obvious this would have been perfect for a sixty-minute *Twilight Zone* episode. *36 Hours* (just as another of Seaton's Hitchcock imitations, *The Gazebo*) could only have benefited from a less talky, far more cinematic approach. ♟♟♟

MIRAGE (1965)

A sudden attack of amnesia and a coworker's mysterious fall from a tall building send a Manhattan accountant spiraling into paranoia. He enlists an old love and a private detective to help untangle the mystery of why he cannot remember the past two years of his life.

THE MACGUFFIN: The hero's sanity

Mirage plays like a movie for which no one involved in its making got what or whom they wanted. After screenwriter Peter Stone's big success with *Charade*, he adapted for the screen Howard Fast's *Fallen Angels*, a 1952 thriller novel with political overtones. Although *Charade* castmates Walter Matthau and George Kennedy signed on, Cary Grant, the star for whom Stone wrote *Mirage*, would not. Rock Hudson got announced instead, only to be superseded by stolid, sober-sided Gregory Peck. Universal reportedly offered *Charade* director Stanley Donen the job after Hitchcock himself turned down the chance to direct it—having already done his amnesia thriller with Peck, *Spellbound*, twenty years earlier and having no wish to repeat the experience.

Instead, Edward Dmytryk (*Crossfire*, *The Caine Mutiny*) got the gig. Universal offered the leading lady role to Leslie Caron, whose boyfriend at the time, Warren Beatty, advised her not to do it; if he *did* advise her to instead do the deadly *A Very Special Favor* (opposite Rock Hudson) or, even worse, *Promise Her Anything* (opposite him), then Caron should have questioned his taste and motives. Instead, Dmytryk cast Diane Baker over (or so suggest some perhaps dubious sources) Alfred Hitchcock discovery Tippi Hedren, who has claimed that the master of suspense sabotaged her career by allegedly refusing to loan her out to Dmytryk or other directors. But out of—what, spite? (Highly dubious since, after Hedren hadn't become the major new star Hitchcock attempted to make her with *The Birds* and *Marnie*, the director was already burning off his exclusive contract with her by farming her out to episodic TV shows. So why not movies?) Anyway, *Mirage* opens promisingly enough with a moody, black-and-white panoramic view of the Manhattan skyline accompanied by Mancini-esque theme music by Quincy Jones (heavy on harps, bongos, and horns). Then all the lights of a skyscraper sputter out and we find Peck hoisting a flashlight while descending twenty-seven flights of stairs; along the way, he encounters the lovely Baker, who apparently knows him intimately but whom he doesn't recognize. In no time flat, more weirdness overtakes Peck's life. He becomes obsessed with stairwells and entire floors of the building that apparently don't exist. Food mysteriously vanishes and just as mysteriously gets restocked in his fridge. An unlikely hitman (Jack Weston) walks into his apartment. Baker grows increasingly inscrutable (or is it merely her emotionless line readings?). Our hero realizes his memories are wiped, leading to him needing to confront that age-old suspense movie conundrum: *Can I trust anyone?* The plot twists grow increasingly convoluted, the flashbacks and flash-forwards pile on the 1960s trendiness, and the Peck-Baker combo generates zero heat. The movie's best stuff is delivered by such supporting players as Matthau, who gives the proceedings a welcome sardonic comedic spin as a newbie private eye. There's also good work by Robert H. Harris as Peck's doubting shrink, George Kennedy as another hitman, and Kevin McCarthy as a skeezy corporate type. It all ends with an exposition dump so tiresome

Can amnesiac businessman Gregory Peck trust mysterious Diane Baker in *Mirage*?
Michael Ochs/Moviepix/Getty Images

that I'll be damned if I cared to hear it out. *Mirage* is good *enough*, just not *good* enough. All it lacks is the hand of Hitchcock, a stronger screenplay, and two far more emotionally accessible stars in the leading roles. ♟♟♙

SECONDS (1966)

A mysterious company coerces a discontented suburban husband and father into undergoing a radical process that transforms him from a jowly sixty-something nonentity into a hunky playboy artist with a Malibu Beach bachelor pad. Unintended consequences ensue.

THE MACGUFFIN: A second chance at life

Alfred Hitchcock never took the plunge into speculative fiction on screen, although before he ultimately decided to follow *Psycho* with *The Birds* he weighed the filming potential of H. G. Wells's *Food of the Gods* and Fredric Brown's *The Mind Thing*. One wonders what he might have done with the equally bleak but more human-centered David Ely novel *Seconds*. Ely's 1963 cult novel concerns bored, unhappily married sixtyish-year-old bank executive Arthur Hamilton being given a chance by a shadowy, exclusive organization to shed his old life, face, and body and—for a Faustian price—emerge "reborn" into an entirely new second life with a younger, substantially upgraded face and body. Think of it as a forerunner of the Oscar-nominated 2024 body horror movie *The Substance*. The film version of Ely's novel, from director John Frankenheimer (*The Manchurian Candidate*) and scripted by Lewis John Carlino (*The Great Santini*) features so many commonalities with Hitchcock's work that at times it almost feels like a Hitchcock movie from a parallel universe. *Almost.* The similarities start with a chilling title sequence by Saul Bass (*North by Northwest*, *Vertigo*, *Psycho*)—extreme close-ups of a man's face with eyes darting fearfully (recalling *Vertigo*) and features stretching and distorting as in a fun-house mirror—while Jerry Goldsmith's musical score strikes chords as ominous and sepulchral as Bernard Herrmann's. The film's art director is Ted Haworth (*Strangers on a Train*), and the unsparing, clinically scrupulous black-and-white cinematography by master of the art James Wong Howe recalls that of *Psycho* but with wild baroque flourishes more akin to *Strangers on a Train* and *Spellbound*.

Seconds stars Rock Hudson (who declined Hitchcock's offer of the male leading role in *Marnie*) as the "second" version of the protagonist and John Randolph as the unfulfilled, morose Arthur Hamilton (version one)—shades of Judy/Madeleine from *Vertigo*. Frankenheimer had wanted Kirk Douglas to play both roles, but he was too busy, and though Laurence Olivier was willing to step in, the studio doubted his box-office appeal. Hudson didn't feel he could handle the older role, but he's effective as the reborn hero relocated to Malibu Beach, where

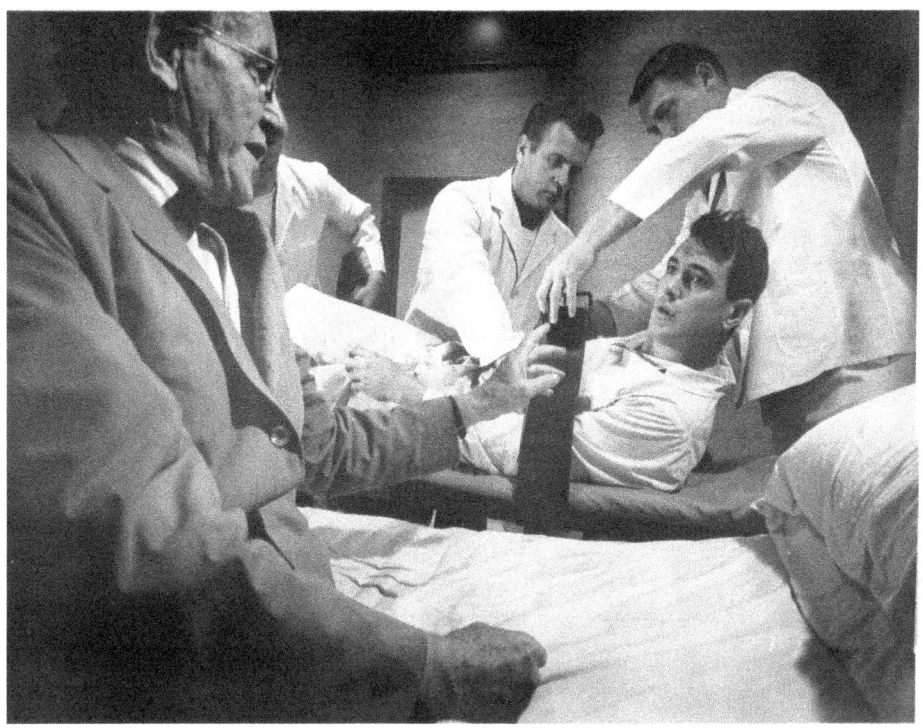

Unhappy, middle-aged Rock Hudson pays a terrible price for wanting a brand-new life in the terrifying *Seconds*.
Michael Ochs/Moviepix/Getty Images

even a romance with free-spirited Nora (Salome Jens) and a Santa Barbara bacchanalian party (so poorly done it is the movie's most unfortunate misstep) leaves him feeling so empty that he demands to be given a whole new identity. This leads to an unforgettably nightmarish and harrowing finale. *Seconds* is so strange, disturbing, and grim that it will probably always remain a specialized, acquired taste. Although it is one of the most striking and singular films of the 1960s, it died in theaters—unlike the financially successful *The Substance* with which it shares many similarities. See *Seconds* while you're in an up mood because it will almost surely ruin your day. 👤👤👤👤

TEN DAYS' WONDER (1972)

A young sculptor, who awakens from nightmares and blackouts covered in blood but no memory of his actions, travels with his former philosophy professor to the manor house of his powerful millionaire adoptive father, whose young wife is one of the sculptor's former lovers. Blackmail and a series of crimes only deepen the mystery.

THE MACGUFFIN: The money

On the heels of Claude Chabrol's four impressive and impeccably Hitchcockian films (*Les Biches, La Femme Infidèle, Que la bête meure,* and *Le Boucher*) came the director's chance to finally realize one of his dream projects, a big screen adaptation of a 1948 Ellery Queen novel about a wealthy, overbearing father, his lovely young wife, a troubled adopted son in love with his stepmother, and a blackmail scheme that unleashes madness and mayhem. Chabrol stalled the start date of production for years because he refused to make it without Orson Welles as the domineering, godlike billionaire Theo (the film is very heavy in theology). Chabrol's whim of iron forced him to wait out Welles's generally chaotic schedule and his often-pressing need for cash. The film, shot in English, begins intriguingly with Anthony Perkins as thwarted poet Charles Van Horn awakening from a religious dream covered in blood. Fearing he may have murdered someone, Charles invites his old college philosophy professor Paul Régis (the ever-elegant, fascinating Michel Piccoli) to join him as his guest at his father's manse—to help him solve the mystery and to keep an eye on his troubling bouts of amnesia. Despite what's described as possessing "an extraordinary analytical brain," Paul proves useless as a detective or a friend as Charles becomes increasingly disoriented while being covertly drugged and deliberately seduced into the sordid atmosphere of his billionaire adoptive father's domain, an eighty-room monument to his favorite era, the 1920s. The master of the house even demands that his young bride Hélène, Charles, and staff of servants adopt hairstyles and apparel appropriate to the home's vintage décor and furnishings from a grander era of the past. In the end, the film Chabrol made, though interestingly cast with Welles, Perkins, Piccoli, and Marlène Jobert (reportedly an eleventh-hour replacement for Catherine Deneuve), never fulfills its aspirations, nor do the acting styles ever mesh. The movie is messy, shot on beautiful French locations, stylistically fussy, weird for the sake of weirdness (the hag in the attic revealed as Theo's mother), although it is packed with playful nods to (and jabs at?) *Spellbound*, *Vertigo*, *Psycho*, and Alain Resnais's *Last Year at Marienbad* and Welles's own *Citizen Kane*. Welles sports a greenish-gray prosthetic nose, and Anthony Perkins seems especially robotic and very much at sea (even worse, his French is dubbed, although he was fluent). The actors seem understandably baffled by their roles and by the film Chabrol is making, but at least it is amusing to watch a melancholy, sometimes manic Welles attack his role as if it were a twenty-pound *jambon de Bayonne*. For fans of Chabrol and his cast, this is a frustrating, fitfully fascinating film that veers from riveting moments (that child on a train as she recites the Ten Commandments) to embarrassing ones (the director's need to explain the ending feels like a sad *mea culpa* from a usually confident moviemaker). In interviews, Chabrol confessed the film was a miss. He also admitted to the press that he chose the filming location, Alsace, simply for its abundance of fine restaurants, at one of which he and Welles dined nightly. We hope they at least enjoyed themselves. ♟♟♟

SHATTERED (1991)

After recovering from facial disfigurement and a coma after a car crash, a man suffers selective amnesia, leading to his insistence that his nightmares are telling him the truth no one else around him will verify.

THE MACGUFFIN: A canister of revealing photographs

German screenwriter-director Wolfgang Petersen (of the masterful WWII submarine thriller *Das Boot*) lost his footing making his clumsy American film debut with *Shattered*, an all-too-obvious attempt to do Hitchcock-style suspense. Tom Berenger, as San Francisco real estate tycoon, abusive bully, hound, and wife-beater Dan Merrick, emerges from a coma after a drunken New Year's Eve car accident that sent him and his wife hurtling over a mountainside. Doctors reconstruct Merrick's mangled face from photos, but he is plagued by recurring nightmares—cue images of breaking glass, crashing waves, a gun!—and is left a psychogenic amnesiac. Meanwhile, it appears his solicitous wife, Judith (played seductively by Greta Scacchi), got hurled from the car before it took the big plunge, walking away from the wreckage with barely a hair out of place—all the better to be able to coach Merrick into "remembering" his old identity while passionately bedding him back to health.

But Dan unearths a hidden roll of film containing highly incriminating sexual photos of Judith with another man. Meanwhile, Dan learns he has been carrying on an affair with the family's very best friend, the discontented wife (Joanne Whalley-Kilmer) of his business partner (Corbin Bernsen). To say any more would reveal the plot twists of a movie that hinges entirely on plot twists, none of them especially new, interesting, or making much sense. There's fun to be had from Bob Hoskins as an asthmatic detective who works out of a pet shop, an only-in-the-movies eccentric whom Dan apparently hired pre-accident for one reason or another. Is Dan the man he thinks he is? Is anyone in this thing what they say they are? And what's with the succession of women who disrobe at the mere sight of Dan? Although *Shattered* looks sleek and stylish thanks to the great cinematographer Laszlo Kovacs, and Berenger plows along, attempting his best impression of Gregory Peck in *Spellbound*, Petersen's screenplay is so convoluted and overstuffed with absurd third act revelations that any interest we had in these thoroughly unpleasant characters dies right along with the suspense. Working from Richard Neely's 1969 novel *The Plastic Nightmare*, Petersen grabs a bit of *Spellbound* here, a piece of *Vertigo* there, tosses in some *Suspicion* and a pinch *Rear Window*, and what do we get? A fine director so lost in Hitchcock's San Francisco fog that he drives himself straight over the cliff of his own muddled ambition. ♟♟

12 MONKEYS (1995)

A convict in postapocalyptic times gets sent back to 1996 to find the manmade virus that nearly annihilated all mankind. Beset by recurring dreams of a foot pursuit and gunfire at an airport, he instead finds himself in 1990 and gets promptly locked in a mental hospital.

THE MACGUFFIN: A deadly manufactured virus

Ambitious, doom-laden, utterly mad, devilishly disturbing, and compelling, *12 Monkeys* was the brainchild of screenwriters David Peoples (*Unforgiven*) and Janet Peoples, who took inspiration from Chris Marker's 1962 French short film *La Jetée*. As directed by maverick Terry Gilliam (*Time Bandits*, *Brazil*, *The Fisher King*), *12 Monkeys* is set in the year 2035 in what's left of the world after a man-made virus has annihilated five billion people and the survivors are forced to live in underground tunnels. A fatalistic air of oppressive dread shadows the convict James Cole (Bruce Willis, rarely better), sent by nefarious creeps to locate the original source of the virus with the hope of finding a sample that might lead to developing a cure. For most of the movie's running time, Cole gets boomeranged back and forth between the 1990s and the 2030s, where he meets people for whom there is no hope, including psychiatrist Kathryn Reilly (Madeleine Stowe) and emotionally explosive eco activist Jeffrey Goines (Brad Pitt, doing so much Acting that he of course got nominated for an Oscar). The face of inescapable

The trippy *12 Monkeys* with Bruce Willis and Brad Pitt has Hitchcock's *Vertigo* on the brain—often.
Universal/Photofest © Universal Pictures

disaster, Cole learns the importance of refusing to surrender to nihilistic despair, even as his life runs in repetitious, ever more confined circles. He and Katherine the psychiatrist find themselves in a theater watching James Stewart and Kim Novak wandering dreamily among the Muir Woods redwoods in *Vertigo*. Against the odds, Cole discovers a measure of grace and joy to be had in what he calls "the right now." And in a dystopian time-travel thriller, and in an ever more dystopian world, that's a very big deal. An unforgettable, one-of-a-kind movie about which the less you know going in the better. ♟♟♟♟

MEMENTO (2000)

A man out to avenge the violent murder of his wife struggles with the fog of his rare posttraumatic condition of short-term memory loss.

THE MACGUFFIN: A Polaroid of the corpse of a rapist-murderer

Adapted for the screen by Christopher Nolan from his brother Jonathan Nolan's short story "Memento Mori," the innovative, mind-bending reverse linear narrative *Memento* immerses the viewer in the jumbled, addled mind of insurance investigator turned enigmatic avenging detective Leonard Shelby (Guy Pearce, compellingly spacey and uber-intense). With Nolan brilliantly telling the story unconventionally both in color in reverse order and in black and white in correct order, we're set up to feel as jumpy and disoriented as this intense young widower who wanders the underbelly of LA navigating red herrings and bizarre plot twists while trying to unscramble the mystery of who violently raped and murdered his wife. Meanwhile, his psyche is being battered by severe short-term memory loss—anterograde amnesia—the result of one of his wife's attackers having brutally clubbed him over the head. The traumas have made Leonard incapable of creating new memories, so he papers the walls of his rundown motel room with Polaroids of people he meets and which he cryptically captions with such notes as "Don't believe his lies" (so we *don't*); more dramatically, he tattoos his body with key phrases and clues that are captured, then lost. Leonard's rare condition makes for dozens of achingly funny/sad moments. He's constantly introducing himself to people he's met repeatedly. Or when he's running madly through a trailer park, spots another guy running, and must figure out who's chasing who. Like Hitchcock, Nolan is in complete control of sound and vision. Cinematographer Wally Pfister's mastery of lighting, framing, and color choices sells us Leonard's shifting, unstable world; the ambient, synthesized musical score by David Julyan (who also scored Nolan's earlier *Following*) and the precise, hallucinatory editing by Dody Dorn (who earned an Oscar nomination) further support and enhance the director's vision and deepen the film's profound sense of unease and disorientation. And I'll now stop revealing story details because Nolan's labyrinthine, haunting film is too good to let anyone spoil by revealing too much about what makes it so good. Just know that *Memento*—meshing a Kafka-like nightmare, a peak-level Rod Serling philosophical puzzler, and a Hitchcockian psychological thriller a la *Spellbound* (but a *Spellbound* where his and Salvador Dali's craziest ideas weren't squashed by the censors or producer David O. Selznick)—is a brainy, challenging, existential thriller, carrying a warning: *Never trust your memories*. Joe Pantoliano is sleazy and superb as Teddy, a hotwired, ambiguous sounding board for Lenny, and Carrie-Ann Moss is impressive as a dangerous dame. Let others argue pointlessly whether this is Nolan's best work so far—topping *Inception*, *The Prestige*, *Oppenheimer*?—*Memento* got there first as the writer-director's breakthrough, with all the craft, creativity, and acting firepower on a fraction of the budget. I saw the movie the week it opened, and two times more that same year. Funnily enough, each time I forget where I parked my car. That's how deeply *Memento* messed with my head. ♟♟♟♟

INSOMNIA (2002)

The murder of a teenage girl sends a burnt-out, unstable veteran police detective to the disorienting land of the midnight sun, where the murder suspect's deadly cat-and-mouse games threaten to send the detective over the edge.

THE MACGUFFIN: The detective's shaky hold on sanity

Wait. You call yourself a fan of all things Hitchcock and Hitchcock-adjacent and you've never seen this one? Come on. It's *only* directed by Oscar-winner Christopher Nolan (*Oppenheimer*, *The Dark Knight*, *The Prestige*), a contemporary giant of film craft and a great admirer of Hitchcock's work. It also stars Academy Award winners Al Pacino, Robin Williams, and Hilary Swank. Okay, some Nolan fans knock points off *Insomnia* for not being a Nolan original but a rethinking of a grittier and, in most ways, weirder and trippier 1998 Norwegian film starring Stellan Skarsgård. Another reason for some Nolan fans' coolness toward *Insomnia* is that Hillary Seitz, not Nolan, gets credit as the screenwriter. But Nolan's fingerprints are all over the redo, an elevated entry into what is now an extinct genre, at least in movie theaters—the psychological suspense thriller procedural. Its premise is simple and intriguing. Temporarily stranded in the disorienting twenty-four-hour daylight of an Alaskan summer in a village called Nightmute, Pacino plays sleep-deprived Will Dormer (close enough to *dormir* for you?), an anguished LA detective with a compromised past. He's been sent with a partner to investigate the especially ugly murder of a teenage girl.

Knocked off-balance by the hallucinatory fog and the puppy dog admiration of a smart young police officer (Swank), Pacino looks like a ravaged, burned-out case beyond flattery, beyond sex, dead inside, and ground down by his job. One gets the sense that the actor responded to this being one of the best of his late-career opportunities, and he's chillingly effective. Dormer's prime suspect is Walter, a local writer who specializes in detective stories. Robin Williams plays him, and he's deeply creepy and, well, superb. Nolan's cat-and-mouse moviemaking finds its most Hitchcockian expression in his superb use of physical environment as a metaphor for Dormer's state of mind; the character's Alaskan hellscape is every bit as apt as James Stewart's haunted-by-the-past San Francisco in *Vertigo*. Nolan, who played so brilliantly with time-slipping narrative in *Memento*, handles things more conventionally here. But his jagged editing of flashbacks to Dormer's past is evocative and, often, chilling. There's a trippy pursuit across logs in a frozen river that even Hitchcock might have envied as a set piece. Is *Insomnia* a paradigm-shifting, mind-bending thriller? No, but it's impeccably made, shot, and scored and well acted. It gets under the skin. Not every film has to be life-altering, not even a Hitchcockian film from Christopher Nolan. ♟♟♟♟

SHUTTER ISLAND (2011)

A widowed US marshal and his new partner go to an isolated hospital for the criminally insane to probe the mysterious disappearance of a patient institutionalized for drowning her three children.

THE MACGUFFIN: Who is Patient 67?

Without having read Dennis Lehane's 2003 novel *Shutter Island* at the time I first saw Martin Scorsese's elegant and blustery movie version, I guessed the twist. I'd chalk that up to a lifetime of reading and watching psychological thrillers—as well as an occupational hazard—except that neither of those applied. It was that I had previously seen William Peter Blatty's 1980 movie *The Ninth Configuration*, which pretty much came to the same conclusions and used similar gimmicks but got there first—and with far less portentous self-importance. Not only that, but the audaciously gifted Scorsese, hardly known for his light touch, hammers down on so many diversionary camera tricks and tony discordant classical music, and so leans into the doom, that he telegraphs that Something Is Very Wrong in This Important Picture. Not that any of this stopped me from appreciating the expensive-looking, awards-baiting *Shutter Island* for what it is, an A-budget prestige movie inspired by livelier, more unruly B-movie bloodlines, including Val Lewton's *Bedlam*, and less anxious-to-impress A movies—especially, Hitchcock's *Spellbound* and *Vertigo*. Spot all the references while you're watching, if you like that sort of thing. For no other apparent reason than to salute the Master of Suspense, Scorsese and ace cinematographer Robert Richardson shoot a scene under a shower head with the water swirling down the drain. Yes, we've seen *Psycho*, too, thanks. How about when he has his hero stare over a soaring cliff that he must climb down, a la Cary Grant at Mount Rushmore in *North by Northwest*? In a movie full of thunderstorms, during one major boom a tree comes crashing through a wall. Remember a similar moment in *Marnie*? So do we. His hero drags his way up a lighthouse like James Stewart does a bell tower in *Vertigo*. Hitchcock several times films Kim Novak in *Vertigo*, Tippi Hedren in *The Birds* and *Marnie*, and Cary Grant in *Notorious* from the back of their heads; villainous Max von Sydow gets introduced in *Shutter Island* this same way.

Though expertly done and brimming with panache, none of these stylistic flourishes feel organic to Scorsese's narrative, which opens with 1950s-era Federal marshal Teddy Daniels (Leonardo DiCaprio, brow furrowed, trench coat flapping in the wind) storming onto the titular remote island off the New England coast to stick his nose into the unlikely escape of child-murdering patient Rachel Solando from ominous Ashecliffe, the fortress-like maximum security mental hospital that looks like equal parts Alcatraz and Dracula's Castle. Before filming, Scorsese apparently asked DiCaprio to study the tight-lipped, deadpan stoic performance of handsome, sad-eyed Dana Andrews playing the cynical and disaffected detective who loses his head while investigating the vanishing of the alluring heroine in *Laura*, whom he has seen only in a painted portrait. Andrews, though a far less gifted actor than DiCaprio, wears his trench coat, fedora, and angst like a second skin; in a tricky role, DiCaprio, chain-smoking, haunted, and out to avenge the murder of his wife at the hands of an Ashecliffe patient, looks uneasy, pose-y, and overburdened. Meanwhile, his watchful, recessive partner Chuck Aule (Mark Ruffalo, fedora and sarcasm tilted at just the right angle) strikes authentic vintage notes and grabs the eye. No wonder Daniels begins to mistrust him.

The narrative gets awfully busy and messy, as prescribed by Lehane's novel and scripted by Laeta Kalogridis. The marshals deal with bureaucratic stalling by the two doctors who rule over the hospital—played by Ben Kingsley and Max von Sydow. You can guess which of the two is the more humane one and which is the sadistic tyrant. Then there's the patient who tells Teddy that the hospital staff regularly lobotomizes inmates in the island lighthouse and routinely subjects others to brutal mind control experiments. As if those weren't enough, there is also a major hurricane, Teddy's migraines, and flashbacks to his army days liberating Dachau. Then there's Teddy believing he saw Chuck's dead body dashed on the rocks below a towering cliff. Scorsese also populates every nook and cranny of Ashecliffe with well-known actors playing patients, guards, or the ghosts that haunt DiCaprio's painful memories. The script gives a few of them Best Supporting Actress/Actor–bait monologues, and the gifted

Emily Mortimer, Michelle Williams, Jackie Earl Haley, Elias Koteas, Patricia Clarkson, Ted Levine, and John Carroll Lynch are all in there pitching for the gold. Honestly, this movie is... well... *a lot*. In a storied career that includes *Mean Streets*, *Taxi Driver*, *Raging Bull*, *Goodfellas*, *Silence*, *Casino*, and more, it is surprising that such a full-blown melodrama as *Shutter Island* would be automatically hailed as peak-level Scorsese. But the movie's fans are legion, and those who take the movie very seriously argue to this day about the bleak finale and what it means. Despite all the talent and effort put into it, *Shutter Island* received no Oscar nominations but became Scorsese's biggest financial success until the much better, more trenchant and entertaining but no less unhinged *The Wolf of Wall Street*. ♟♟♟

On remote, windswept Shutter Island, the lighting on stars Leonardo DiCaprio and Mark Ruffalo always screams 1940s crime melodrama.
Paramount Classics/Photofest © Paramount Pictures

SIDE EFFECTS (2013)

Prescribed a series of experimental antidepressants by her psychiatrist, the wife of a man recently released from prison violently assaults her husband while she is sleepwalking. Her psychiatrist battles for his client's acquittal in court but begins to wonder if he is being conned.

THE MACGUFFIN: An experimental antidepressant that causes sleepwalking as a side effect

This neo-Hitchcockian psychological thriller from unpredictable director-screenwriter Steven Soderbergh (*Traffic*, *Erin Brockovich*, *Ocean's Eleven*) has a chilly, modern vibe all its own yet bears unmistakable traces of Hitchcock's *Suspicion*, *Spellbound*, *The Paradine Case*, and *Marnie*. Spooky-lovely, supernaturally composed Rooney Mara (who replaced Blake Lively, a more likely candidate to play a contemporary version of a possibly dangerous Hitchcock blonde) stars as depression-plagued socialite Emily, whose investment banker husband (Channing Tatum) gets sprung from prison after serving jail time for insider trading. Mandated to attend therapy sessions after deliberately ramming her car into a parking garage wall, she begins treatment with a respected, tightly wound psychiatrist and academic (Jude Law) who consults with Emily's whispery, spooky former shrink (Catherine Zeta-Jones); once they decide to try Emily on an experimental drug, her world goes haywire. Sleepwalking, stabbing, bloodshed, police investigations, courtroom scenes, psychiatric hospitalizations, treachery, ruined lives, and an unlikely finale are the aftermath. Emily's psychiatrist begins wondering whether he—and his clients—are being deliberately duped, as his own life and career unravel. It's a very Soderbergh kind of movie written by Scott Z. Silver (*The Bourne Ultimatum*, *Contagion*), so expect filmmaking expertise and sharp commentary on our society's hunger for "quick-fix" pharmaceuticals and the sway that drug reps hold over some doctors. It's also a high-style potboiler, so expect well-calibrated performances (from Law, especially), beautifully shot two-hander scenes, and many,

many plot turns. The most glaring area in which the movie falls short of a top-shelf would-be Hitchcock movie is that the characters are given almost no reason to exist beyond being driven by the plot. They're too self-absorbed to engage the viewer, and even the expertise of the actors and the immense skill of the director don't compensate for the distancing chill they and *Side Effects* emit. ♟♟♟

4 Las Hijas de Carlotta Valdez

Lovers reincarnated or lovers being cruelly scammed. These are the hallmarks of films made in the shadow of the deliriously swoony and profoundly dark masterwork *Vertigo*. The 1958 Hitchcock film starred James Stewart as a commitment-averse retired detective crippled by a debilitating fear of heights, and Kim Novak as the bewitching, potentially suicidal woman he is being paid to follow. It was crowned the greatest film of all time by the British Film Institute's once-every-decade poll in 2012, supplanting *Citizen Kane* from Orson Welles. (In 2022, *Jeanne Dielman, 23 quai du Commerce, 1080 Bruxelles*, weighing in at three hours and twenty-two minutes, kicked *Vertigo* to the curb.) The dreamlike, despairing *Vertigo*—part detective story, part ghost story, part metaphysical love story, part story of erotic obsession and necrophilia (Hitchcock once jokingly referred to it as *To Lay a Ghost*)—still polarizes film fans, even fans of Hitchcock's work. Some complain about its languorous and hypnotic pace, its obsession with the male gaze, its perceived misogyny. Some insist on viewing it as Hitchcock's uncomfortably confessional autobiography. Some recoil at the age gap between its costars. Some identify too deeply with either the character played by Stewart or the character played by Novak. But few can deny its emotional impact, nor the grip it holds on the psyches of moviemakers, who keep reimagining it again and again and again and…

For decades, Hitchcock himself tried to interest various female stars (Nova Pilbeam, Ingrid Bergman, Audrey Hepburn, Grace Kelly, Tippi Hedren) and movie studio bosses in helping him realize a different dream, a film version of Sir James Barrie's disturbing and haunting 1920 play *Mary Rose*. He described it, variously, as a "sentimental ghost story" and "a kind of sad, melancholy *Twilight Zone* tale." In it, the childlike, titular heroine—who, as a young child, vanishes for days on a mysterious Outer Hebrides island—returns to that island as a young wife and mother only to vanish again; decades later, completely untouched by time, she is a ghostly presence in her abandoned childhood home, in which her parents have grown old and the lost child for whom she's been searching is now a world-weary young soldier. Hitchcock described the film's dilemma thusly: "If the dead were to come back, what would we do with them? I see it as a horror story. A beautiful young ghost returns to find her handsome young husband is now a paunchy, middle-aged man. Can you imagine anything more horrible?"

To Hitchcock's enduring frustration and sadness, no studio executive—from Darryl F. Zanuck at 20th Century Fox in the 1940s to Lew Wasserman at Universal in the 1960s—would finance the project. The director envisioned it as either a *Vertigo* precursor or a companion piece. After the outsized financial success of *Psycho*, Hitchcock's wife and collaborator, Alma Reville, keenly aware of her husband's fascination with the unusual material, tried to convince him to instead direct a movie version of the somewhat similar *Trap for a Lonely Man*, a French play about a new groom whose newlywed wife disappears mysteriously on their honeymoon; while the police search in vain for the missing wife, she returns to her husband—who insists the woman is not his wife at all. Somehow, Darryl F. Zanuck agreed to make that one, but Hitchcock abandoned the idea. It wasn't *Mary Rose* after all, the Hitchcock ghost story he always hoped would be.

THE UNINVITED (1944)

A brother and sister buy a long-abandoned seaside house marked by a tragic past. Soon supernatural occurrences trouble the siblings and are connected to a troubled, grieving young beauty with whom the brother falls in love.

THE MACGUFFIN: Why is a female ghost haunting a brother and sister's coastal mansion?

In 1943, the great writer-producer Charles Brackett, who collaborated with Billy Wilder on thirteen films—among them *Ninotchka*, *A Foreign Affair*, *The Lost Weekend*, and *Sunset Boulevard*—brought to Alfred Hitchcock *The Uninvited* script, on which he had previously worked with Dodie Smith (*To Each His Own*) and Frank Partos (*Stranger on the Third Floor*, *The Snake Pit*) in hopes of persuading the suspense maestro to direct his project based on Dorothy Mcardle's romantic supernatural thriller novel *Uneasy Freehold*, published in England in 1942. Unfortunately, Hitchcock and Brackett could not come to a deal on the project—which shared many common elements with the director's hugely successful screen version of *Rebecca*. But Hitchcock responded to the project's potential, enough to at least provide Brackett with a considerable number of script suggestions. One wonders whether it was Hitchcock's work schedule that stopped him from accepting Brackett's invitation. Or was it simply that, if Hitchcock was going to try his hand at the supernatural at all, he preferred to hold out for the chance to make the one ghost story he talked most about doing, Sir James Barrie's sentimental and mournful play *Mary Rose*. In any case, lots of *The Uninvited*—the movie debut of Broadway director Lewis Allen (*Suddenly!*, *Desert Fury*)—has the feel of a Hitchcock-style ghost tale. It takes a witty, classy, intelligent approach to ghosts and hauntings with no detective or psychiatrist on hand to explain it all away in the finale. It is also disarmingly odd and suggestive.

Adult siblings Pamela and Roderick Fitzgerald pool their money to buy a dirt cheap (1,200 pounds!) windswept old, abandoned Cornwell coast house. These roles are performed with breezy intelligence and dash by Ruth Hussey (*The Philadelphia Story*) and Ray Milland (*The Lost Weekend*, *Dial M for Murder*). The two impulsively move into the house with their adorable squirrel-chasing dog Bobby, who refuses to go upstairs to the second floor and soon after vanishes. Neither will their cat venture those stairs. Animals always know when a place is *bad*. Fresh-cut flowers wither and die on contact with the house, and at times the scent of mimosa hangs in the air. Plaintive moans cry out in the night, and the former artist's studio earmarked as Roderick's music room is plagued by cold spots.

A Mrs. Danvers–type figures in the melodrama, and as played by actress-playwright Cornelia Otis Skinner, she's a glowering, domineering piece of work. Meanwhile, also lurking and watching the Fitzgerald siblings is the sad-eyed Stella Meredith (composer Victor Young's romantic classic "Stella by Starlight" is introduced instrumentally in the film, and it suits her). Stella (played by the hauntingly lovely but tragic Gail Russell) is the granddaughter of Commander Beech (Donald Crisp), the austere, unwelcoming gentleman from whom the Fitzgerald siblings have bought what is obviously a house with a dark past; it's where Stella's mother, Mary (who is as idealized as the dead first wife in *Rebecca*), died tragically. The backstory of Mary (who either committed suicide or was murdered by her artist husband, who carried on a tempestuous love affair with a gypsy) is about as muddled and byzantine as all that Madeleine Elster/Carlotta Valdez backstory hocus-pocus in *Vertigo*.

The Uninvited has inspired filmmakers for decades since—Martin Scorsese, Guillermo del Toro, Robert Wise, and Steven Spielberg are among those who have expressed their admiration. And the movie's influence on *The Haunting*, *The Innocents*, *The Others*, and *Poltergeist* (remember the line about the scent of mimosa?) is apparent. To contemporary viewers who prefer to be beaten into submission by jump scares, booming musical soundtracks that instruct them when and how to react, and wall-to-wall special effects, *The Uninvited* may seem like weak sauce. For those who still appreciate restraint and subtlety, here is a rainy-night movie that delivers quietly creepy thrills.

Ray Milland and Ruth Hussey learn more about ghosts than they ever planned, thanks to the troubled young woman played by Gail Russell.
LMPC via Getty Images

And, as good as it is, we still wish that we could have seen what Hitchcock would have made of it. ♟♟♟♟

OBSESSION (1976)

A wealthy New Orleans widower haunted by the kidnapping and murder of his wife and young daughter eighteen years previously falls hopelessly in love with his wife's doppelganger in Italy.

THE MACGUFFIN: A real estate fortune

Even as an unabashed fan of Brian De Palma's *Sisters*, *Carrie*, *Blow Out*, and *Phantom of the Paradise*, few things strike me as sillier than the argument that the director's amusingly overheated, over-the-top melodrama *Obsession* is in any way greater than *Vertigo*.

If Hitchcock had not made *Vertigo*, would *Obsession* even exist? Scripted by Paul Schrader and directed feverishly but with curious emotional detachment by De Palma, the movie opens nicely as Vilmos Zsigmond's camera glides through a posh New Orleans mansion anniversary party celebrating wealthy lovebirds Elizabeth (Geneviève Bujold, terrific) and Michael Courtland (Cliff Robertson, awkwardly cast). Waiters with silver trays swan around proffering drinks to the guests, but with Bernard Herrmann's music grumbling so threateningly, we know things are about to go badly. Sure enough, a smash close-up reveals one of those butlers is packing a gun in his belt. Suddenly, Elizabeth and her young daughter get violently abducted. Good stuff. But then the movie jumps the track. We're supposed to believe that shock and grief would make the rapacious and conniving Courtland agree to the police's moronic scheme of catching the bad guys by stuffing half a million dollars in fake ransom cash into a briefcase wired with a device that will alert them to the whereabouts of the kidnap victims. The dim-witted cops botch the extraction, losing Courtland his beloved family in a fiery getaway car crash. Eighteen years later, the morose widower revisits the ancient church in Florence, Italy, where he and Elizabeth first met. Guess who he sees helping with the restoration of the venerable ancient structure? Yes, an intriguing young woman named Sandra who sports a 1970s shag hairdo and a sort-of Italian accent yet looks exactly like Courtland's wife who died eighteen years ago. Is Sandra merely a lookalike? A ghost? Were she and Michael destined to meet, or was that carefully orchestrated? Too lovestruck to ask even the most obvious questions, Michael immediately forgets his business obligations and begins courting this hallucinatory doppelgänger apparently emerged from among the dead. With Herrmann's glorious musical score thunderously and deliberately evoking *Vertigo*, what viewer could possibly be so dense as not to immediately figure out exactly what's going on? From here on in, Schrader's utterly humorless script keeps pulling fast ones and twists, but they're not clever or fast enough. Nor is Robertson (sporting a terrifying hairpiece made of what resembles recycled Brillo pads) a compelling enough tragic figure to keep us from ignoring the crater-size plot holes. Fortunately, the splendid Bujold replays the Kim Novak

Obsession is so much like *Vertigo* that Geneviève Bujold could be telling Cliff Robertson the tale of Carlotta Valdez.
United/Hulton/Getty Images

dual roles with just the right note of mockery underneath her conviction, even when the script's Electra-complex dramatics go in a decidedly cringey direction that wouldn't fly today. And with John Lithgow laying it on thick as Robertson's oily southern lawyer, who except a De Palma diehard could possibly mistake *Obsession* for anything more than a cynical, derivative, tongue-in-cheek hoot? ♟♟♙

DEAD AGAIN (1991)

A private eye discovers his bizarre and potentially fatal past-life connection to an amnesiac woman who dreams she is the reincarnation of a singer murdered decades before by her composer husband.

THE MACGUFFIN: The anklet

One can't fault *Dead Again* for a lack of chutzpah. After all, here's a movie that dares to mess with our collective memories of *Rebecca*,

Spellbound, *Dial M for Murder*, *Psycho*, *Vertigo*, Alfred Hitchcock, Old Hollywood, Orson Welles, and—hey, why not?—Laurence Olivier and Vivien Leigh, too? Made back when Kenneth Branagh's thrilling version of *Henry V* (previously an Olivier directing-acting 1944 milestone) had some British and American critics tripping over themselves to hail the actor-director-showman as the second coming of Olivier, its star-director became intrigued by the gifted Scott Frank's audacious, floridly romantic screenplay set in parallel timelines, *Dead Again*. Why not star in and direct it himself?

In post-WWII and glorious black-and-white Los Angeles, a once-in-a-lifetime tragic romance erupts between internationally renowned German composer Roman Strauss (Branagh) and a rising singer, Margaret (Emma Thompson, wonderful). They marry, but jealousy and doubt poison their relationship, leading to Margaret being stabbed to death; the emotionally destroyed Roman, vowing his innocence, gets executed for the murder. The parallel story, in shadowy, stylized color, is set in 1991 Los Angeles and revolves around cynical gumshoe Mike Church (Branagh again, of course, criminally miscast) getting hired to aid a lost soul (Thompson again, terrific) who has been robbed of her memory and speech. A hypnotist/antique dealer (Derek Jacobi, having a high old time in a Maria Ouspenskaya–worthy role) insists on hypnotizing the woman, hoping to uncover a dark trauma from a past life. Sure enough, she regains her ability to speak, and as an inevitable romantic relationship evolves with Mike, she suspects that he is a reincarnation of Roman and that she must be the reincarnation... well, you get the point.

Hitchcockian themes of fate, guilt, and obsession to right wrongs by repeating the past lend to a showy, shallow movie the illusion of depth. *Dead Again* is rubbishy pulp, swooningly romantic, completely bananas, and often enjoyable on so many levels, yet it falls so far short of the films its participants keep reminding us about, films they so clearly love and, possibly, envy. The quirky supporting cast members—Andy Garcia, Robin Williams, Hanna Schygulla, Campbell Scott, Obba Babatundé—do their damnedest to help put over the hocus-pocus with conviction. They're so good that they, and the ambitious Branagh, almost succeed. *Almost.* It isn't great, but it certainly isn't dull. An A for effort, at least. ♟♟♟

FINAL ANALYSIS (1992)

A psychiatrist involves himself romantically with two beautiful, deeply troubled sisters—with disastrous results.

THE MACGUFFIN: The bad sister

Hitchcock loved the element of romantic triangles in his thrillers, and this gonzo pseudo-Hitchcock psychological thriller offers a promising setup. There's handsome San Francisco psychiatrist Richard Gere (in merely passing-through mode) caught between two gorgeous blondes, twisted sisters with bizarre and traumatic pasts. These femmes fatales are played by Uma Thurman (as suicidal Diana plagued by horrific family trauma) and older, badly married, and equally unwell sister Heather, played by Kim Basinger, who looks glorious and vulnerable but whispers all her lines and strikes sultry poses as if she were the new Lana Turner. In no time at all, the shrink and Heather are locked in a secret love affair in a gorgeously shot (by Jordan Cronenweth) movie crammed with multiple double-crosses, heated trial scenes, and frantic attempts to generate a hothouse erotic ambience. On the sidelines lurks Eric Roberts (outlandishly scary) as Basinger's sadistic, jealous, abusive Greek millionaire husband. And there's quintessentially 1990s production design dazzle by Dean Tavoularis; this is a Hitchcock tribute where the money looks well spent. But it all rises or falls on the story by Robert H. Berger and Wesley Strick (*Wolf, Cape Fear* [1991]), who is also credited with the final script. I suppose if one has never seen *Vertigo, Double Indemnity, The Postman Always Rings Twice,* or *Body Heat, Final Analysis* might impress as gripping, torrid stuff. Solidly directed by Phil Joanou (*State of Grace, The Veil*), the movie features lots of spectacular vistas of a prime Hitchcock locale, San Francisco (*Vertigo, The Birds*), sites in and around and under the Golden Gate Bridge, where the filmmakers decided to add a nonexistent lighthouse, only as an excuse to stage a goofy, unearned finale during which characters face off on a catwalk and dangle off it while waves crash below. There's a better film trying to break out of this one, but, as it is, *Final Analysis* is preposterous, convoluted, pretty, and dunderheaded. 👤👤

PERFECT BLUE (1997)

A pop idol turned actress goes insane when she is stalked by an obsessive fan who invades her life.

THE MACGUFFIN: An online diary

Whether enjoyed as a paranoid psychological suspense thriller, as an indictment of celebrity-obsessed culture and toxic fandom, or as a mold-breaking animated film that influenced such works by director Darren Aronofsky as *Requiem for a Dream* and *Black Swan* and peppered with thematic and visual references to Hitchcock films, director Satoshi Kon's *Perfect Blue* is a fascinating, confounding, and transfixing piece of work—especially for an animated film. Can an animated film be Hitchcockian? This one can and *is*. Besides, stylized animation is prominent in key moments in Hitchcock's *Sabotage*, *Spellbound*, *Vertigo*, and *The Birds*.

Sadayuki Murai's screenplay, loosely based on Yoshikazu Takeuchi's novel *Perfect Blue: Complete Metamorphosis*, centers on rising J-pop singer Mima Kirigoe (voiced by Junko Iwao), whose decision to abandon music and shed her cutesy image for a grown-up acting career triggers shockwaves among her fans, who'd prefer her to be trapped in the amber of her innocently girlish image.

The rage is most apparent in an obsessive stalker who photographs her in secret and runs a creepily invasive website reporting his fallen idol's every move, even with a bogus online diary he writes. Mima shoves down her own rage when she reports her stalker's obsession but is ignored and gaslighted by those who run her career. Mima's manager (Rica Matsumoto) lands her star client a showy role for which she's pressured into filming a violent rape scene for a worthless cop drama; although warned against doing the scene, she persists and the shooting proves to be degrading and deeply traumatic. The scene is so intensely staged and filmed that it is painful to watch. Abused by predatory photographers and TV makers, Mima loses her bearings and comes undone.

Then comes a sudden spate of brutal and vengeance-driven murders aimed at those responsible for Mima's acting career. That is when the heroine's—and the film's—line between reality and dreams vanishes. Is Mima experiencing a psychotic break? Is she an innocent victim? Is she a murderer? It's when a specter begins to appear—a dreamy, white-hued Mima double who announces herself as the *real* Mima—that the film truly delivers its most beautiful, disturbing, mind-bending passages. We're talking about a deep dive into highly unorthodox script construction, bizarre twists and turns, and cinematic head games that might have been influenced by Hitchcock's *Vertigo*. The less one knows going into *Perfect Blue* the better, but it made a stunning directorial debut for the late Satoshi Kon (*Paprika*, *Tokyo Godfathers*), whose life was taken by cancer in 2010 at only age forty-six. But be warned. A feel-good Disney animated movie it isn't. ♟♟♟♟

MULHOLLAND DRIVE (2001)

An aspiring actress befriends a mysterious amnesiac in surrealistic Los Angeles.

THE MACGUFFIN: An amnesiac's lost identity

I've always loved *Mulholland Drive*—David Lynch's ultrasurrealistic, hypnotic, bewildering and beautifully batshit crazy celluloid fable. The film—which Lynch called a "a love story in the city of dreams"—is almost impossible to describe logically. But isn't that almost always true about dreams—and life itself? Let's just say that this isn't a movie for viewers who demand strict logic or linear storylines. Hitchcock always insisted logic is dull, remember? In 2001, I remember leaving the theater after a press preview of *Mulholland Drive*. When a friend waiting in line for the next screening asked me to describe it. I flippantly said,

"A fresh-faced Hitchcock-blonde-type Hollywood newbie befriends a post-car-accident amnesiac Rita Hayworth type and they search the high and low life of Tinseltown trying to solve the mystery of Rita's lost identity. They become lovers, then they swap identities. Ann Miller is their landlady. Then things get much weirder."

Twenty-five years later, I still can't come up with a more coherent description. Nor do I want one. The first chunk of the movie is highly stylized and deliberately dreamlike as Naomi Watts (in a stunner of a dual performance) gets introduced to us as Betty, a smalltown dance contest winner arriving at Los Angeles International Airport. Dewy with stars in her eyes and naïve to Hollywood's backbiting ways, she's just itching for movie stardom; Watts told the press that the look and style of Tippi Hedren (*The Birds*, *Marnie*) was an inspiration for playing her roles. But Watts's deft, chameleonlike performance as Betty/Diane is utterly original; that said, surely her Hedren-esque look and vibe in Lynch's movie helped account for Watts being rumored to star in a mid-2000s redo of *The Birds* that never achieved liftoff. Opposite the blonde Watts in *Mulholland Drive* is sultry, ravishing brunette Laura Harring as the amnesiac, duplicitous, mysterious Rita—an iconic Hollywood movie star's name she borrows from a movie poster for *Gilda*, the breakthrough 1940s film that turned Rita Hayworth into a star and legendary femme fatale.

A search for Rita's lost memories sends Betty and Rita on increasingly weird adventures through the Hollywood underbelly, including a quest for a woman named Diane Selwyn that ends up in finding a rotting corpse in the bed of a bungalow court dwelling, followed by an unnerving encounter with a demonic feathered entity living in a cloud of smoke behind a Sunset Boulevard greasy spoon diner, followed by a knockout musical sequence staged in a theater/nightclub called Club Silencio. Onstage, a seedy multilingual master of ceremonies keeps announcing, "No hay banda" (There is no band) and introduces a singer (Rebekah Del Rio) who spellbindingly performs Roy Orbison's classic "Crying" in Spanish before collapsing while her prerecorded vocals continue. There's no band; there is only illusion. The movie ascends to the realm of the fully surreal when Lynch takes us from a dream state to a dark reality: the two women, whose roles reverse, get torn apart by rivalry over film roles and by Camille's romance with a glib, mercurial movie director (Justin Theroux) for whom Betty auditions but whom Camille (formerly Rita but really Diane Selwyn—are you getting all this?) is about to marry. That triggers the emotionally strung-out blonde to hire a hitman to kill the woman she loves. Almost every character and incident we've seen in the first half of the film gets doubled and darkened in the second half. Allusions to Hitchcock (shifting identities, donning a blonde wig to look like another woman, subjective tracking shots, dream sequences, sexual tension and rivalries between blondes and brunettes, etc.) abound. So do references to such Hollywood-set films as *Sunset Boulevard*, *All About Eve*, and more. As a Hollywood exposé, as a dissection of the rotting of the so-called American Dream, as a darkly comedic Hitchcockian nightmare nightmare only the visionary David Lynch could conjure, *Mulholland Drive* is singular and singularly brilliant. ♟♟♟♟

DÉJÀ VU (2006)

An ATF agent travels back in time to undo a domestic terror attack while preventing the death of a woman with whom he has fallen in love.

THE MACGUFFIN: A time travel and surveillance program

There is no big mystery why *Déjà Vu* is my favorite movie directed by Tony Scott (*True Romance*, *Crimson Tide*, *The Hunger*). Underneath its big, sleek, frantically paced, gleefully ridiculous science-fiction-cum-forensic-crime-thriller-cum–suspense-thriller plot and special effects whiz-bang-ery is a surprisingly moving *Vertigo*-adjacent time-travel love story. Denzel Washington plays super competent, highly intuitive ATF Special Agent Doug Carlin, recruited to investigate the terrorist bombing of a ferry carrying US Navy sailors on leave and their families to Mardi Gras, leaving 543 people dead. (Of course, given the year the movie was made, the fictional event serves as a therapeutic stand-in to help assuage America's ongoing unresolved PTSD over the tragedies 9/11 and Hurricane Katrina.) New Orleans native Carlin is the smartest, most prepared, articulate guy in the room, which rankles some of his big-city coworkers (played by Adam Goldberg, Erika Alexander, and Bruce Greenwood). But Carlin is too impressive to ignore, so an FBI special agent (Val Kilmer) invites him to be part of a top-secret elite team probing the bombing using a time-bending crime prevention surveillance program that allows them to view events from the previous four days and six hours.

That's where Carlin gets the chance to study the movements of a stunning young woman named Claire Kuchevar (Paula Patton) reported dead in the ferry bombing. But hadn't he previously viewed Claire's decimated body during a forensic exam—and hadn't her corpse turned up *before* the bombing? As Carlin and the team study the satellite footage of the enchanting Claire in her home, his bristly, guarded pose weakens and, like James Stewart in *Vertigo* or, even more, like Dana Andrews in *Laura*, he develops a necrophiliac's romantic obsession for the dead girl murdered by the terrorist (Jim Caviezel, convincing as a sullen, unhinged Timothy McVeigh stand-in crackpot). When Carlin's efforts help track down the bomber and the case is to be closed, our hero convinces his colleagues to let him go back in time to prevent Claire's murder and the deaths of those aboard the doomed ferry.

Screenwriters Bill Marsilii (*The Wubbulous World of Dr. Seuss*) and Terry Rossio (*Pirates of the Caribbean*), who were paid a whopping five million dollars for their spec script, later called director Scott the wrong man for the job because he altered their "airtight" time-travel script to suit his preoccupation with making another of his governmental overreach, surveillance-obsessed movies rather than an action-packed science fiction flick. *Déjà Vu* won mixed reviews but connected with audiences due in large part to the performance of Washington, who exuded command, humor, and bristliness as his character navigates subtle and not-so-subtle racism and intra-agency bureaucracy. Even more impressive, he sold the painful longing of an impossible love story and helped finesse some of the plot absurdities. Watch the play of emotions wash over his face as he stares at that massive screen of Patton in the fleeting hours before her death—masterful movie star stuff. *Déjà Vu* delivers a touching romance along with its pyrotechnics. ♟♟♟

In *Déjà Vu*, ATF agent Denzel Washington itches to go back in time to rescue a dead beauty with whom he falls hopelessly in love.
Corbis Historical/Getty Images

PHANTOM THREAD (2017)

The regimented existence of a celebrated 1950s couturier gets upended by his fascination with a young waitress who becomes his lover, inspiration, and, perhaps, potential murderer.

THE MACGUFFIN: The mushrooms

Paul Thomas Anderson's exquisite and perverse psychological thriller wrapped around a love story is a Hitchcockian art film for connoisseurs. Conceived, directed, photographed, costumed, designed, acted, scored, and edited to a standard too rarely seen in contemporary American films, *Phantom Thread* rivals Hitchcock at his most delirious and opulent. In fact, although the writer-director told the press he took inspiration from Hitchcock's *Rebecca*, those who resonate with Hitchcock's work on a deeper level, as Anderson clearly does, will also feel the pull of undercurrents from *Suspicion*, *Notorious*, *Vertigo*, and *Marnie*. The film revolves around the relationship between a famed couturier named Reynolds Woodcock (is that close enough to Alfred Hitchcock for you?) and an enigmatic country inn waitress named Alma, embodied by Vicky Krieps (Alma was the name of Hitchcock's film collaborator and wife of over five decades).

The fastidious, impeccable Woodcock is a consummate creator—obsessively workaholic, a fanatic for detail, image, brand, and celebrated for rearranging the world (and, especially, women) to align with his aesthetic standards of beauty and perfection. It's a portrait of an artist as imperious, emotionally remote, selfish, moody, temperamental, full of hubris, and as Day-Lewis and Anderson subtly show us, fragile beneath his fanatically maintained persona. He also has major issues regarding his dead mother. Hmmm, does he sound a bit like any other artist depicted in films and theater (not named Alfred Joseph Hitchcock, that is)? The two main characters meet when Woodcock has just completed a creation for a longtime client of whom he's grown weary and dismissive. He takes an early morning jaunt in his aubergine-colored roadster and orders breakfast from country girl Alma at a cozy inn where she is a server. She wryly watches as he, instantly smitten, orders with comically absurd fussiness "a not-too-runny poached egg" atop a Welsh rarebit, "scones with butter, cream, and jam—not strawberry," a pot of lapsang tea, and sausages. The moment not only tells Alma (and us) exactly who Woodcock is but also who he wants others to think he is. It is also an act of seduction. The act works. Alma presents the bill with a written note, "For the hungry boy."

Soon, he sweeps the unlikely Alma into his obsessively curated life, transforming her into his mannequin, muse, and live-in lover. (Hitchcock performed similar Svengali-Trilby transformations with leading ladies Madeleine Caroll, Joan Fontaine, Grace Kelly, Vera Miles, Tippi Hedren—minus the lover aspect.) Initially, the more earthy Alma seems like someone of whom Woodcock will soon tire and then cruelly instruct his imposing, fiercely protective sister Cyril (Lesley Manville, predictably brilliant in a role analogous to Mrs. Danvers) to send packing. (Hitchcock's assistant Peggy Robertson and others performed this function in real life.) Cyril wants Alma gone too, but slowly Alma impresses her with her steely spine and ability to cut Woodcock down to size. When Alma prepares Woodcock a sumptuous feast as a token of love and wears for the occasion a frock she designed herself (see the mortifying costume party in *Rebecca*), Woodcock boorishly rejects her and her declaration of love. She reacts by picking poison mushrooms and knowingly feeding them to Woodcock before he is to present a princess's wedding gown. The power dynamic will shift more than once in the course of this audacious, bizarre evocation of a deeply complex pair of lovers who, in another era, could have been played by Ingrid Bergman and Cary Grant in the land of Hitchcock. And yet *Phantom Thread* is a gorgeous, darkly funny, deeply messed-up original contemporary masterwork from the heart and mind of the brilliant Paul Thomas Anderson. ♟♟♟♟

5 Tight Spot

A lifeboat in the middle of the Atlantic. A posh Manhattan apartment that initially seems large until violence, suspicion, and betrayals turn it stiflingly claustrophobic. A speeding car driven by someone too drunk or reckless to be trusted. The privacy of a shower stall invaded by an unhinged psycho with a butcher knife. An attic invaded by marauding birds. The fragile shelter of a public telephone booth during a massive avian attack. An innocent man confined to a prison cell; shown from a God's-eye point of view, the walls of the tiny cell appear to be closing in. These are just some of the confined spaces in which Hitchcock traps his characters not only to test their mettle and explore their capacity for loyalty and betrayal but also to assess their humanity – all the while allowing Hitchcock to demonstrate his technical prowess and psychological acuity.

According to Hitchcock, this obsession with confined space could be traced to a childhood trauma:

> I have a vague recollection of being four or five years old and being sent with a note to the local police station. After reading the note, a policeman took me to a cell and locked me in as a punishment for some mishap. I don't even know what it was for. The policeman never told me. I was probably unjustly incarcerated at the time. But, of course, a psychiatrist will always tell you that if you have a fear that is rooted in you and comes from something in your childhood, the moment you can go back to it and release it, all is well. It doesn't apply to me. I'm scared of everything.

As a character says in *Rope*, one of Hitchcock's most impressive experiments in the use of confined space, "Nobody ever feels really safe in the dark. Nobody who's ever a child, that is." That's the key. In his confined-space films, Hitchcock attempts to exorcise his own fears—fears that just happen to be universal.

THE FALLEN IDOL (1948)

The innocence of a lonely ambassador's son is shattered when he thinks he sees his beloved friend—the embassy's butler—killing his wife.

THE MACGUFFIN: The telegram

The life of eight-year-old Phillippe (Bobby Henrey), son of the French ambassador installed in the austere splendor of an embassy in London's famed Belgravia, looks posh from the outside looking in. Except he is achingly lonely because his busy father is often absent and his neglected mother is beset by various maladies, leaving Philippe mostly cared for by the embassy's spit-and-polish butler Baines, who enthralls his admiring young charge with tall tales of his supposedly adventurous and heroic past. Slipping away from the cloistered world of the embassy, Philippe spies Baines at a tea shop with Julie, the lovely embassy typist, who is in the process of breaking off their secret love affair. Philippe fully accepts Baines's explanation that Julie is his niece; later, Phillipe accidentally exposes the affair to cold, nasty Mrs. Baines, who impulsively scrambles to a high ledge to spy on Julie but, by fluke, leans against a window and plummets to her death. Young Phillippe believes Baines has murdered his wife and, desperate to protect his friend and father figure, inadvertently causes the police to doubt the butler's innocence. *The Fallen Idol*, scripted by William Templeton and Lesley Storm and based on Graham Greene's 1935 short story "The Basement Room," is told from Philippe's perspective. In this way, it becomes an exquisitely heartbreaking depiction of the loss of childhood innocence, that inevitable moment when exalted authority figures get exposed as betrayers—deceptive, frail, imperfect, all too human.

When one experiences the great works of Carol Reed—and *The Fallen Idol* is right up there with his *The Stars Look Down*, *Night Train to Munich*, *Odd Man Out*, and *Our Man in Havana*—one marvels at the director's craftsmanship, skill with actors, taste, and compassion. In *The Fallen Idol*, note how he builds palpable tension and suspense in such scenes as the hide-and-seek game with that mysterious woman who watches from the shadows. Or when Philippe escapes the embassy and wanders the night streets alone. Or that excruciating business with a possibly incriminating telegram. These are moments that make one wonder why Reed has not been as exalted and celebrated as Hitchcock. One probable reason is Reed's never having been championed by the *auteurists*, who prefer directors whose output is primarily confined to specific genres, identifiable by repeated visual signatures and motifs and an apparent worldview. After all, what to do with Reed's six-Oscar-winning musical *Oliver!* or the dull nobility of his much-nominated historical epic *The Agony and the Ecstasy*? But being difficult to box in and file away should not disqualify Reed from being acknowledged as a master filmmaker. It's hard to imagine

The innocence of an ambassador's lonely young son (Bobby Henrey) is betrayed by callous, self-absorbed adults as a revered butler's estranged wife (Sonia Dresdel).
Hulton Archive/Moviepix/Getty Images

CHAPTER 5 TIGHT SPOT

performances any greater than those of his handpicked cast, including Bobby Henrey (who made only one other film) as Phillipe, Ralph Richardson as the idealized butler, and the exquisite Michèle Morgan as the butler's lover. *The Fallen Idol* is suspenseful, atmospheric, touching, unmissable Hitchcockian viewing. ♟♟♟♟

THE WINDOW (1949)

No one takes a highly imaginative young latchkey kid seriously when he tries to get the police or his parents to believe that he saw a neighbor couple kill a man. Is he the couple's next victim?

THE MACGUFFIN: A lonely boy's overactive imagination

Ten-year-old Bobby Driscoll (*So Dear to My Heart*) is excellent as Tommy Woodry, a twelve-year-old tenement kid who has witnessed the couple upstairs, the Kellersons (*Citizen Kane's* Paul Stewart and *Strangers on a Train*'s Ruth Roman, both effective), kill a man, but because of his reputation as a fanciful tale teller, Tommy can't even convince his parents (Arthur Kennedy, Barbara Hale) to believe him, nor, when mom gets called away to tend to a sick relative, to help them realize that their own son may be the couple's next victim. Shot on a tight budget on gritty New York locations, *The Window* is a taut, no-frills, heart-in-your-mouth melodrama that keeps one hoping that its likeable, lonely lead character will survive the dangers that get thrown at him for almost the film's entire seventy-three-minute running time.

The movie has several Hitchcock connections. Its director, Ted Tetzlaff, was Hitchcock's cinematographer on *Notorious*, Roy Webb (*Notorious*) composed the musical score, and the magazine story on which it is based, "The Boy Cried Murder," is by Cornell Woolrich, whose "It Had to Be Murder" Hitchcock turned into *Rear Window*. Its screenwriter, Mel Dinelli, adapted *The Spiral Staircase*, a project that producer David O. Selznick envisioned for Hitchcock and Ingrid Bergman until both turned it down. Those aspects aside, *The Window* features several expertly effective, claustrophobia-inducing suspense sequences—set in a dangerously tumbledown tenement building, another on a fire

Overly imaginative city kid (Bobby Driscoll) runs afoul of a murderous adult (Paul Stewart) out to make him his next victim in *The Window*.
Michael Ochs/Moviepix/Getty Images

escape. Perhaps the most frightening and persuasive element of *The Window* lies in how ruthlessly it piles so much jeopardy onto a poor, sad little kid. But the most crushing aspect of the only child's life is the cycle of poverty that grinds down him, his family, and the other tough, hardscrabble neighborhood kids who ridicule him. This strong, unpretentious little movie packs a punch, delivers its thrills, and moves on, leaving us to contemplate the aftermath. ♟♟♟

WITNESS FOR THE PROSECUTION (1958)

The verdict in a man's trial for the murder of a wealthy woman who made him her beneficiary hinges entirely on the testimony of the man's secretive wife.

THE MACGUFFIN: The dead woman's fortune

In the hands of the wrong moviemaker, a courtroom melodrama can be deadly dull cinema. As Hitchcock would have it, "They're a prime example of photographs of people talking." Overrun by the constant imposition of terrible ideas from producer David O. Selznick, Hitchcock lost the battle that reduced *The Paradine Case* to a turgid, talky, overproduced legal tribunal as the producer wanted, not the labyrinthine, erotic exercise in sexual obsession Hitchcock envisioned. The only other courtroom drama Hitchcock had previously directed was *Murder!* seventeen years earlier, and after *The Paradine Case* he never did another. The director also avoided whodunits of the Agatha Christie variety because he considered them more appealing to the intellect than to emotion. So it is peculiar that when the great Billy Wilder chose to direct a movie version of Christie's play *Witness for the Prosecution* he talked about it as his experiment in wading into Hitchcock territory that, in the end, so bored him that he never wanted to do another either. *What???*

In any case, you'd hardly detect any hint of Wilder's ennui in the superbly atmospheric and claustrophobic scenes set in Old Bailey as an apparently innocent young Brit (Tyrone Power, convincing neither as young nor English) on trial for the murder of a widow. The movie features all the pitfalls of the genre—the (mostly) single set, one witness after the other questioned by showy lawyers, and endless talk. But Wilder stages the action like a pro, and cinematographer Russell Harlan (*Red River*, *Gun Crazy*) and editor Daniel Mandell (*The Best Years of Our Lives*) never let the proceedings drag. Christie's play offers surprise after surprise, but the script by Wilder and Harry Kurnitz is razor sharp, loaded with biting dialogue delivered with verve and old-time star power by the likes of Marlene Dietrich (of Hitchcock's *Stage Fright*, as Power's wife), three-time Hitchcock scene stealer John Williams (as a lawyer), Una O'Conner (a Scottish maid), Elsa Lanchester (a ferocious nurse), and best of all *Jamaica Inn*'s Charles Laughton as Power's lecherous, cigar-and-brandy-loving defense attorney afflicted with a faulty heart. On the movie's theatrical release, ticket buyers were warned against entering the theater during the final ten minutes. As movie material goes, *Witness for the Prosecution* may not have exactly been Hitchcock's cup of tea, but Wilder's version is so smooth and satisfying that it is difficult to see how even Hitchcock could have done it much better. ♟♟♟♙

23 PACES TO BAKER STREET (1956)

An embittered, blind American playwright in London overhears what sounds like a kidnap and extortion plan involving a child. The police doubt his story, so he convinces his estranged fiancée and manservant to help him foil the plan.

THE MACGUFFIN: A perfume-wearing nurse

This London-set thriller was scripted by Nigel Balchin (*The Man Who Never Was*) based on the 1938 novel *Warrant for X* by Philip MacDonald, a screenwriter on Hitchcock's *Rebecca*. It tries clumsily to rework elements of *Rear Window* and *The Man Who Knew Too Much*, elements that Hitchcock and company appeared to do so smoothly and seamlessly. Competently but unimaginatively directed by legendarily hard-edged veteran Henry Hathaway (*Niagara*, *Kiss of Death*), nicely acted, handsomely mounted, the film is populated by such delightful supporting cast eccentrics as Estelle Winwood as a barmaid and Isobel Elsom as a grande dame who supplies the hero a clue or two. What the movie cries out for is the brilliance of Hitchcock putting his spin on a screenplay by, say, John Michael Hayes working at the level of *Rear Window* or Ernest Lehman giving it the impeccable plotting, polish, and acidic wit of *North by Northwest*. So often does *23 Paces to Baker Street* (spoiler: this movie has nothing to do with Sherlock Holmes) recall Hitchcock movies that it's almost impossible to keep oneself from imagining the short-fused, combative playwright role in the hands of Cary Grant or even James Stewart, rather than stolid, ever-grumpy, self-enchanted Van Johnson, who hardly radiates intelligence, wit, or literary prowess. And, as for the movie's Grace Kelly role—the underappreciated, underestimated girlfriend—how fascinating might it have been to see Grant matched with the female star of *23 Paces to Baker Street*, Vera Miles (whom Hitchcock directed on TV and in supporting roles in *The Wrong Man* and *Psycho*, but whose pregnancy cost her the starring role in *Vertigo* and "the new Grace Kelly" big-star buildup the director planned for her), costumed in true "Hitchcock blonde" mode by Edith Head and accompanied by a romantic and suspenseful Bernard Herrmann score? *23 Paces to Baker Street* has some good things going for it aside from Miles—handsome color cinematography by Milton R. Krasner (*All About Eve*), elegant art direction by Maurice Ransford (*Lifeboat, Laura*) and Lyle Wheeler (*Gone with the Wind, Rebecca*). The movie also boasts several decent suspense sequences, including a vertiginous one in which the hero is lured high up into a bombed-out building and another, a showdown with the villain in the blind hero's dark apartment, a kind of dry run for a similar moment in *Wait Until Dark*. But unlike *Rear Window*, *23 Paces to Baker Street* too often feels stodgy, talky, and stage-bound. With so many characters constantly knocking on the hero's door, saying their piece, then leaving, how can the action ever break into a run instead of a crawl? And without an unforgettably nasty villain to jeer, where's the tension and suspense? We don't want our Hitchcockian thrillers to merely pace their way to Baker Street, we want them to run headlong. ♟♟♟

CHASE A CROOKED SHADOW (1958)

A man claiming to be her brother descends on a diamond heiress living in Spain. The only hitch—her real brother died in a car crash and this one is trying to drive her mad.

THE MACGUFFIN: The missing brother

This one has an intriguing setup, anyway. Handsome, mysterious Ward Prescott (Richard Todd of Hitchcock's *Stage Fright*) turns up at the swank Costa Brava Spanish villa of the woman he claims is his sister, diamond heiress Kimberly Prescott (the ever breathy, earnest Anne Baxter of Hitchcock's *I Confess*). Although Ward is charming, persuasive, and has letters of reference and a valid passport—why, his framed photo even sits on the heroine's bedside nightstand!—Kimberly alerts the police inspector Vargas (Herbert Lom) that that a car crash claimed the life of the real Ward, her race-car driver brother, a year before. Meanwhile, Ward protests to Lom that Kimberly, who also lost their diamond-mine-owner father to suicide a year previously, is not acting like herself. Besides, Ward knows exactly how to fix Kimberly's choice of morning pick-me-up drink, owns a cigar box his sister gifted to him, and even drives the correct car like a champion—her *brother's* car. Ward, who explains his long absence as due to his having spent months in a coma after his car crash, even gets positively identified by Kimberly's favorite Uncle Chandler (Alexander Knox). Vargas thinks Kimberly is unstable, to put it delicately. Who's gaslighting who? The more Ward piles up his proof, the more suspicious, melodramatic, and overwrought Kimberly grows (and the more scenery Baxter chews). While the suspense, contrivances, and suspects (including Faith Brook as Ward's mysterious friend Mrs. Whitman) multiply—some of them painfully obvious to anyone who's ever sat through such a thoroughly sub-Hitchcockian B-level lady-in-peril thriller as this one—there are giggles and pleasures to be had. Many of the giggles come when Kimberly absconds to a beach house below her villa when she fancies her enemies plan to drown her and steal her millions. Among the pleasures is a white-knuckle speeding car sequence obviously shot without tricks or stunt doubles but with Todd at the wheel and Baxter appearing genuinely frightened in the passenger seat. At the end the film's producer, Douglas Fairbanks Jr., addresses the audience, Hitchcock style, announcing, "In Northern Spain, there's an old proverb, 'To keep a secret is to keep a friend.' So we would appreciate it very much if you'd join with us and not tell anybody how *Chase a Crooked Shadow* ends." He forgets to add, "Even if you figure it all out way before the movie ends." Michael Anderson (*Around the World in 80 Days*, *The Naked Edge*) directs indifferently, and the fatally humorless dialogue and dramaturgy must be blamed on David Osborn (*Murder, She Said*) and Charles Sinclair (*77 Sunset Strip* episodes). This one wants to be like Hitchcock but lacks a powerhouse script and the directorial know-how to put it over. If you want to see what this film might have been, then get your hands on a copy of the hauntingly beautiful, deeply mysterious 1964 Hindi film *Kohraa* (*Fog*), which melds elements of *Rebecca*, *Gaslight*, and even *Cast a Crooked Shadow* into a singular work of art. ♟♟

THE SERVANT (1964)

Perverse mind games between a newly hired manservant and his lazy, wealthy employer spiral into role reversals and mental collapse, especially ignited by the arrival of the sensual housemaid masquerading as the servant's sister.

THE MACGUFFIN: The class system

In the mid-1960s, Alfred Hitchcock was reportedly eager to work on an original thriller with brilliant and notoriously prickly playwright Harold Pinter (*The Birthday Party*, *The Caretaker*) but it was not to be. One can easily envision what Hitchcock might have done with Pinter's claustrophobic, horrific, darkly malicious *The Servant*; that said, it is difficult to imagine anyone else making a more menacing—let alone better—film from Pinter's screenplay based on Robin Maugham's confessional novella than director Joseph Losey did, armed with the ideally cast and perfectly matched Dirk Bogarde (at the top of his estimable game) and James Fox (in a powerful movie debut) in the starring roles. The impeccable Bogarde *is* Barrett, a professional manservant who becomes the live-in valet, housekeeper, tastemaker, nursemaid, and de facto wife to Tony, a good-looking, lazy, aristocratic, day-drinking cipher recently moved into a London townhouse and living comfortably off a private income from his insane and wealthy parents. Tony feels superior to Barrett because of unearned privilege and is launching a vague plan to build low-cost housing that will involve destroying a swath of a jungle in Brazil.

Two women stand between Barrett and Tony's undercurrent of studiedly repressed flirtation and sadomasochistic homoeroticism, although Robin Maugham's personal tale of sexuality has been straightwashed and rendered as subtext, apparently to protect the sensibilities of 1960s audiences. There's Tony's posh, nasty, oddly asexual fiancée, Susan (Wendy Craig), who loathes/lusts-after Barrett as much for his lower social class as for her envy of his unhealthy hold on Tony. Then there's Vera (Sarah Miles, sultrier and even spookier than usual), whom Barrett introduces as his sister and invites her to become Tony's live-in maid… with benefits. Once Vera calculatedly seduces Tony and lets him make love to her atop the island in his kitchen, the film gets exponentially stranger and more nightmarish. Barrett and Vera's seductive, parasitic plan becomes clear as Tony devolves into alcoholism, helplessness, codependency, and self-loathing.

As with the more recent *Parasite* and *Saltburn*, *The Servant* offers a scathing critique of the decaying class system. Losey's film, spectacularly shot by Douglas Slocombe (*The L-Shaped Room*) with a heavy emphasis on mirrors, Dutch angles, and a Diane Arbus–esque view of its side characters, manages to conjure not only Hitchcock but also Buñuel and Fellini. It's a film emblematic of what critic Pauline Kael derided as the "Come-Dressed-As-the-Sick-Soul-of-Europe Parties" arthouse movie genre of the 1960s and 1970s (see *L'Avventura*, *La Notte*, *La Dolce Vita*); it's certainly one of the more depraved examples. It operates on the level of a psychological horror film, a pitch-black comedy, a satire, a meditation on the codependence of predators and prey, and the weird interplay of sadomasochistic master and servant games. By those standards, *The Servant* is pretty much untouchable. ♟♟♟♟

DUEL (1971)

After a businessman passes a truck on a two-lane road, his trip becomes a nightmare because the truck driver seems hell-bent on getting revenge.

THE MACGUFFIN: The anonymous truck

The young Steven Spielberg's most Hitchcockian movie is his first. Made as a TV movie-of-the-week but released after its TV run with padded footage in some theaters in the United States and Europe, *Duel* is most compelling as an example of how energetic, relentless, and resourceful the fledgling director could be in executing the promise of a primal, no-frills survivalist premise. Dennis Weaver plays David Mann, a dweeby businessman cruising along in a red Plymouth Valiant on a two-lane desert highway who decides to zoom past a mammoth grunge-covered tanker truck. Big mistake. Caught in a classic battle of incredible shrinking man versus toxic Macho man, our beleaguered everyman hero spends the rest of the movie in a deadly cat-and-mouse death race fighting the truck's (we never see much of the driver) aggressive tailgating, attempts to force him off the road, and shoving him right into the path of an oncoming speeding train.

That's basically the long and the short of the movie, scripted by Richard Matheson from his story first published in *Playboy* magazine. And yet, so long as Spielberg keeps his foot jammed on the pedal and he and cinematographer Jack A. Marta ramp things up with tricky camera angles and sharp editing, *Duel* works like gangbusters, especially when it stays in its Hitchcockian lane by letting sound and image speak louder than dialogue. Less successful are those interludes given over to Mann's inner dialogue musing on such matters as the thin line between civilization and "the jungle." They sound preachy and overwrought, in the style of some of the more dated *Twilight Zone* episodes.

Duel is pretty much a one-man show for Weaver, until the script forces him to make a detour or two en route—including a humdinger when a shaken Mann pulls into a roadside café thinking he's rid himself of that menacing truck and its maniacal trucker. The camera tracks him into the café, into the rest room, and back out toward the diner's front window: the hulking truck looms large across the street. (Recall fugitive secretary Janet Leigh nervously trading in her old car at the used car lot in *Psycho* when she spots across the street the menacing highway patrol cop who has been trailing her.) Meanwhile, Mann nervously appraises the diners at their tables, a moment that tingles with the unspoken question: which of these people wants to kill me? Spielberg has talked of *Duel* being "like *Psycho* or *The Birds*, just on wheels." That probably sounded great during a studio pitch meeting, but *Duel* plays closer to *Straw Dogs* on wheels. It's when *Duel* veers off-road that it tends to go off-kilter. There's a phone call to his wife, for instance, that reveals Mann as browbeaten—Dennis Weaver's presence and astute performance already convey this quality—but Spielberg and Matheson hammer home the point by depicting the parents bickering about Mann's passivity when another man hassled his wife; meanwhile, we see the Mann kids preferring the company of space-age toys. Anyway, the filthy, scary, villainous monster truck is the real star of the movie. So it's only when the hero stands up to the bully and reclaims his pride that we become fully caught up in Spielberg's wild ride into a peculiarly American brand of darkness. ♟♟♟

BLOW OUT (1981)

A sex worker who witnesses the assassination of a presidential candidate and a sound recordist who accidentally tapes that assassination find themselves in grave danger.

THE MACGUFFIN: An audio recording of a political assassination

Brian De Palma takes inspiration from Hitchcock's *Rear Window*, Antonioni's *Blow-Up*, and a movie inspired by both of those, Coppola's *The Conversation* but comes up with something so perfectly cinematic, stylized, and artificial that it's positively movie mad. It's a suspense thriller featuring John Travolta as Jack Terry, a Philadelphia-based soundman for sleazy softcore porn hits with such titles as *Blood Beach Two* and *Bordello of Blood*. Jack's current task is to record the blood-curdling scream-of-a-lifetime for a new skin flick titled *Coed Frenzy*—a soul-shaking, wall-rattling howl from a young beauty at the moment of her death. One night finds Jack on a bridge recording hooting owls and other ordinary evening sounds.

Along comes a car, a tire blows out, and the car swerves wildly, sending it plummeting into the river. Jack leaps over the bridge railing and rescues from the car a young woman named Sally (Nancy Allen), and it turns out that the car's driver was a rising-star potential presidential candidate. When Jack listens to his recording of the incident, he hears a gunshot, then the blowout. All signs point to a Watergate-level assassination scandal, a murder cover-up that riffs on the unfortunate events surrounding the drowning of twenty-eight-year-old political campaign strategist Mary-Jo Kopechne when she was a passenger in a car Senator Ted Kennedy drove off a bridge in Massachusetts. Considering the movies that inspired *Blow Out*, the signs also point to its being a serious paranoid thriller.

I mean, *Blow-Up* not only questioned whether a photographer saw a murder but whether all reality is an illusion. *Blow Out* isn't that at all, which isn't to say that it's not superbly made (just watch the scene in which Travolta pieces together what happened when he looks at photos of the fatal car crash against his sound recordings of the event). What's more, the Hitchcockian elements are strong and organic—especially a breakneck chase through Philadelphia during a celebration of the Liberty Bell. It's De Palma's best screenplay to date, a big help to the rising star that was Travolta (in one of his standout performances), Nancy Allen (warm and delightful), and the lowlifes

A fashion photographer accidentally films a murder in Antonioni's *Blow-Up*. A movie soundman (John Travolta) accidentally records a murder in De Palma's *Blow Out*.
Corbis Historical/Getty Images

played delightfully by John Lithgow and Dennis Franz. For once, De Palma seems so self-assured that he has fun *with* his audience and his characters, not despite them. More of this, please. ♟♟♟♟

ROAD GAMES (1981)

Suspicious that a man in a van is killing young women and dumping their bodies en route, a truck driver, helped by a hitchhiker, entices the murderer into cat-and-mouse games to catch him out.

THE MACGUFFIN: Guitar strings as a murder weapon

Road Games is a well-made, nicely acted, straight-ahead *Rear Window* on wheels—or is it Spielberg's *Duel* meets *Rear Window?*—from Hitchcock devotee and Australian director Richard Franklin (*Psycho II*). Stacy Keach stars as an amiably quirky, poetry-quoting American truck driver named Pat Quid, assigned to deliver a freezer full of pork along the Nullabor Plain, a flat, desolate stretch of Outback desert running from Melbourne to Perth, Australia. Passing the time by cracking jokes and inventing tales of the lives of people in passing cars, to amuse himself and Boswell, his beloved dingo road mate, the deeper Quid drives into the isolated desert, the more certain he grows that the driver of a green van is killing young female hitchhikers.

Unable to prove anything to the police, he finds an ally in a feisty and intelligent American hitchhiking vagabond (Jamie Lee Curtis) who joins Quid's cat-and-mouse attempts to catch out the murderer. But both characters appear to be holding their cards close to the chest. Can they possibly trust each other? Screenwriter Everett de Roche (*Patrick*) skillfully leans into many recognizable Hitchcockian hallmarks—paranoia, obsession, deadpan conversations about various forms of violent murder, voyeurism, slow-burning sexual tension between the male and female characters, and sustained suspense—building up to an oddball, funny, yet satisfying payoff.

Despite how *Road Games* was made during the "slasher mania" era of moviemaking, Franklin and de Roche build their film through tension not bloodletting, peppering the narrative with cleverly integrated allusions to *North by Northwest*, *Psycho*, and *Frenzy*. The movie's stunt coordinator, Stunt Rock, doubles as the murderer, and he's aces. The chemistry between Keach and Curtis (not only the daughter of *Psycho*'s own Janet Leigh but whose character is named Hitch) only adds to the enjoyment of this stripped-down, no-nonsense thriller, which at 101 minutes wisely does not overstay its welcome. Even so, we find ourselves asking such distracting questions as, why are the two stars of this Australian movie both American? Mostly, though, the performances and the film's buoyant sense of humor keep us amused and distracted. And, when all else fails, that dog playing Boswell is a natural-born scene stealer. ♟♟♟

BODY DOUBLE (1984)

House-sitting for a friend, a struggling, claustrophobia-afflicted actor engulfs himself in a murder plot after spying on and stalking a beautiful neighbor. An adult film star helps him uncover a conspiracy.

THE MACGUFFIN: The identity of the voyeur/stalker/murderer

Brian De Palma has directed some technically impressive Hitchcock-style suspense movies. *Body Double* is one of the lesser of those. De Palma has also directed and written some movies that are as emotionally exhilarating as they are visceral and technically dazzling. *Body Double*, scripted by De Palma, is also not one of those. Brian De Palma could, in fact, drive a movie lover (let alone a Hitchcock lover) psycho. On the one hand, *Body Double* displays the director's love of excess and Day-Glo visual pizazz. This movie is one of his more delirious deep dips into Hitchcockian style—it's as though *Rear Window*, *Vertigo*, and *Frenzy* snorted coke and threw a *giallo* party on 1980s-era Cinemax After Dark. On the other hand, the movie's obsession with sleazy, performative, S&M-lite sex is as adolescent and goofy as its plotting. Craig Wasson (*Four Friends*) plays Jake Scully, a struggling actor and slow-witted dupe who lands himself in serious trouble when house-sitting a modernist Hollywood Hills home for a fellow actor (Gregg Henry) whom he barely knows. With way too much time on his hands, Jake, a recovering alcoholic who suffers from acute claustrophobia, becomes obsessed with peering through a telescope into the bedroom window of a sultry neighbor across the way, Gloria Revelle (Deborah Shelton, most assuredly not playing any relation to Hitchcock's life mate Alma Reville), who performs a ritualistic, seductive nightly striptease. When Jake spots another creep who is also peeping on this modern-day "Miss Torso," he impulsively follows her, eager to play Sir Galahad by warning and protecting her. Or something.

De Palma's technical virtuosity and his curiously stunted concept of screen sexuality are simultaneously on display in a well-filmed and -choreographed sequence of Jake stalking Gloria around a luxe Beverly Hills boutique mall while this second weird dude is also following her. Another of De Palma's more effective moments involves the choreographed movements of several characters on the beach in the foreground while, in the background, other characters move around various balconies of a Santa Monica hotel; it recalls Hitchcock's direction of James Stewart in his wheelchair in the foreground while he spies on the fellow tenants of his Greenwich Village courtyard in *Rear Window*. But, when Wasson and Shelton finally lock lips, those 360-degree pirouettes done by De Palma and cinematographer around the two actors have aged poorly; they're cheap and unearned, a bratty film student's wank rather than the profoundly emotional moment they mark in *Vertigo*. Terrific performances from charismatic players might have compensated for the film's shortcomings. But although Wasson is good in other films, here, with his countless furtive side-to-side glances, he is a wet blanket, Shelton is merely spectacularly decorative, and the wig and makeup worn by the other voyeur, the mysterious Native American, are dead giveaways. But everything clicks when Melanie Griffith (the voluptuous, expertly comic lookalike daughter of Tippi Hedren of Hitchcock's *The Birds* and *Marnie*) arrives on the scene to deliver a star-making turn as X-rated film queen Holly Body. Griffith said yes to a role spurned by Jamie Lee Curtis, Carrie Fisher, Linda Hamilton, and even such porn film performers as Annette Haven; that's a good thing because it is difficult to imagine those others being as sexy, innocent, hilarious, and droll, especially when Griffith applies her patented baby doll spin on such dialogue as "I have a routine that's a sure 10 on the Peter Meter.... I'm known far and wide for that little bit of business."

A pity that things didn't work out for Kurt Russell, an early candidate to play Scully, because he and Griffith might have lifted the whole movie, which progressively becomes more ludicrous when you want it to become savagely satirical. But De Palma can't seem to get out of his own way. He reportedly wanted *Body Double* to be Hollywood's first mainstream movie to feature unsimulated sex; Columbia Pictures not only slammed the brakes on that notion but also, when *Body Double* tanked, the studio canceled two additional films de Palma was contacted to make under a multifilm deal. After this and the calamitous *The Bonfire of the Vanities*, De Palma's career never quite recovered, and he hasn't been able to get a movie financed since 2019. That's our loss. Because when the guy cooks, he's really onto something wild. ♟♟♩

Playing adult film star Holly Body, Melanie Griffith steals the show in De Palma's *Body Double*.
Corbis Historical/Getty Images

APARTMENT ZERO (1988)

The sexually repressed manager of a struggling Buenos Aires revival movie theater becomes obsessed with his mysterious, charismatic roommate when he begins suspecting him of being a cold-blooded political assassin.

THE MACGUFFIN: The roommate's secret bag

Although almost entirely (and unfairly) forgotten today, Argentinian screenwriter-director Martin Donovan and coscreenwriter David Koepp's (*Panic Room*, *Black Bag*) delightfully perverse, tense, and claustrophobic psychological thriller—a heady mélange of Hitchcock, Polanski, Almodóvar, and Pinter, with undercurrents of Patricia Highsmith–style homoeroticism and overtones of *Kiss of the Spider Woman*—created a stir on the arthouse circuit back in the day. Colin Firth plays Adrian LeDuc, an introverted, sexually conflicted lover of Golden Age stars and films. For him, the walls are closing in. At the Buenos Aires revival movie theater he manages, such films he worships as *Rebel Without a Cause*, *Touch of Evil*, and *Seven Samurai* are no longer drawing big crowds. With his mother hospitalized and losing her sanity, loner Adrian struggles to put food on the table and to make the monthly rent on his apartment filled with movie memorabilia and portraits of such Hollywood gay icons as Montgomery Clift, Elizabeth Taylor, and James Dean. Meanwhile, he annoys and intrigues his nosy neighbors—a transvestite, a lonely young wife, an eccentric pair of British sisters—who find him stuffy and standoffish. Enter the Oscar to his Felix, the charismatic, mysterious, carnal Jack Carney (Hart Bochner), his new roommate who, announces Adrian, possesses "a certain James Dean *je ne sais quoi*." Instantly, the sexy and more than slightly creepy Jack—armed with a sociopath's ability to appear to be all things to all people—hopelessly beguiles Adrian and seduces, sometimes literally, several of his fellow tenants. Unfortunately, the movie's grip on the viewer wobbles just when it ought to shift into overdrive; Adrian begins to shield Jack from the police and obsesses over him even more intensely when his seductive roommate is revealed as a stone-cold mercenary killer and full-on psychopath.

(More than a bit like Joan Fontaine's character overlooking Cary Grant's unsavory and selfish characteristics in *Suspicion*). Slow and sometimes awkwardly directed, *Apartment Zero* falters and frustrates when it reminds one of other, better movies. Still, it is wonderfully acted by Firth who sparks palpable screen chemistry with Bochner, who has rarely been better cast. ♟♟♟

MISERY (1990)

A novelist, rescued by a former nurse from a car crash and brought to a backwoods cabin to recuperate, discovers the controlling, violent nature of the nurse, who calls herself the writer's biggest fan.

THE MACGUFFIN: The subject of a popular writer's next novel

Long before *Baby Reindeer*'s obsessive, terrifying, and pitiable stalker Martha Scott (brilliantly portrayed by Jessica Gunning) came the also brilliant Kathy Bates as the fictional Annie Wilkes in the popular film version of Stephen King's bestselling novel *Misery*. King's novel is about a famed gothic romance writer (his heroine's name is, satirically, Misery) getting imprisoned and tortured by an insane superfan. With its simple, intriguing premise, nearly one-location setting, claustrophobic snowbound backwoods Colorado cabin, and enigmatic heroine, this might have been the kind of slam-bang, straightforward material that—had the book been published back in, say, the 1970s—might have captured Hitchcock's attention. Especially if he were "running for cover," tackling the sort of material he said he would turn to "when your batteries run dry, when you are out creatively, and you have to go on. That's what I call running for cover. Take a comparatively successful play [or novel] that requires no great creative effort on your part and make it. To keep your hand in, that's all." Now, *Misery* hounds, don't get us wrong. This is a movie made to a highly satisfying professional standard by director Rob Reiner (*Stand by Me*) from a William Goldman screenplay. It is difficult to imagine an any more satisfying version of King's tale of a former nurse Annie (Kathy Bates) who digs out her all-time favorite author Paul Sheldon (James Caan) from a snowbank after he's crashed his car, nurses him back to health, but turns obsessively volatile and dangerous when she learns that Paul is killing off her most beloved character in the financially successful but creatively stultifying series of hack, mushy historical potboilers that have made him a success. With Paul's world of fans, his Manhattan agent (Lauren Bacall), and a local sheriff and his wife (Richard Farnsworth, Frances Sternhagen) believing him dead, the balance of the movie is pretty much no more or less than a sadistic two-hander hinging—like *What Ever Happened to Baby Jane?*—on the imbalance of power between the emotionally unstable nurse and her irritable, beefy but physically dependent, almost passive captive. The character's inherently passive predicament—the maiden-in-distress aspect—may have been one of the reasons the role got turned down by many young leading men of the day, including William Hurt, Kevin Kline, Michael Douglas, Harrison Ford, Robert De Niro, Al Pacino, Robert Redford, Dustin Hoffman, and more. Or perhaps some of these gents hoped *Misery* might be reworked, Hitchcock style, into something more complex than just a cracking good horror thriller. Nevertheless, the movie became a financial hit and a fan classic and won the then little-known Kathy Bates a Best Actress Oscar for her terrifying but nuanced portrayal of toxic fandom. For most viewers, *Misery* didn't need to be anything more than one hell of a horror thriller, but in Hitchcock's hands, it could have been. ♟♟♟♙

PANIC ROOM (2002)

Spending their first night in their Manhattan brownstone mansion, a wealthy recent divorcée and her teenage daughter face off against a trio of home invaders.

THE MACGUFFIN: Three million dollars hidden in a brownstone's underground safe

Jodie Foster nabbed one of the better opportunities of her adult career when a knee injury forced Nicole Kidman to bow out of this thriller from director David Fincher, whose *The Game*, *Se7en*, and

Zodiac announced him as, arguably, modern Hollywood's foremost Hitchcockian. Fincher himself described *Panic Room* as "*Rear Window* meets *Straw Dogs*." He knows whereof he speaks. The setup of *Panic Room*, which opens with Saul Bass–style titles floating against the sides of Manhattan buildings à la *North by Northwest*, exemplifies Hitchcockian simplicity itself. On their first night in the historic multistory Manhattan brownstone that is their new residence, newly divorced Meg Altman (Foster) and her diabetic teen daughter Sarah (Kristen Stewart) call it a night when they can't figure out how to switch on their state-of-the-art home security system. Out of a thunderous rainstorm emerge three contentious thieves (Forest Whitaker, Jared Leto, and Dwight Yoakam playing variations on the home invaders familiar from *Lady in a Cage* and *Wait Until Dark*); expecting to find the house empty, they easily break in hoping to steal the three million dollars supposedly stashed in the paranoid previous owner's safe buried in the floor of a concrete-and-steel-clad fortress within the house, a "safe room," stocked with a bank of surveillance monitors revealing views of every room in the house (think of it as another *Rear Window* callback), unfortunately not yet connected. There is water, fire blankets, food supplies, and, yes, a phone—also not yet connected. Once the thieves begin trashing the townhouse with hammers and drills, their increasingly violent, bloody bickering sends mother and daughter to seal themselves in the panic room, screenwriter David Koepp's (*Apartment Zero*, *Jurassic Park*) contemporary equivalent of Hitchcock's one-location exercises in psychological tension. That's when Fincher and his cinematographers (Conrad W. Hall replaced Darius Khondji when the latter and Fincher disagreed over the film's look) go wild with the bravura camera flourishes, gliding up and down three levels of the townhouse in one go, zooming through keyholes, burrowing though walls to chase crucial electrical and phone wiring. Fincher also ratchets up the vibe of immersive terror with such ambient sounds as creaking floors, torrential rainfall, and breaking glass. Even if we tire of the gamesmanship between home defender Foster and her ruthless attackers, we can revel in those long takes when the camera prowls through the gloomily lit brownstone, which becomes a gorgeous melancholy character all its own. Considering the movie's

David Fincher's home invasion robbery thriller *Panic Room* leaves only one hiding place for mom Jodie Foster and daughter Kristen Stewart.
Moviepix/Getty Images

relatively thin and limited premise, Foster and Whitaker are especially good. She excels as the wily, sad, frazzled, intelligent, angry ex-wife of a pharmaceuticals giant and fiercely protective mother. He is the basically decent, financially strapped home security systems expert and father trying to get in and out of this heist gone sideways without inflicting human harm but caught between two violently unhinged (but not especially compelling) cohorts. And with the meticulous Fincher constantly raising the stakes and filming the narrative like a maestro, though *Panic Room* may only be a popcorn movie, at least its gourmet popcorn. ♟♟♟

PHONE BOOTH (2003)

A psychopathic assassin threatens to shoot a man if he steps out of a phone booth in the middle of Times Square in New York City.

THE MACGUFFIN: A sniper's obsession with a lowly show-business publicist

A man waits expectantly by a midtown Manhattan phone booth. He's Stu Shepard (Colin Farrell, radiating raw talent and charisma), a fast-talking, narcissistic, low-level publicist who regularly uses this booth to make the calls that he doesn't want his wife to detect on their cell phone bill. The pay phone—apparently one of the last phone booths standing in a city of cell phones—jangles. Stu grabs the receiver. But it's not one of his actor or musician clients like the budding actress (Katie Holmes) he's trying to get into bed. Instead, the voice on the other end is a psychopathic serial sniper (an impressive Kiefer Sutherland, better heard than seen) who knows all about Stu and his side chick(s), his wife (Rhada Mitchell), his daily routine, even his private phone numbers.

Croons the mellow-voiced, utterly bonkers assassin, "I'm someone who enjoys watching you.... Don't even think about leaving that booth.... I'm aiming at you right now." If Stu hangs up, he's a dead man; to prove he isn't bluffing, the sniper shoots dead a random passerby in a way that fingers Stu as the prime suspect. Once Stu is forced to deal simultaneously with an NYPD negotiator (Forest Whitaker), his wife (Mitchell), his girlfriend-client (Holmes), and the sniper, the movie becomes a morality play. Farrell is more than up to the task, and Joel Schumacher directs with economy and energy, although with an unfortunate penchant for split screens and hyperkinetic editing.

Still, *Phone Booth*—for which screenwriter Larry Cohen and director Joel Schumacher devise some ingenious, some ludicrous ways to trap its leading character and keep him squirming for eighty-two minutes until his defenses crack—is entertaining. According to its screenwriter, it is also one of the very few Hitchcockian movies that might have become an actual Hitchcock movie. In the late 1960s, writer Larry Cohen personally pitched the concept to Hitchcock, with whom he later spent hours struggling to devise the right plot device to keep the hero confined to the phone booth. No wonder. Hitchcock loved creating tension and terror in such confined spaces as a shower stall (*Psycho*), an attic, and, yes, a phone booth (*The Birds*). But the sniper idea didn't dawn on Cohen until he revived the project, long after Hitchcock's death. Alas. What sets apart *Phone Booth* from other

Hitchcock imitations, though, is that even when its script and direction bow to the master, it's done with a maximum of breezy impudence and swagger and a minimum of clumsiness or pretense. *Phone Booth* is no masterwork, but it's an entertaining rediscovery. Imagine the field day Hitchcock might have had with it. ♟♟♟

TRANSSIBERIAN (2008)

Returning from doing church-sponsored volunteer work, an American couple traveling from China to Moscow on the Transsiberian Express *get befriended by another young couple who send things spinning dangerously out of control.*

THE MACGUFFIN: A suitcase full of heroin-filled Russian nesting dolls

The tension and claustrophobic settings of such "innocents abroad" Hitchcock films as *The Lady Vanishes*, *The Man Who Knew Too Much*, *Rich and Strange*, *Torn Curtain*—laced with doses of the nastier elements of *Strangers on a Train* and *North by Northwest*—are qualities alive and well in this eight-day-train-trip thriller from writer-director Brad Anderson (*The Machinist*). Woody Harrelson is Roy, a hyperfriendly, openhearted doofus midwesterner and railfan jazzed by the sight and sound of vintage trains; he has just completed a stint as a church missionary in China. Emily Mortimer is Jessie, sharper, solemn, more guarded and observant than her husband, photographing the weathered faces of locals and the bleak, austere beauty of the landscapes through which their train passes. Like Hitchcock's stalemated couples in the aforementioned thrillers, Roy and Jessie, stuck at a sexual and emotional impasse, will be shaken to their foundations by life-altering experiences. Enter new train cabinmates glib, dashing Spanish bad boy Carlos (Eduardo Noriega) and his watchful, edgy, twenty-year-old Seattle runaway girlfriend Abby (Kate Mara).

Compared to blond, cornfed Roy—whom worldly Carlos schools on surefire ways to finesse passport trouble and elude suspicious customs officers—these two radiate the survival instincts of born hustlers and the too-easy familiarity of narcissists. The gullible Roy appears oblivious, bringing along with him the opportunistic charmer Carlos on a trek to an eerie, isolated snowy repository of abandoned coal trains. The scene fades out mysteriously on one of the two men ominously hoisting a wicked looking iron rod he finds in the debris. What happened between them? Director Anderson draws the veil, creating a teasingly ambiguous Hitchcockian touch that makes one wonder—especially considering where the movie is heading—whether everyman Roy is as squeaky clean as he appears to be. Jessie quickly recognizes Carlos and Abby's types; as we'll learn, though she's now clean and sober, before meeting Roy she led a wilder, more eventful life than her face and manner suggest. She resists, for a while anyway, the sexual current that flows between her and Carlos with his shameless seductive glances and come-ons. She's been there before. Director Anderson takes his sweet time laying the groundwork and developing the characters, almost unheard of in today's TikTok-addled audience attention spans.

But the stage has been set for the unspeakable things that are about to happen, beginning when only three of the four reboard the train after a stop at Irkutsk. Roy goes missing (like the whimsical-seeming Miss Froy in *The Lady Vanishes*), and the frantic Jessie gets little help from the Russian functionaries beyond vague assurances that Roy must have missed the train and will arrive surely on the next one. But did he? Will he? During their layover, Carlos exploits Jessie's emotional state—and her past. She travels with him to a deserted snowscape leading to a ruined Orthodox church decorated with lovely, fading murals. Only one of them lives to take the bus back to their hotel. Roy reappears, with a new friend, a Russian narc detective named Grinko (Ben Kingsley, properly pragmatic and unsettling) who prods Jessie with insinuating questions she evades. The rest of the film is violent, absurdly improbable, but absolutely thrilling. Entire sections of the train vanish. Roy reveals hidden talents and ferocious protective instincts toward his wife as bloodshed, several gruesome deaths, grim laughs, and a bang-up action train track finale coincide, revealing writer-director Anderson and script partner Will Conroy as a duo completely familiar with Hitchcock's paranoid classics. Can we please have more of this? ♟♟♟

BURIED (2010)

A truck driver in Iraq awakens to find he's been kidnapped, buried alive in a coffin, held for ransom, and left with only a cell phone and a cigarette lighter.

THE MACGUFFIN: Military secrets

Anyone who has broken out in a sweat from reading Poe's horrifying "The Premature Burial" or from seeing the Hitchcock-directed "Breakdown" (1955) episode of *Alfred Hitchcock Presents* (featuring a virtuosic Joseph Cotten performance as a businessman appearing to be dead while trapped behind his car's steering wheel after a crash) will spot them as inspirations for the minimalistic, highly efficient, claustrophobic thriller *Buried*. For the entire ninety-five-minute running time of this nail-biter, director and cowriter Rodrigo Cortés confine us to a coffin with an ordinary man named Paul Conroy (Ryan Reynolds, effective and relatable), a civilian contractor and truck driver in Iraq who awakens in total darkness and slowly learns that he's been kidnapped and buried alive for ransom by Iraqi insurgents for five million dollars. His only sources of light and hope? A partially charged cell phone and a Zippo lighter. We hear only disembodied voices as Conroy tries phoning his wife and son, struggles vainly to enlist the aid of State Department functionaries, and deals with his uninterested employer; often, he is stalled or put on hold.

As his time is ticking down, he fights anger, panic, and terror that he will run out of oxygen and power before anyone bothers to help him. Considering what a harrowing viewing experience Hitchcock made of the twenty-six-minute "Breakdown" episode, it is fascinating to speculate how terrifying he might have made *Buried* for the big screen by exploiting the scary sense of confinement and by keeping the audience riveted by the performance of a single actor for the length of a feature film. Still, the talents behind *Buried* do an impressive job of gripping the viewer in a tense, ever-twisting situation and moving us with empathy for the central character. As an exercise in suffocating, stifling horror, it works. ♟♟♟

THE GIRL ON THE TRAIN (2016)

A depressed alcoholic commuter gets rebuffed by the police when she reports shocking information on learning that a woman she views daily from her train window is feared dead. She launches her own investigation, courting potential danger.

THE MACGUFFIN: The heroine's memory

Adapted by Erin Cressida Wilson (*Secretary*) from the airport and supermarket favorite murder mystery international bestseller by Paula Hawkins, *The Girl on the Train* is what happens when a *Gone Girl*-style unreliable female narrator thriller gets directed by someone less exacting and scrupulous than David Fincher. The 112-minute movie, capably directed by Tate Taylor (*The Help*), is, like Hawkins's novel, of more ordinary stuff than *Gone Girl*; it's a kind of ersatz, unconvincing *Rear Window* meets *Gaslight* riding the rails. In it, Emily Blunt (painfully raw and sympathetic) plays Rachel Watson, a former public relations hotshot, now a dissolute, broken alcoholic writhing in self-loathing and pointlessly riding the train back and forth from Manhattan to fill her time.

Completely lacking guardrails, the untethered Rachel becomes voyeuristically obsessed with the residents of two handsome neighboring suburban Hudson Valley homes she passes daily. Her fellow train travelers give her a wide berth; she looks like what she is, a virtually unhoused wreck, quickly careening toward bag lady status. But Rachel once lived in one of those two enviably cool, catalogue-ready Upstate New York houses before she was divorced by icy Tom (Justin Theroux), who wanted a family; we learn that when Rachel realized she couldn't have children, she began hitting the bottle hard and is now reduced to crashing on a friend's couch and living vicariously through the lives of two female strangers who look as if they have it all as she once did. There's Megan Hipwell (Haley Bennett), a poised, radiant blonde whom Rachel spies standing (as if posing for a TV commercial or a photo shoot) on the balcony of her woodsy suburban home. The artsy Megan nannies for neighbor Anna (Rebecca Ferguson), the bored, patrician beauty now married to Rachel's ex-husband. Rachel, more and more unhinged, slips into her former home and, in secret, heartbreakingly but creepily clings to Anna's and Tom's baby Evie as if it were hers.

She spirals even more dramatically, triggered by spotting Megan secretly kissing a man (Luke Evans) she's seeing on the side. Things get even darker when Rachel turns up at night, covered in blood and mud. Megan has gone missing; our heroine has suffered one of her many blackouts but keeps envisioning (remembering?) herself creeping up on Megan with a shiny sharp object. Rachel may be guilty as sin—that's how the cops see it, according to the sardonic, unimaginative detective played by Allison Janney. But is something bigger at play here? Yes, but mostly no.

The movie hurtles toward a laughable, violent finale straight out of something made for Showtime or Starz. The terrific, always watchable Blunt (and the obligatory Hitchcock allusions to *The Lady Vanishes*, *Rear Window*, *Psycho*, and *Vertigo*) are the only reasons to bother with this one. ♟♟♙

THE WOMAN IN THE WINDOW (2021)

An agoraphobic former therapist now living alone begins spying on her neighbors and witnesses shocking domestic violence she believes she must stop.

THE MACGUFFIN: The murder across the street

The kindest thing one can say about *Atonement* director Joe Wright's film of Daniel Mallory's (pseudonym A. J. Finn) bestseller, scripted by Tracy Letts (*August: Osage County*) is that no one should ever confuse it with Fritz Lang's 1944 classic of the same name. But no one can say that the trashy, big-budget, visually handsome 2021 film isn't a determinedly wannabe neo-Hitchcock movie. The movie has barely begun when flickering images of James Stewart in *Rear Window* appear on the screen—the troubled heroine is a fan of old movies she watches on TV; a glimpse of Ingrid Bergman and Gregory Peck in *Spellbound* is soon to follow. Yes, we understand the meta of it all. But is it a brilliant idea to remind an audience that they could be watching those much better movies instead?

Anyway, those flashing images are just the beginning of the dozens of Hitchcock references in *The Woman in the Window*; instead of James Stewart as the irascible, housebound, injured photojournalist spying on his neighbors while convalescing from a job-related injury in *Rear Window*, this movie gives us Amy Adams as a slovenly, self-loathing, wine-guzzling agoraphobic former child psychologist Anna Fox, whose psychiatric problems have kept her housebound for nearly a year. With nothing but time on her hands to spy on her neighbors, she comes to believe that she has witnessed through the window of her swank Harlem brownstone the stabbing murder of an abused wife and mother named (just like the old-time sex symbol) Jane Russell (played by Julianne Moore, unmoored) at the hands of her brooding husband Alistair (Gary Oldman), whose thick shock of snow-white hair invites us to recall the white locks of murderous Raymond Burr in *Rear Window*.

Pitiable Anna, who has—to put it mildly—let herself go, is apparently friendless and, though she rarely opens the door for anyone but her psychiatrist (Tracy Letts), she somehow permits occasional visits from her neighbors, the abused wife who lives across the street and her twitchy, sensitive, intelligent fifteen-year-old son Ethan (Fred Hechinger, *The White Lotus*, *Gladiator II*), who acts like a beaten puppy. Anna receives a warning visit from a policeman (Brian Tyree Henry), who remains sympathetic despite having dealt with her brand of crazy all too often. But everyone else in Anna's orbit—including her shifty, parole-violating millennial basement tenant (Wyatt Russell) and neighbor Jennifer Jason Leigh, who claims that she (not Julianne Moore) is Ethan's mother, the real Jane Russell—writes her off as delusional because of her rampant paranoia and volatile temper exacerbated by her constant boozing and prescription pill popping. She gets little support from the estranged husband (Anthony Mackie) and her young daughter, both of whom we are shown only in Anna's reveries but whom we hear during their regular phone calls.

What's quite good about the movie is Wright's skillful manipulation of ambient sounds, distorted visuals, and Amy Adams's febrile, wholly committed performance; they help sink us into Anna's socially anxious and debilitating mania. What's not good is how obviously jerry-rigged the movie is, so much so that we can't help but ask questions when we should be at the edge of our seats. Exactly how does the unemployed Anna afford to keep living in such a snazzy New York house? Why would a die-hard fan of classic old movies never comment on the name "Jane Russell," an actress who appeared in more than a few films Anna surely would have watched? If Anna is so paranoid, why does she let her ornery, unreliable tenant have his run of the place? Why do the actors in the movie speak so solemnly and with such long pauses as if they're acting in a Harold Pinter play revival? (If *only*.) But when the much-reshot *The Woman in the Window* fully jumps the track and goes embarrassingly full-on De Palma–style *Psycho* in its final stretch, the only mystery left to unravel is how did such impressive talents manage to play those scenes with such straight faces? An embarrassment. ♟♟

LOCKED (2025)

A wealthy psychopath locks a young small-fry carjacker in his remote-controlled luxury SUV and sends him on the nightmare ride of his life.

THE MACGUFFIN: A remote-controlled luxury SUV

Locked is a "big idea" concept unconcerned with depth or resonance. It's the kind of gimmicky thriller that Larry Cohen (*Phone Booth*) might have tried to peddle to Hitchcock, but it is, in fact, a variation on the 2019 Argentinian thriller *4x4*. This English-language version features Bill Skarsgård as well-intentioned but downbound Eddie Barish, whose ratty van needs repairs he can't afford, which means he can't work his gig as a delivery driver nor even give his charming daughter, Sarah (Ashley Cartwright), a lift home from school when she needs one.

Up against a wall and seeing no other options, Eddie spots in a parking lot a gleaming black luxury SUV, a new model Dolus (Latin for "trick" or "hoax"). Finding the tempting car unlocked, he climbs in, makes himself at home, and while he's scrounging around the tricked-out interior for anything he can sell for a quick buck, the doors lock him inside. He then gets a Bluetooth call from the owner, warning him that having messed around with the wrong person, he is about to suffer the consequences. The FAFO man is Anthony Hopkins; he plays William, a self-righteous superrich right-winger, spouting hatred and revulsion toward the economically disadvantaged and choosing to live out whatever time he has left in his life by setting an elaborate trap for any poor soul who followed the six others who tried carjacking his SUV in the last year alone.

Soon, the moralizing, sadistic SOB—Hopkins' presence is mostly confined to an anonymous voice and a face on the van's dashboard screen—puts working-class Eddie (and the audience) through the ringer by alternately cranking up the car's heat, then dialing to eleven the blisteringly frigid air-conditioning. He also relies on torture by starvation, toilet challenges, breaking out into yodeling, taser shocks (is there *anything* one can't get on the auto aftermarket these days?), and shaming his captive as a deadbeat dad way overdue with his child support payments. Confined to such tight quarters, Eddie can't use his cell to call for help because the car blocks WiFi; he can't even scream for help while pounding the bulletproof windows because they are so darkly tinted. Most nightmarish of all, William starts driving the car by remote control, warning Eddie he might send the car plunging over the roof of a parking garage or careening straight into the path of a bunch of unsuspecting little kids. How is Eddie expected to atone and to stop these diabolical games? Well, he could slice off four of his fingers in sacrifice, as William suggests. Or use the pistol Williams has helpfully provided for Eddie to blow his brains out.

Director David Yarovesky (*Brightburn*) and screenwriter Michael Arlen Ross have all the ingredients for a tight, claustrophobic, single-setting thriller. Even at only ninety-five minutes of running time, *Locked* wears out its welcome by being overly repetitive and sadistic. In his day, Hitchcock surely would have worked with his writers to deepen and complicate the associations between the two characters—making them like distorted fun-house mirror images or linking them by their shared pathologies. Instead, the moviemakers aim for a fair and balanced approach to class conflict—the older character smugly complacent and insulated by wealth and power, the younger character doing what he can to stay afloat while barely scraping by financially and emotionally. In our time of growing rage against oligarchs, *Locked* hints at a potentially resonant and explosive theme it wants to explore, but only uses it as window dressing. But it is also true in these posttruth, postguilt days that deep explorations and stinging explorations of culpability and morality seem lost on many viewers. There's no faulting the compelling and impressive Skarsgård, though, who holds the screen throughout and is so hapless and endearing that it makes us root for him. As for Hopkins, he's funny, menacing, loathsome, sounds appropriately intelligent, and knows exactly what sort of cat-and-mouse games he's playing, having played them earlier and often in better movies. ♟♟♟

6 Psychos

There are psychos and then there are *psychos*. What sets apart Hitchcock's most dangerously and terrifyingly unhinged characters from madmen in the films of others is their veneer of normalcy and attractiveness. Think of lovestruck, mother-dominated Nazi spy Alex Sebastian in *Notorious*. Or the charming, cosmopolitan "Merry Widow Murderer" Uncle Charlie in *Shadow of a Doubt*. Coddled, wealthy wastrel and vicious Bruno Antony in *Strangers on a Train*. World-weary traveling salesman and wife murderer Lars Thorwald in *Rear Window*. Debonair art connoisseur and espionage agent Phillip Vandamm in *North by Northwest*. Bashful, stammering mama's boy motel keeper Norman Bates in *Psycho*. Fruit monger, flashy dresser, and secret necktie strangler Robert Rusk in *Frenzy*.

Most of them also tend to be charming, well groomed, appealing—and Hitchcock deliberately cast his villains that way right from the first. After all, in his highly influential 1927 silent-era thriller *The Lodger: A Story of the London Fog*, he cast as the Jack-the-Ripper-inspired multiple murderer no less than Ivor Novello, the Welsh playwright, singer, composer, actor, and bona fide matinee idol. As the director himself explained, "In the old days, villains in pictures and on stage twirled their moustaches and kicked the dog. Audiences are smarter today. They don't want their villain to be thrown at them with green limelight on his face. They want an ordinary human being with failings."

Later in his career, the director—who seriously pursued for villainous or morally ambiguous roles such magnetic stars as Montgomery Clift, William Holden, Marlon Brando, Yul Brynner, Robert Redford, Terence Stamp, Richard Harris, Michael Caine, Steve McQueen, and Burt Reynolds. "Villains should be very attractive, persuasive, even charming men. Otherwise, they'd never get anywhere near their victims. I like contrast in my pictures, which is one of the reasons I like to cast against type." Aiding their ability to manipulate, deceive, and mask their villainy, Hitchcock's antagonists—who often ran away with the best reviews of any other actor in their films—tend to be polished, articulate, persuasive, and poised. More importantly, though, through writing, costuming, lighting, performance, direction, they emerge as memorable and resonant due to the glimpses of humanity, vulnerability, and relatability Hitchcock always insisted they show.

M (1931)

For their own reasons, police and the criminal underworld separately race to find a homicidal pedophile terrorizing Berlin in the 1930s.

THE MACGUFFIN: The murderer who whistles Grieg's "Hall of the Mountain King"

Darker than dark, visually and aurally stunning, magnificently acted by its central star, and hugely influential, *M* is a pioneering masterwork that wears it age exceedingly well. Of course, *M* is probably most celebrated for being a subtly blood-freezing yet surprisingly humane psychological thriller about Hans Beckert (Peter Lorre), a sexual predator with an uncontrollable compulsion to molest and murder children in Berlin. *M* also stands out as an early, expertly done police procedural manhunt featuring parallel searches for the predator by the law, the criminal underworld, and a frightened public whipped into a lynch-mob frenzy by the manipulative media. With these disparate elements in play, *M* also displays the grace—and the courage—to be a searing indictment of the vilification of the poor as well as a damning portrait of the disintegrating life of Berlin in 1931, just before the full-on horrors inflicted by Hitler with the full support of his deluded followers and lackeys.

Directed and cowritten (with Thea von Harbou) by Fritz Lang, *M* opens chillingly and never flags. A careworn mother (Ellen Widmann) performs housework while awaiting the arrival of her little girl Elsie

(Inge Landgut), due home from school. Lang cuts to Elsie bouncing a ball against a grim "wanted" poster reporting the atrocities of the child killer and the reward for his capture, just as the killer's shadow slithers across the broadsheet and a male voice asks the child her name. The unseen man buys little Elsie a balloon, then leads her ominously away. As the hour grows late, the mother's anxiety moves her to throw open a window and repeatedly cry out Elsie's name as the camera lingers on an empty staircase, a vacant storage space, and Elsie's plate and silverware waiting atop the dining table. Then, the dreaded inevitability: the child's ball rolls out from some undergrowth and her balloon flies up toward utility wires. It is a devastating sequence, perfectly shot, nearly wordless, and paced so that the audience is left to imagine unspeakable horrors Lang never needs to show.

Paranoia, suspicion, and mass hysteria run rampant among all levels of German society as Lang depicts masses of train travelers and haughty members of a men's club alike devouring lurid details of the murders that have everyone pointing accusing fingers at each other and scapegoating possible culprits. The fear and horror build until the final entrapment and capture of Beckert, who during a harrowing kangaroo court trial reveals to an underground roomful of criminals the inner torment of the "monster" inside that overtakes and compels him to kill again. The complex mix of emotions expressed by the twenty-six-year-old Lorre, making his film debut, is justifiably legendary: "Don't want to—*must!* Don't want to—*must!*" The film's finale pulls a switch on the inevitability of vigilante justice and instead ends, where it should, focusing on the grieving mothers of the innocent young victims, warning us all to protect the children. Hitchcock's and Lang's rivalry (sometimes spilling over into bitter animosity on Lang's part) and mutual influence is apparent. Peter Lorre's powerhouse performance in his first big film role helped lead to Hitchcock's casting him as a paid assassin three years later in *The Man Who Knew Too Much*, and the director often said that he learned much from Lang's work. *M* was neither a major financial nor critical success but gained recognition over time as a cinematic landmark and surely a milestone in the careers of Lang and Lorre. Once you have experienced *M*, you will never be able to hear Edward Grieg's "In the Hall of the Mountain King" the same way again. ♟♟♟♟

NIGHT MUST FALL (1937)

When a boyish psychopath scams his way into the home and good graces of a hypochondriacal dowager, the woman's wary niece tries to reveal the intruder as a multiple murderer.

THE MACGUFFIN: The hatbox

Alfred Hitchcock might have been the ideal director for *Night Must Fall*, the quietly chilling film version of the 1935 London and New York stage success written by and starring Emlyn Williams (who worked on the script for Hitchcock's 1934 version of *The Man Who Knew Too Much* and acted in his 1939 film *Jamaica Inn*). Still, even without the Hitchcock touch, this unjustly forgotten 1937 psychological shocker is something strange and special. Consider the elements that might have intrigued Hitchcock, who was still building his reputation in England when MGM bought the film rights from Williams. First, there is the inciting incident: the shattering of the cozy complacency of an English hamlet when a wealthy woman hotel guest disappears mysteriously; when the woman's body gets found, it is headless. By moonlight, a shadowy figure buries something or other in the forest while jauntily whistling "Mighty Lak' a Rose." By daylight, a cocky young Irish immigrant bellboy named Danny (thirty-three-year-old Robert Montgomery, who later starred in Hitchcock's *Mr. & Mrs. Smith*) gets summoned to a remote homestead to answer to the tyrannical, hypochondriacal, highly entitled dowager Mrs. Bramson (Dame May Whitty, "Miss Froy" of *The 39 Steps*), who intends to question his intentions now that he has impregnated one of her young housemaids. Enter Danny, a charm monster with a dubious Irish brogue and a manic, mechanical twinkle in his eye.

Too slick and studied by half, Danny imitates emotions he obviously does not feel, switching expressions on and off at will, as if he's performing for an audience, revealing his inner self only when he thinks no one is watching. He so thoroughly disarms and flatters the fearsome Mrs. Bramson that, instead of her thrashing Danny for the swaggering, soulless cad he is, she treats him like a long-lost son, shows him where she keeps her money, and offers him a job as a handyman. The single person *not* entranced by Danny is Mrs. Bramson's starchy, bookish niece and companion Olivia (Rosalind Russell, miscast but soldiering on). Olivia, bored silly by her nice dull boyfriend (Alan Marshal), sets out to entrap and reveal Danny for the manipulative fraud (and far worse) she suspects he is. When Danny decides to seduce her, Olivia's repressed sexuality bubbles to the surface; her smoldering sexual attraction to Danny makes her act irrationally, virtually his accomplice in murder.

Alas, when the conservative, family-friendly MGM and suave light comedian Robert Montgomery decided to tackle the film version of *Night Must Fall*, Hitchcock had not yet emigrated to America. Instead, workmanlike MGM contract director Richard Thorpe (*Tarzan Escapes*) took on the film (apparently with major directorial intervention by an exasperated Montgomery), making it a bit stodgy and verbose and missing the perversity Hitchcock would have teased out of the material. (And since we're speculating, is it so far out of the realm of fantasy to suspect that Hitchcock might have tried persuading thirty-three-year-old Cary Grant to play the sexually magnetic psychotic Danny?) Still, even as the film exists (despite several major sequences entirely cut before the first preview), when *Night Must Fall* works, it's deeply unnerving and creepy, due largely to the skills of Montgomery, nominated for a Best Actor Oscar; his rubbery features and dead eyes make him resemble a malevolent ventriloquist's dummy. If you think the role is an easy one, though, have a look at Albert Finney in the far less effective 1964 remake, or perhaps you were unlucky enough to see how the 1999 Broadway revival collapsed because star Matthew Broderick brought the charm but none of the required heat.

On release in 1937, *Night Must Fall* won critical acclaim, including the National Board of Review's Best Picture of the Year. Today, it has yet to be sufficiently championed, even by the if-it's-in-black-and-white-and-shadowy-it's-film-noir brigade. Which is just, well, weird and arbitrary. Even with its failings, *Night Must Fall* is *far* more twisted, dark, and *better*

In *Night Must Fall*, breezy, young Danny (Robert Montgomery) seems so sweet a boy—until women turn up decapitated.
LMPC via Getty Images

than the enjoyable but overpraised *The Spiral Staircase* (embraced because the excellent, more *noir*-identified Robert Siodmak directed that one?) or *Sorry, Wrong Number* (ditto, its brilliant, tough-as-nails star Barbara Stanwyck and hit-or-miss director Anatole Litvak?). ♟♟♟♟

HANGOVER SQUARE (1946)

In turn-of-the-century London, an awkward, lonely classical musician suffers blackouts that reveal him to be responsible for a string of murders triggered by loud sounds and discordant music.

THE MACGUFFIN: Sudden loud sounds

Hitchcockian elements abound in this fogbound, brooding thriller set in turn-of-the-century gaslit London and made to capitalize on the 1944 box-office success of *The Lodger*, the 1927 silent version of which marked a career-making success for the twenty-seven-year-old Hitchcock, who called it the "first true Hitchcock film." *Hangover Square* is based on a strong novel by Patrick Hamilton, perhaps best known for his plays that became the George Cukor–directed *Gaslight* in 1944 and, four years later, Hitchcock's *Rope*. *Hangover Square* also not only features a powerhouse musical score but also a centerpiece "Concerto Macabre" by Bernard Herrmann, who famously worked on nine Hitchcock film projects. The movie revolves around sensitive young George Harvey Bone (Laird Cregar) as he gets crushed under the pressure of completing a concert piece commissioned by his wealthy fellow Hangover Square neighbor (Alan Napier, *Marnie*), whose kindly daughter Barbara (Faye Marlowe) is attracted to the intense, otherworldly George. Barbara tries helping Bone puzzle out the recent blackouts and memory losses that send him seeking help from psychologist Dr. Alan Middleton (George Sanders, *Rebecca*, *Foreign Correspondent*) when he begins to wonder if his bloody dagger and blood-drenched cloak mean that he's responsible for the recent murder of an antiques dealer. The doctor prescribes immediate R&R, so Bone haunts a pub where ambitious strumpet Netta Longdon (Linda Darnell, at her lustrous and venal best) lures the poor composer into thinking she's attracted to him. What Netta really wants is for Bone to write her some popular ditties that could lift her out of playing local dives and into the legitimate theaters of London's West End. Nasty Netta nearly bleeds Bone dry, and when he learns she is about to hitch her wagon to a theatrical producer (Glenn Langan), Bone strangles her. In a visually virtuosic sequence, he carries Netta's corpse through the streets and tosses it into a Guy Fawkes Day bonfire. There's an equally lurid finale involving Bone playing Herrmann's "Concerto Macabre" that literally burns down the house. While one can easily imagine how Hitchcock might have treated all this floridly histrionic melodrama—though he came to mock the costume movies he made—some of the big reasons that *Hangover Square* endures are its music score, Joseph La Shelle's (*Laura*, *Fallen Angel*) atmospheric cinematography, and Linda Darnell's lustrous allure. Greatest of all, though, is the unique talent and otherness of Laird Cregar's screen presence. Tragically, the scene-stealing actor died at age thirty-one, having seriously

Starving himself for stardom cost the life of tormented Laird Cregar two months before the release of *Hangover Square*.

John Kobal Foundation/Moviepix/Getty Images

compromised his health by undertaking an unsupervised crash diet to boost his career by losing one hundred pounds in order to win this, his first and last motion picture starring role. *Hangover Square* makes quite an epitaph. ♟♟♟

THE NIGHT OF THE HUNTER (1955)

A diabolical preacher terrorizes two small children and their widowed mother to steal their dead father's stolen fortune.

THE MACGUFFIN: Ten thousand dollars in stolen money

Alfred Hitchcock directed—or at least *tried* to direct—the idiosyncratic, famously self-tortured, but often brilliant actor Charles Laughton in *Jamaica Inn* and *The Paradine Case*, films that rarely appear on lists of *anyone's* favorite or best-ever Hitchcock films. But it *is* surprising that the one directed by Laughton rarely turns up on lists of the most frightening and powerful films of all time. Maybe because no one knows how to slide it into an easy slot. Is *The Night of the Hunter* an allegorical fairy tale? A horror movie? A bleak comedy? A commentary on America's fatal weakness for con artists who cloak their grift in religion? A suspense thriller? Yes, it is. And more.

Based on a 1953 novel by Davis Grubb, the film is indisputably strange, hauntingly beautiful, poetic, expressionistic, and dreamlike. It focuses on traveling preacher Harry Powell (based on real-life Harry Powers, who murdered at least five people, including three children), a predatory backwoods grifter who learns from a former prison cellmate—now a freshly hanged bank robber and killer—that he had stashed ten thousand dollars somewhere for his young children John and Pearl and widow. Laughton shows us Powell driving a stolen car through the Deep South while talking to God—a God who apparently assures Powell that he's fully entitled to that ten thousand dollars so he can build his own church with it. Then, we catch Powell eying a rural burlesque-show blonde dancing on stage; this guy's misogynistic vengeful God is also fine with killing "sinful" or otherwise obstructive women. Instead of casting a more respected, actor-y actor, Laughton apparently surprised Hollywood by choosing the underestimated, untamable Robert Mitchum to play Powell—"Love" tattooed on the fingers of his right hand, "Hate" on the left. Mitchum nails every twisted, hypocritical facet of this silver-tongued devil; he's chilling, weirdly funny, seductive, obscene, and, yes, charismatic, the equal or better of any screen bogeyman. Michael Myers? Freddie Kreuger? Small potatoes. Mitchum is so good that one can only imagine the voltage he might have delivered had Hitchcock wanted him, say, in the role of the murderous traveling salesman Thorwald in *Rear Window* or, against type, as the stalked tennis player in *Strangers on a Train*.

Things go intensely gothic once the Bible-thumper homes in on the dead convict's children John and Pearl (Billy Chapin, Sally Jane Bruce, with whom Laughton could not bear to work) and widow (when Mitchum heard that Shelley Winters was cast, he said, "The only bit she'll do convincingly is to float in the water with her throat cut"). Powell (and his version of God) want the money. As played by Winters, the easily deluded pseudo-religious Willa, no mental or moral giant, can barely contain her lust for the phony preacher; on the other hand, her solemn-eyed children, who know where the cash is hidden, immediately see right through Powell. Willa desperately marries the man of the cloth; their wedding night, set in a bedroom that looks part church, part tomb, is pure grotesque Germanic expressionism worthy of *The Cabinet of Dr. Caligari* or *Nosferatu*, thanks to the set design by Hilyard M. Brown (*Creature from the Black Lagoon*) and cinematography by the great Stanley Cortez (*The Magnificent Ambersons*). Harry demands a chaste wedding night; after all, his holy mission is solely to save Willa's mortal soul, which he does by hoisting a phallic switchblade as the terrible swift sword that sends Willa to kingdom come. Laughton and Cortez give Winters one of the all-time great cinematic kiss-offs. We see her dead body, looking like a bizarre aquarium ornament, seated behind the wheel of a car at the river's bottom, her long, bottle-blonde locks undulating with the seaweed.

The Night of the Hunter is at its most visually poetic when the orphaned kids drift downriver by night in a little boat as innocent wildlife watch from the shore. And always, the demonic Powell pursues them. John knows their psychopathic stepfather isn't joking, having been threatened at knifepoint: "Speak or I'll cut your throat and leave you to drip like a hog hung up at butchering time." The poor kids finally find a surrogate mother—and the devil finds his undoing—in Rachel Cooper, the embodiment of pure, powerful faith as played to perfection by the protean silent-era star Lillian Gish. Despite its glories, scripted by novelist-poet-film-critic James Agee, the film met with critical derision and died at the box office on release. As with so many great nonconformist films, this one took decades to find its champions, though it was and clearly remains not to everyone's taste.

Robert Mitchum gave the performance of his life as a vicious "man of god" in Charles Laughton's nightmarish *The Night of the Hunter*.
Herbert Dorfman/Corbis Historical/Getty Images

Charles Laughton never got to direct another film, but he hit such a high level with this one, perhaps he never needed to try again. ♟♟♟♟

PEEPING TOM (1960)

By night, a lonely, awkward film studio employee films documentary footage of women while he murders them. A friendship with a sympathetic young woman who lives in the same building leads to his exposure and capture.

THE MACGUFFIN: The portable camera equipped with a knife blade

In 1960, two world-class directors shocked audiences with dark, bold, violent, troubling movies unlike anything they had ever done previously. Those films forever altered their careers. *Psycho* triumphed over mixed reviews to become a box-office sensation that put Hitchcock on top of the world. Critics and audiences were so repulsed by *Peeping Tom* that Michael Powell, despite his track record of codirecting with Emeric Pressburger such masterpieces as *The Red Shoes*, *Black Narcissus*, *I Know Where I'm Going!*, and *The Life and Death of Colonel Blimp*, instantly became a marginalized figure in the film business, a pariah.

Today, *Peeping Tom* is a cult favorite and considered one of Powell's most fascinating experiments. That doesn't make it any easier to watch. As with all Powell-Pressburger color films, *Peeping Tom*—right from its opening frames—startles us with bold compositions and heated hues. We watch the film's central figure, Mark Lewis (German actor Carl Böhm, billed as Karlheinz Böhm), a bland, baby-faced camera assistant who moonlights by photographing half-dressed women sold clandestinely at magazine and tobacco shops, trails a weary prostitute (Brenda Bruce) to her flat where he films her with his hidden camera. In her squalid apartment, he films her dying moments while stabbing her with a knife embedded in his camera tripod. Later, he kills a vivacious dancer-actress (Moira Shearer, star of *The Red Shoes*) at a film studio. And we suspect he may have a similar fate planned for kindly fellow redhead Helen Stephens (Anna Massey, who later appeared in Hitchcock's *Frenzy*), who rents a flat with her blind mother in the rambling house owned by the socially stunted, damaged Mark; Mark also hides away there and obsessively pores over his snuff films in his darkroom.

The milieu is seedy, the worldview bleak, the color scheme lurid and highly saturated, and—with Powell deliberately filming the murder scenes from behind Mark's camera peeping through the viewfinder—the accusation that filmmakers and filmgoers are essentially voyeurs is hardly subtle. But neither is it necessarily untrue. Hitchcock made similar observations years before in both *Rear Window* and *Vertigo*, but Powell gets more vicious, bringing in themes of child abuse (Mark shows Helen films in which his sadistic psychologist father staged or exploited situations triggering fear, horror, grief while filming his young son's reactions), sexual deviance, and the hero's fetishistic relationship with the camera so intense that he can barely function without holding it in his hands. We ought to look away, we often want to, but, after all, we like to watch. It isn't hard to see why repertory cinemas once kept double-bills of *Psycho* and *Peeping Tom* in heavy rotation.

In truth, Powell's film feels more akin to *Frenzy*, prefiguring Hammer Films and Italian *giallo* horror by several years. On the other hand, Powell's great film suggests what might have happened had Universal Pictures not squelched Hitchcock's plans to film *Kaleidoscope*, an experimental, modest-budgeted, European-influenced late '60s project in which a disarmingly boyish, mother-dominated psychopath's killer instincts get triggered by his proximity to large bodies of water. ♟♟♟♟

HOMICIDAL (1961)

A murderous blonde stabs a justice of the peace, unleashing the dark secrets of a troubled Southern California family.

THE MACGUFFIN: The homicidal blonde

For years, director William Castle and screenwriter Robb White told interviewers that they hadn't seen *Psycho* when they concocted their bargain-basement knockoff, *Homicidal*. *Right.* A blonde heroine on the run with cash and with crime on her mind, often filmed in tight, tense close-ups while driving? Janet Leigh in Hitchcock's movie *and* Jean Arless/Joan Marshall in Castle's. Lack of money as the motive for desperate acts? The heroine of *Psycho* impulsively embezzles cash from her employer so that she and her boyfriend can be married; in *Homicidal*, the murder victims stand in the way of a psychopath out to claim a ten-million-dollar family inheritance. In both, the heroines have hunky, stolid, blue-collar smalltown boyfriends. It's Hitchcock's John Gavin versus Castle's Glenn Corbett in the "Battle of the Blands." In each film, startlingly violent, out-of-the-blue stabbing scenes erupt. Each film also features an old dark house inhabited by a mysterious elderly woman and a very strange young man. Both flicks feature climactic scenes in which the supporting female character (Vera Miles in *Psycho*, Patricia Breslin in *Homicidal*) intrepidly searches the scary house and uncovers hair-raisingly weird sexual revelations (for 1961, anyway).

Castle's film is shot in moody black and white by Burnett Guffey (Oscar winner for *From Here to Eternity*) imitating the vibe and the style of John L. Russell (Oscar nominee for *Psycho*). Fabulous showman Hitchcock promoted *Psycho* with a whopper of a publicity gimmick—Pinkerton guards stood at movie house doors to enforce the director's edict broadcast over loudspeakers: "No one will be admitted to the theater after the start of each performance of *Psycho*!" The delightfully shameless carny huckster Castle even promoted *Homicidal* with an ad campaign that echoed *Psycho*'s; *Homicidal* featured an audience participation gimmick, a "Fright Break," merely an on-screen ticking clock with Castle in voice-over advising scaredy cats to flee the theater before the climax and to get their blood pressure checked by a "nurse" waiting to attend them in the lobby's "Coward's Corner." (And risk being mocked mercilessly by ticket buyers on their way out or in.)

It'd be a fool's errand to relate the joyous lunacy and nonsense entailed in the plot of *Homicidal* that begins once the crazy-eyed, frozen-faced leading lady wearing a dubious blonde wig boldly picks up a hotel bellhop (the insolently sexy Richard Rust), offers him two thousand dollars to marry her, and immediately hustles him off to a justice of the peace in the middle of the night, with a sharp, gleaming knife stowed in her handbag. To say more would spoil the fun of this pulpy, tabloidy, whacked-out movie. Make no mistake: *Homicidal*, set in and partially filmed in the quaint California village of Solvang ("The Danish Capital of America")—where Hitchcock's daughter Patricia once resided—and in the city of Ventura, California, is a deeply weird, enjoyably oddball psychosexual head trip offering performances ranging from amateur theater–worthy to unnervingly and fascinatingly bizarre (looking at you, Jean Arless, the fascinator who starred as Lily in the pilot for TV's *The Munsters*, was briefly wed to director Hal Ashby, and served as an inspiration for Ashby's smash hit 1975 Oscar-winning comedy scripted by Robert Towne, *Shampoo*). Once lampooned as a poor man's *Psycho*, *Homicidal* now enjoys cult status. What doesn't? ♟♟♟

CHAPTER 6 PSYCHOS

EXPERIMENT IN TERROR (1962)

A bank teller and her sister are terrorized by an asthmatic maniac who forces the teller to steal from her employer. A sympathetic FBI agent tries to protect the young women from their predator.

THE MACGUFFIN: One hundred thousand dollars in stolen money

In the opening moments of this effective excursion into Hitchcock-style thrills from director Blake Edwards (*Breakfast at Tiffany's*, *The Pink Panther*), the perils of beautiful young bank teller Kelly Sherwood (Lee Remick) begin when she gets grabbed by the gloved hand of a intruder hiding in her shadowy garage. Wheezing into Kelly's ear, the gruff-voiced asthmatic psychotic warns that if she doesn't steal one hundred thousand dollars from her bank, he will kill her and her younger sister (Stefanie Powers). He cautions her against informing the police; he's got her house under surveillance. It's a promising setup, and for the brief time Edwards focuses on the interactions of the sisters—ordinary people in extraordinary circumstances, as Hitchcock put it—the movie is at its tense, nerve-jangling best. But all too soon, the FBI pros (personified by a fine Glenn Ford) take over as Remick's helpmates, it devolves into a procedural of wiretaps and cat-and-mouse chases, and the air goes out of the whole thing. It's as if Edwards knew it, too, so to jazz things up, he goes heavy on the kinky psychology, shock cuts, and sudden bursts of loud noise or blaring music as if such gimmicks could prove his cred as a hip 1960s director.

More impressive, though, is the use of offbeat San Francisco locales against which to play out the chases and to trap the extortionist—there are gritty nightclubs, a space filled with spooky fashion mannequins, a movie theater, a hospital, and a finale in Candlestick Park during a Giants game. It's a shallow, showy, but undeniably creepy movie with a jangly, superb Henry Mancini score, immaculately creepy Phillip Lathrop cinematography, and first-class performances from Remick, Ford, and Ross Martin (unforgettable and oddly sympathetic as madman "Red" Lynch).

CAPE FEAR (1962)

A psychopath released from prison targets one of the lawyers—and his family—who put him away. When the legal system fails him, the lawyer defends himself and his family from the vengeance of the seductive madman.

THE MACGUFFIN: The blind revenge of a psychopath

Of all the invectives hurled at Hitchcock as a director, even his harshest critics rarely accused his films of being basic or crude. For 1962, *Cape Fear* is a brute-force psychological thriller in ways that Hitchcock films never are. The screenplay by James R. Webb (*The Big Country*), based on John D. MacDonald's 1957 novel *The Executioners*, details the chaos unleashed by psychopath Max Cady after he gets sprung from prison and becomes hell-bent on terrorizing attorney Sam Bowden, the lawyer whose court testimony sent Cady up the river for rape. The lewd conman Cady, radiating sexual menace equal to his badassery, mercilessly kills the Bowden family dog, stalks the lawyer's wife, and tries seducing his teenage daughter, then descends on their summer home intending to slaughter the whole family. Gregory Peck, who worked twice for Hitchcock in the 1940s and bought the film rights to MacDonald's novel from actor-filmmaker Cornel Wilde, became the producer, cast himself as the beleaguered lawyer, and handpicked Webb to write the screenplay. Peck is rumored to have tried to interest Hitchcock in the material, but whatever he thought of the material, the director was preoccupied with deciding on a follow-up project to *Psycho*. Instead, Peck turned to the more malleable, workmanlike J. Lee Thompson (*Tiger Bay*, *The Guns of Navarone*), who, as a Hitchcock fan, promised to apply a similar approach to what was considered pulpy, potentially explicit material. Making good on his intentions, Thompson hired Hitchcock's composer Bernard Herrmann, Hitchcock's superb and innovative editor George Tomasini, Hitchcock's frequent production designer Robert F. Boyle, and actor Martin Balsam (*Psycho*). He also chose to film in black and white rather than color, the better to *suggest* rather than show. And then Peck personally chose Robert Mitchum to play Cady, and he is so brilliantly menacing, that he's virtually blowtorching everyone and everything around him. Mitchum is electrifying in his moments brutalizing Barrie Chase as a pickup who chooses the wrong man with whom to trifle; similarly, his cat-and-mouse games with Polly Bergen as Peck's emotionally distraught wife and Lori Nelson as Bergen and Peck's young daughter suggest the depths of Cady's sadism, perversion, and taste for vengeance.

It's Mitchum's show, but the stolid, dignified Peck is also fine as the "good" man capable of surprisingly monstrous acts in the name of saving his family. But Mitchum owns his role, for life—something that became apparent when Martin Scorsese directed Robert De Niro in an overblown remake that in spelling out and underlining everything became much less frightening. While the original *Cape Fear* could have benefited from Hitchcock's humor and expertise, it didn't need to be a Hitchcock movie to be terrifying. It had Mitchum. ♟♟♟

It's family man and lawyer Gregory Peck versus malicious ex-con Robert Mitchum in the shocker *Cape Fear*. It's Mitchum's show, all the way.
LMPC via Getty Images

WHAT EVER HAPPENED TO BABY JANE? (1962)

An aging, self-deluded ex-vaudeville child star torments her wheelchair-bound former movie star sister in their faded Hollywood mansion as she plots a show business comeback.

THE MACGUFFIN: The guilt of a troubled sister

If Hitchcock hadn't made Robert Bloch's *Psycho* from Joseph Stefano's screenplay and director-writer Billy Wilder (with coscreenwriters Charles Brackett and D. M. Marshman) hadn't made *Sunset Boulevard*, would director Robert Aldrich (*Kiss Me Deadly*) have gotten his turn at bat with *What Ever Happened to Baby Jane?* Maybe not, but this macabre, baroque Gothic shocker about two long-feuding sisters forced to live together way beyond their show business glory days—their saga equal parts *Sunset Boulevard*, *Gypsy*, and *Psycho*—became a big hit back in its day. The two central performances are justifiably legendary. Bette Davis, only thirteen years earlier the highest paid woman in the United States but now being kicked to the curb by Hollywood for the unpardonable sin of aging, has the juicier role and plays it straight up to the third balcony. She is Jane Hudson, a once-popular child star on the vaudeville circuit, where rube audiences adored her for cloyingly saccharine pre–Shirley Temple charm and brittle "sincerity," while offstage she is a spiteful, ungrateful little tyrant who emotionally batters and belittles her shy sister, Blanche. But the worm turns when, as twentysomethings, Blanche (played by Joan Crawford) blossoms into a glamorous movie star and box-office queen while Jane's movie career nose-dives and leaves her a vengeful, embittered alcoholic, a terminal case of arrested development.

A hushed-up 1935 automobile accident leaves Blanche paralyzed from the waist down, ending her career and leaving her confined to a wheelchair and, over the decades, reduced to a reclusive existence in the second-floor bedroom of the grand manse she shares with her begrudging caretaker, Jane, who grows crazier and more volatile as she prepares to make a show business comeback. The balance of the movie is a harrowing and sadistic exercise in spider versus fly torture games—with Jane serving her sister a rat and her own pet canary for din-din and deliberately bludgeoning to death one of Blanche's few sources of kindness and only reliable lifeline to the outside world. Aldrich revels in cruel close-ups of two of Hollywood's most iconic faces, inviting audiences to feel smugly superior to the grim spectacle of seeing once desirable, unattainable movie idols cut down to size by time. Then and now, some consider *What Ever Happened to Baby Jane?*, scripted by Lukas Heller from a 1960 Henry Farrell novel, a shrieking exercise in high camp. And sure, Davis, slathered in white powder makeup, a slash of lipstick, a blonde fright wig of banana curls, and antiquated dresses, knowingly makes a grand spectacle of herself as she wallows in her enjoyably over-the-top acting excesses. But she and Crawford—as egotistical, petty, and envious of each as they might have been offscreen—deliver fierce commitment and undeniable Old Hollywood charisma to what is, in its black heart, an exploitation film *about* exploitation, sibling rivalry, aging, and the pernicious effects of familial abuse.

The two stars are well matched by Victor Buono, that Laird Cregar of the 1960s, wonderful as the sleazy, opportunistic Edwin Flagg, a pianist whom Jane hires (and deludes herself into considering a potential beau) and for whom she memorably reprises "I've Written a Letter to Daddy," the tear-jerking signature song of her days as a child performer. The scene is as grotesque as it is heartbreaking. By the finale of the movie, when it is fully revealed which sister did what to the other, the big mystery no longer matters. These pathetic siblings, who might have been friends all along, are exposed as living anachronisms on a ruthlessly sunny beach, where they are mocked and gawked at as freaks, exactly the way some viewers have been watching the entire movie. *What Ever Happened to Baby Jane?* became such a hit that it spawned a glut of psychological thrillers featuring famed and half-remembered female stars of Hollywood's Golden Age whose bank accounts or egos wouldn't permit them the luxury of saying no. Few pack the power or pathos of this one. And to think, Bette Davis tried

In *What Ever Happened to Baby Jane?*, Joan Crawford and Bette Davis play out a sibling-rivalry-fueled dance of death in their faded Hollywood mansion. The film set the template for dozens of imitators.

Moviepix/Getty Images

getting Hitchcock to direct it, but he declined, ostensibly because of his ongoing work on *The Birds*. ♟♟♟♟

PARANOIAC (1963)

Though believed to be dead, a long-lost brother suddenly materializes just when his explosive alcoholic brother and his emotionally fragile sister are days away from coming into an inheritance.

THE MACGUFFIN: The mysterious brother back from the dead

One of the better reasons to track down this Hammer Films exercise in Hitchcockiana is for the pleasure of watching the young, blazingly charismatic Oliver Reed act up a storm as Simon Ashby, the boozy, devious, and bonkers orphan son of rich parents who, along with his lovely, emotionally fragile sister, Eleanor (Janette Scott), is salivating at the prospect of finally inheriting his long-dead parents' money and property. Simon and Eleanor's brother, Tony (Alexander Davion), committed suicide after their parents' deaths in a plane crash, and now, if only Simon can push their stern, odd live-in Aunt Harriet (Sheila Burrell) to agree to commit Eleanor to an asylum, the fortune would all go to Simon, who spends most of his days indulging his violent mood swings and many of his nights bedding Eleanor's comely French nurse (Liliane Brousse). Imagine poor Eleanor's freakout when she keeps seeing her dead brother Tony popping up here and there. Is she hallucinating? Is Tony back from the Great Beyond? Answers begin to emerge when he finally strolls back into the family manse, bold as brass and obviously very much alive.

What the *Psycho*-meets-*Diabolique* is going on here? Not much beyond the standard cat-and-mouse antics of several dozen other, better drive-the-wealthy-heroine-crazy melodramas. Still, there are pleasures to be had from the polished cinematography of Arthur Grant (*Quatermass and the Pitt*) and from Freddie Francis's straight-faced direction of Jimmy Sangster's screenplay based on the famed 1949 novel *Brat Farrar* by the estimable Josephine Tey (Hitchcock based his 1937 film *Young and Innocent* (a.k.a. *The Girl Was Young*) on Tey's *A Shilling for Candles*). The movie is also full of such stuff as its characters being menaced by a bizarre figure waltzing around the Ashby mansion wearing an unforgettably spooky mask. The storyline offers loads of plot switchbacks and endless opportunities for hammy acting, and the whole thing is hinged on the Hitchcockian notion that no one is exactly what they appear. It's all fun and games if you're a fan of Reed, but lots less so for fans of first-class psychological suspense shockers. ♣♣♪

STRAIT-JACKET (1964)

An outbreak of ax murders casts suspicion on a middle-aged woman trying to rebuild a life with her daughter after a twenty-year psychiatric hospital stay for the ax murders of her unfaithful husband and his lover.

THE MACGUFFIN: Which character has an ax to grind?

"From the creator of *Psycho*, the director of *Homicidal* and the co-star of *What Ever Happened to Baby Jane?*," shouted the advertisements for *Strait-Jacket*, another of *Homicidal* director William Castle's futile attempts to chase Hitchcock's shadow. The director even went so far as to hire *Psycho* novelist Robert Bloch to pen the original screenplay. Bloch was a seminal figure in crime and horror literature. A powerful novelist and short story writer he was, but a great screenwriter he was not, and the sledgehammer approach Castle took to Bloch's clumsy, obvious script makes for a howler, not a screamer. Toward the mid-1960s, Columbia Pictures began squelching Castle's ideas for gleefully hokey promotional gimmicks that made him rich and famous—insuring movie patrons through Lloyd's of London against death from fright, or flying life-size plastic skeletons over audience's heads—so he somehow sweet-talked Joan Crawford, hot off the success of *What Ever Happened to Baby Jane?*, into playing ax-murderess Lucy Harbin (any resemblance to Lizzie Borden is purely intentional) in a script likely cobbled from scraps of such classic Crawford yesteryear melodramas as *Possessed*, *A Woman's Face*, and *Mildred Pierce*.

Crawford told the press that when she read Bloch's original screenplay, she warned Castle he must make changes: more mother-daughter conflict like *Mildred Pierce*, fewer gimmicks. But any pretense of Castle's or Crawford's leveling up to a psychological thriller aimed at grown-ups flies straight out the window when *Strait-Jacket* introduces sixtyish-year-old Crawford in a soft-focus flashback supposedly playing Lucy at forty. She steps off a train ("bad girl" saxophones blaring) smoking up a storm, eyes hungrily scanning the horizon for action, helmeted in a dubious black *Mildred Pierce* wig, her gaudy charm bracelets a-jangling and hips a-swaying. As if we didn't get the point that Crawford—oops, we mean Lucy—is a 12 o'clock gal in a 9 o'clock town, the narration (by Diane Baker, whom Crawford insisted play her daughter when the grand diva had Anne Helm fired) describes her as "very much a woman—and very much aware of the fact." Moments later, Lucy discovers her studly horndog husband (Lee Majors) in bed with a bosomy hussy (Patricia Crest), so she grabs a handy ax (as one does) and in a vengeful rage and a fury of keening theremin music gives them forty whacks that decapitate them. And her poor three-year-old daughter, Carol, wide awake in a bedroom across the way, saw what she did.

Lucy, sprung twenty years later from the nuthouse and supposedly rehabilitated, tries to pick up the pieces by going to live on a remote farm with her brother (Leif Erickson) and sister-in-law (Rochelle Hudson), who've adopted and brought up Carol far away from prying eyes. Carol, now a talented "sculptress" and a languid beauty (Baker), blandly confesses to her fiancé, "My mother… a murderess. And now you know," as if she were reading from a grocery list. Her super wealthy, handsome, even blander fiancé (John Anthony Hayes) reassures her, "Don't you see it doesn't matter?" *Wait, what now?* Oh, but it starts to matter a lot when folks down on the farm—a grimy hired hand (George Kennedy), a nosy doctor (Mitchell Cox)—start losing their noggins, too.

Crawford, despite her surroundings, is *in* it, delivering every twitch, grimace, honeyed smile, and scream in old-time, grand movie star style. When the script gives her a rare breather from being hounded by nightmares or being cruelly gaslighted by tactics straight out of, well, *Gaslight*, she's so fully committed, sympathetic, and touching that anything and anyone around her seems strictly second rate. The film overflows with typical Castle weirdness… the slack pacing that alternately feels scarily dreamlike or just plain inept. That blatant Hitchcock "homage" of the God's-eye view of Crawford freaking out in a claustrophobic dressing room, apparently triggered by that alarmingly hideous vertical-striped wallpaper. Crawford putting sexual moves on her daughter's fiancé and running her fingers over his lips. Okay, high art it's not, but, boy, is it entertaining. Warning: The final reveal of the film's true meanie will only startle those who either haven't been paying attention or have never seen a movie directed by William Castle, the man who would be Hitchcock. 🗡🗡🗡

"Lucy Harbin took an ax…" and Joan Crawford took a tawdry Hitchcock imitation by storm in William Castle's shocker *Strait-Jacket*.
LMPC via Getty Images

THE NANNY (1965)

Cat-and-mouse games turn ugly between a young boy believed to have drowned his little sister and the new nanny his parents hire after his discharge from a facility for emotionally troubled children.

THE MACGUFFIN: The little sister

In the 1950s and 1960s, the British production company Hammer Film Productions Limited was known best for its popular series of lurid

Technicolor, bodice-ripping, gory Gothic horror shockers (*Curse of Frankenstein*, *The Horror of Dracula*, *The Devil Rides Out*). Hoping to replicate the freak success of Hitchcock's modestly budgeted 1960 masterwork *Psycho*, the British studio quietly launched its own Hitchcockian subgenre known unofficially as "mini-Hitchcocks." Arguably the best of them is this eerie, restrained, and ultimately surprisingly moving thriller based on a 1964 novel by Evelyn Piper (*Bunny Lake Is Missing*), scripted by Hammer regular Jimmy Sangster (*Paranoiac*), and directed by Seth Holt (*Scream of Fear*). The bleak and broody movie—less *Grand Guignol* than grand melodrama—revolves around ten-year-old Joey Fane (William Dix), fresh from a two-year stint in a facility for troubled children, where he had been placed after being accused of drowning his younger sister, Susy. His grieving parents are workaholic Bill (James Villiers) and Virginia (Wendy Craig), who are, understandably, struggling to keep it all together. That leaves the newly hired Nanny (Bette Davis) in charge of the bright, bratty Joey, who immediately refuses to sit next to her in the car, to sleep in the bedroom she has prepared for him, or to eat the meals she serves him.

What's most Hitchcockian about *The Nanny* is that it is a character-driven psychological thriller that keeps the audience in a constant state of suspense and dread. The mere casting of Davis in her immediately post–*What Ever Happened to Baby Jane?* and *Hush... Hush, Sweet Charlotte* incarnation signals that Joey may be an unfairly accused, emotionally scarred kid who is silently screaming to alert his parents that they have left him at the mercy of a caregiver whose spit-and-polish professionalism may mask something very sinister and life-threatening. The cat-and-mouse interplay between Nanny and Joey (his barbs are especially cruel) keeps us off-balance, and both Davis and Dix play things relatively subdued (well mostly, anyway). Of course, the cast and director's refusal to treat the material as high camp probably prevents *The Nanny* from being more known and beloved than the more florid movies of Davis's late career.

REPULSION (1965)

While her housemate sister is away on holiday, a shy manicurist who is pathologically terrified of men experiences bizarre hallucinations and succumbs to madness.

THE MACGUFFIN: A straight-edge razor

Director Roman Polanski's first English-language film is as bleak, disturbing, nerve-wracking, and brilliant a psychological thriller as they come. Catherine Deneuve (the great "Hitchcock blonde" that never was) stars as Carol, a reticent manicurist who shares a rambling, broken-down South Kensington flat with her sexy, cosmopolitan sister (Yvonne Furneaux). Carol, an impassive, doll-like beauty who abhors men and fears sex, is simultaneously disgusted and aroused by the sexual insinuations of her sister's loathsome, married boyfriend (Ian Hendry), a salesman given to such obnoxious behavior as troubling Carol's sleep with his show-offy groans of sexual ecstasy in the adjacent bedroom and dropping his razor into her toothbrush glass. Carol spends her workdays in a zombielike state punctuated by facial twitches and the occasional accidental (or is it?) stabbing of a customer's finger with her nail clippers. Her boyfriend seems genuinely caring but ineffectual against Carol's alarming signs of incipient schizophrenia. Carol becomes obsessive about dust, dirt, and grime. And when her sister runs off on holiday with her lover, Carol gets left with the rent money for the lusty landlord and a roasted rabbit for her meals. Neither of those fares well. Agoraphobic and hallucinating that the apartment walls are literally cracking open and dissolving into mud, the heroine's psychological problems spiral into wild paranoia. Hands jut out of the walls to grab at her breasts. A rapist lurks under her bedsheets. The cooked rabbit is left out to rot and attract flies. Carol envisions the choreographed slashings of a razor. These and other hallucinations are handled by Polanski with hair-raising brilliance. *Psycho*, *The Servant*, and Ingmar Bergman's *Persona* may be the most obvious influences. But *Repulsion* delivers shocks and horrors all its own. Powerful stuff, and an early indication that Deneuve was much more than a beautiful face and an icy presence. ♟♟♟♟

A manicurist (Catherine Deneuve) descends into schizoid violence and fantasy in Roman Polanski's *Psycho*-influenced *Repulsion*.

Photo by ullstein bild/ullstein bild via Getty Images

THE COLLECTOR (1965)

A bland butterfly collector uses his lottery winnings to buy an isolated country home in which he keeps captive a beautiful art student.

THE MACGUFFIN: A shy man's psychosis

By the mid-1960s, three-time Oscar winner, twelve-time Oscar nominee William Wyler, the very definition of a classicist, had directed some of Hollywood's most celebrated and varied films, including *The Best Years of Our Lives*, *Roman Holiday*, *Wuthering Heights*, *Ben-Hur*, *The Letter*,

The Heiress, *Detective Story*, *The Little Foxes*, *Dodsworth*, *Mrs. Miniver*, *Friendly Persuasion*, *The Big Country*, and *Jezebel*, let alone directed thirty-six actors to Oscar nominations and fourteen wins. But after three decades of excellence in so many genres—dramas, romantic comedies, melodramas, westerns, biblical epics, and more—he had never made a Hitchcock-style suspense thriller. Not until, that is, he dropped out of directing *The Sound of Music* to make a stark about-face by instead tackling the movie version of the disturbing debut best-selling novel by John Fowles, *The Collector*. In it, a socially and sexually stunted, colorless bank clerk and obsessive butterfly collector named Frederick Clegg wins a fortune in a football pool, buys a remote English country house, and turns its basement into a well-appointed prison for one particular captive; for months he has been stalking and growing obsessed with a beautiful art student, Miranda Grey, who doesn't know he exists.

As cruelly and efficiently as this Caliban captures and kills one of his rare butterflies, he grabs his unsuspecting Miranda in an alley, chloroforms her, yanks her into his van, drives her to his lair, and locks her in the stultifyingly cozy tomb he's created for her. He plies her with bouquets of fresh flowers and trays of food, deluding himself into thinking that she will come to love him one day. It's this sad, strange man's bizarre way of trying to make a human connection. The initially frightened and baffled Miranda disabuses Freddy of his fantasies of entrapment and domination; as her imprisonment drags on, she proves she is not some docile storybook princess pining for rescue but a sharp, resourceful, and snobbish young woman who criticizes her jailer for being uneducated, lacking in taste and refinement, and even being incapable of sexual intimacy.

Their intricate balance of power, a dance of death—sometimes tender, sometimes not—is the stuff of a deeply twisted fable, part *Rapunzel*, *Phantom of the Opera*, and *Beauty and the Beast*. "Almost a love story" indeed, as the movie posters read. Dark, sad, queasy-making, and dryly dispassionate in the Wyler manner, *The Sound of Music* it wasn't. To play Miranda, Wyler first thought of his *Roman Holiday* star Audrey Hepburn (at age thirty-eight?); she, like many other stars, turned down the opportunity. But when the director instead cast rising newcomer Samantha Eggar, he took one of more significant gambles of his career. According to the actress and others with whom she made the film, Wyler isolated and made Eggar miserable during preproduction rehearsals until he finally fired her; before rehiring her (once she agreed to Wyler's demand that she work with an acting coach), the director seriously considered replacing Eggar with one of his original choices—Julie Christie, Natalie Wood, Susannah York, or Sarah Miles. Luminously photographed by Robert Krasker and Robert Surtees, Eggar, who went on to receive an Oscar nomination and a Cannes Film Festival award, is not only stunningly beautiful but also radiates emotional directness, cruelty, intelligence, strength, and more. For his Frederick, Wyler went the Hitchcock route by avoiding such more obvious physical choices as, say, Tom Courtenay or David Warner, choosing another of the best young British actors of his day, Terence Stamp. Then he and Stamp conspired to strip away the charisma, charm, and physical grace that put the devilishly handsome actor on the map in the first place. Attempting to personify the banality of evil, Stamp is studiedly stilted and sometimes chilling. Switching off his usually compelling gaze, slackening his jaw, hunching his shoulders and tilting his head oddly, Stamp appears to be giving Wyler all he asked for, and he won the Best Actor prize at Cannes; still, neither the director nor his star succeeded in making repressed, understated psychopath Frederick Clegg unforgettably compelling. And, for all their tricks, there's just no avoiding how staggeringly beautiful Stamp and Eggar look together. Further distancing the intended audience for a psychological horror thriller, Maurice Jarre's double-harpsichord score underlines the melancholy fairy-tale quality of the work; after all, thriller lovers generally prefer their scares punctuated by now-clichéd screechy orchestral stings. These qualities of restraint may explain the relative obscurity of the impeccably made but emotionally chilly *The Collector*, and why Clegg isn't mentioned in the same breath as such fellow psychos Norman Bates and Hannibal Lecter, who are, admittedly, far more entertaining. All of which makes it frustrating but highly unlikely we will one day get to see a restored version of Wyler's original three-hour version of the film, for which the director said he'd done some of the finest work of his entire career. ♟♟♟

In director William Wyler's screen version of *The Collector*, an art student (Samantha Eggar) gets kidnapped by deceptively mild-mannered psychotic Terence Stamp.
Michael Ochs/Moviepix/Getty Images

TWISTED NERVE (1968)

Rejected by a girl with whom he is obsessed, a deeply troubled, mother-dominated young man with an alternate personality goes on a homicidal rampage.

THE MACGUFFIN: The whistling psychopath

The reputations of respected, socially conscious British filmmaking twin brothers Roy and John Boulting (*Seven Days to Noon*, *I'm All Right Jack*, *The Family Way*) took a beating in the press for this grim, *Psycho*-influenced thriller that somehow conflates psychopathic murderers with people with Down syndrome (or "mongolism" as they are offensively called in the film). That dated, spurious, and rubbishy notion alone helps account for the film's being a box-office pariah

CHAPTER 6 PSYCHOS

kept off the legal home video market for years. The movie, now widely available, benefited from its absence. Not only did it gain a reputation for being a fearless, non-PC shocker (it is, but that doesn't mean it's a suppressed gem), but its Hitchcock associations also helped. After all, Hitchcock privately screened *Twisted Nerve*, and for 1972's *Frenzy*, he cast in prominent roles *Twisted Nerve* actors Billie Whitelaw and Barry Forster (who also earlier appeared in the Boultings' *The Family Way*). Additionally, Hitchcock's most frequent musical composer, Bernard Herrmann, whom the director (understandably but lamentably) fired from *Torn Curtain* in 1966, scored *Twisted Nerve*, from which frequent Hitchcock detractor Quentin Tarantino appropriated the eerie, shrill whistling theme for his own *Kill Bill: Vol. 1*. Assuming one can push past the movie's shameful, primitive premise promised by the title—that a genetic condition giving someone an extra copy of chromosome 21, not a "nerve," could cause violent and sinister tendencies—*is Twisted Nerve* worth your time? I watched it so you don't have to. But if you must, it's best to try seeing it with an understanding of the context of the time during which it was made.

Hywel Bennet (*The Family Way*, *Loot*) is intriguingly odd and effective as Martin, an intense, brooding type who is disliked by his wealthy businessman stepfather (Frank Finlay) and cosseted and sexualized by his mother (Phyllis Calvert), who has stashed away into a London private school Martin's older brother, Pete, who has Down syndrome; she lavishes her repressed emotions on pretty boy Martin. At a children's store, Martin watches a lovely librarian, Susan (Hayley Mills, exceptionally good), buy a toy and follows her out the door while pocketing a rubber duck. Two store detectives drag Susan and Martin back into the shop for questioning by the manager. Martin avoids arrest for shoplifting by calculatedly slipping into his alter ego persona—of childlike, mentally challenged Georgie. (In a film as bizarre as this one, the scene equates to Martin and Susan "meeting cute.") Smitten with the sympathetic Susan, who even pays for the toy "Georgie" stole, the self-conscious and insecure Martin maintains his identity as Georgie to win over Susan.

Meanwhile, we spend private "me" time with Martin, who is into men's bodybuilding magazines (as also was the psychopathic leading character in Hitchcock's never-filmed late 1960s psychological thriller *Kaleidoscope*). He's also given to snuggling a stuffed animal while rocking in a chair under which he smashes a framed photo of his stepfather, scrutinizing his naked physique while preening in a mirror, and in private holding hair-raising two-way conversations with his shadow self, Georgie (like Norman Bates and his mother). The tensest section of the film unfolds at the home of Susan's mother (Billie Whitelaw), who rents rooms to guests, including, eventually, Martin, who pursues Susan as she grows increasingly suspicious of her mother's newest lodger. Things get queasily sexual between Susan's lonely, frustrated mother and Martin, who uses scissors and hatchets on anyone who angers or arouses him, especially those who stand between him getting to Susan. The final scene is an awkward and embarrassing retread of *Psycho* minus the brilliance or the pathos, although writer-director Roy Boulting at least hints at genuine compassion for his central character. You've been warned. ♟♟♟

PLAY MISTY FOR ME (1971)

A disc jockey's life goes haywire when a one-night stand with a troubled listener turns into a dark and violent obsession.

THE MACGUFFIN: The radio show caller who nightly requests the song "Misty"

A young woman with a smoky, seductive voice nightly calls an all-night small-time Carmel, California, radio station jazz disc jockey and always requests him to play Erroll Garner's "Misty." The jockey—a good-looking hound (and a bit of a jerk) named Dave Garver (played by Clint Eastwood at his Clint-iest)—humors her. When Dave's shifts end, he sops up free drinks at local bars; as a local celebrity and himbo, he's accustomed to women coming on to him. One night he and Miss "Misty"—Evelyn (played by Jessica Walter)—meet (*not* by accident) and share a one-night stand. For Dave, it's strictly a one-and-done, and he tells Evelyn so. Evelyn doesn't take it well, and soon she's pushing herself into every corner of the disc jockey's messy life, moving in, clinging, intruding, demanding *more*. Evelyn's craziness escalates when Dave's old girlfriend Tobie (Donna Mills) resurfaces and our hero suddenly pumps the brakes on his tomcatting to settle down with his ex. And that's when things (and people) start getting slashed to ribbons.

In 2025, the plot mechanics of *Play Misty for Me* are old news to anyone who has seen such successors as *Fatal Attraction* or the brilliantly harrowing, tragic *Baby Reindeer*. But in 1971, by flipping the script on a hoary movie trope—this time, it's the macho, naïve man getting terrorized by a transgressive woman—the Jo Heims–Dean Reisner screenplay attracted Eastwood, who chose it for his directing debut. Macho Steve McQueen reportedly turned down the male lead because, for once, the girl had the great role. Universal, meanwhile, wanted Eastwood to cast a big name like Lee Remick to play Evelyn, but he passed her over—as well as, reportedly, *The Group* stars Joanna Pettet and Elizabeth Hartman (Oscar nominated for *A Patch of Blue*). But it was Jessica Walter, another costar in that female-centered 1966 Sidney Lumet-directed movie, who sparked Eastwood's attention.

Play Misty for Me wants to be a big-time shocker on the level of *Psycho* or *Repulsion*. Not a chance. It's too crude and jerkily paced, but damned if it doesn't grab you and only rarely loses its grip (looking at you, dippy, overlong Eastwood/Mills Monterey Jazz Festival love montage). Eastwood is nicely understated in what would traditionally be "the girlfriend role," but it's Walter—nerve-jangling, edgy, go-for-broke, and deeply sympathetic as a pitiful, terrifying avenging angel—who haunts the memory. ♟♟♟

SISTERS (1973)

After witnessing her fashion-model neighbor brutally kill a man, a journalist gets in way over her head while unearthing the bizarre truth about the case.

THE MACGUFFIN: The missing twin

Brian De Palma made this queasy, shockingly effective mystery thriller on bended knee to Hitchcock. But, unlike others of the director's deep dives into Hitchcockiana, this one feels fresh and idiosyncratic because of its rivetingly weird vibe, tabloid sensibilities, and ragged indie movie nerviness. The setup is strong. Actress-model Danielle Breton (Margot Kidder) and newspaper writer Phillip Woode (Lisle Wilson) throw romantic sparks while they are contestants on an exploitative quiz show called *Peeping Tom* (triple hat tip to Michael Powell, to Hitchcock's *Rear Window*, and to the voyeurism theme investigated by both Hitchcock and De Palma). Danielle's prize is a set of shiny stainless-steel knives and forks; Phillip's is a fancy dinner for two at the African Room. They decide to use his prize that night and, after dinner—which gets interrupted by a creepy man (William Finley) who declares himself Danielle's ex-husband before getting escorted out of the place—they spend the night together. We get flashes of things being awry (the ex-husband standing outside Danielle's place, a glimpse of a troubling scar on Danielle's leg). Sure enough, the next morning, we learn that the model is half of a matching set of well-known conjoined Siamese twins, Danielle being the apparently nice one; the other, not so nice, is named Dominique. Example? Dominique arrives to celebrate their shared birthday and, during the strained festivities, viciously knifes Phillip in the crotch. Phillip struggles to scrawl "Help" in blood on a window, then dies.

The brutal murder has been witnessed from across the way (just like in *Rear Window* and its imitators and remakes) by Grace Collier (a nod to Hitchcock's ideal leading lady Grace Kelly?), an intrepid news reporter and amateur sleuth (a very good Jennifer Salt) who reports the crime to the police; they mistrust and disbelieve her due to her series of newspaper stories in which, decrying police brutality, she referred to cops as "pigs." They also seem disinclined to care much because Phillip, the "alleged" victim, was black while Danielle is white. De Palma delivers one hell of a split-screen sequence here: one side features Salt and two policemen heading toward the scene of the crime; on the other side, we see Kidder and Finley cleaning up all traces of the murder and stuffing Wilson's body into the sofa bed. The characters intersect at the front door. The cops find Danielle but no evidence of a crime at all, although, as in *Rope*, the corpse is right under their noses. Now the killer knows about Grace—who hires a sly private detective (Charles Durning, always a pro) to help her prove Danielle's guilt. There's little more one can say about this wicked, nasty little suspense horror flick without spilling the beans, so I won't.

De Palma wrote the screenplay in the 1960s with college classmate Louisa Rose; they took inspiration from a *Life* magazine story about a pair of conjoined Russian twins who were subjected to unspeakable cruelty at the hands of doctors under Stalin, suffered tragic emotional problems, and harbored extreme personality conflicts. The writers conspired to write a shocker that would salute both Hitchcock

In De Palma's *Sisters*, the twisted relationship between formerly conjoined twins played by Margot Kidder makes for queasy viewing.
Michael Ochs/Moviepix/Getty Images

(especially *Spellbound, Rope, Rear Window, Vertigo*, and *Psycho*, but not neglecting *North by Northwest* and *The Birds*) and Roman Polanski (*Repulsion*). They succeeded. Even today, *Sisters* has the power to startle and nauseate. Its brooding, churning Bernard Herrmann score, especially during a wild finale set in an asylum, helps make it the stuff of nightmares. It's a ballsy, nasty little affair revealing the young De Palma daring to try and one-up the master, going deliciously nutso with languid tracking shots, flashbacks, documentary-style footage, and split screens. Little of what happens in *Sisters* makes sense, and unlike Hitchcock, De Palma doesn't seem interested in weaving a compelling story. Still, it's fun to experience the young De Palma back when he was gleeful and full of bratty bravado, a quality too often absent once he moved on to bigger-budget moviemaking. He and *Sisters* are unhinged. In the most entertaining way possible. ♟♟♟

HALLOWEEN (1978)

On Halloween night, an escaped psychiatric hospital patient—the personification of pure evil—goes on a killing spree of teenage girls in a small midwestern town.

THE MACGUFFIN: The man behind the mask

Horror, stripped of anything more than a relentlessly simple premise—an escaped madman with a kitchen knife roams a tiny midwestern town on Halloween night—can be startlingly effective. Working on a shoestring indie budget from a bare-bones script he cowrote in ten days with his producing partner Debra Hill, John Carpenter created a massively successful scare machine that, like it or not, helped launch the entire teen slasher flick genre, changed the face of horror movies, and birthed a title, heroine, and killer that have spawned thirteen movies (so far). All due credit to Carpenter and Hill. On the release of *Halloween*, Roger Ebert is one of several critics who declared *Halloween* so "merciless… violent and scary… terrifying and creepy" that he likened it to *Psycho*. Look, no one expects a film as influential, analyzed, dissected, imitated, and (pointlessly) sequelized as *Halloween* to feel as potent, fresh, and revolutionary today as it did forty-seven years ago, any more than one expects *Psycho* to stun and unnerve viewers with the same power it did sixty-six years ago. But revisiting *Halloween* today through grown-up eyes can be disconcerting. And instructive.

The movie is exceptionally well shot by cinematographer Dean Cundey, who employs every square inch of the frame to scare, disorient, and unsettle us; it felt innovative and unnerving to use Steadicam for those long tracking shots from the masked killer's point of view. Something horrible could happen at any second. Throughout his career, Hitchcock used subjective tracking shots to put viewers in the position of characters with whom he wanted us to identify—late in *Psycho*, we approach and explore the forbidding Bates house from the viewpoint of Vera Miles, who plays the dead heroine's inquisitive sister. Norman Bates gets no such shots. But today, Carpenter's subjecting tracking shots—and even his now famous, nerve-jangling music score—seem overused. Caustic and brilliant film critic Pauline Kael accurately noted that "the camera also tracks subjectively when [the madman] isn't around at all; in fact, there's so much tracking you begin to think everybody in the movie has his own camera." She also suggested that Carpenter did nothing in *Halloween* that hadn't already been done better by Hitchcock (of whom she was no fan), Brian De Palma (whom she championed), and Val Lewton. (And she didn't even mention that, in 1946, director Robert Siodmak briefly used the killer's POV in *The Spiral Staircase* as later did *Psycho* and *Peeping Tom*.) As taut and frantic as I'd remembered *Halloween* being, revisiting it today doesn't give the same effect—because its characters are either fatuous and annoying (Nancy Loomis as the wild-haired teen babysitter, P. J. Soles as the giggly horny teen) or bloviating blowhards (the usually peerless Donald Pleasence, campy as the psychiatrist). And it teases for so long the explosion of violence we know is coming that it becomes a little dull.

What still makes *Halloween* such a gut punch, though, is the utter anonymity and unknowability of the silent, enigmatic Michael Myers. All we know about him is that, as an eight-year-old, he stabbed to death his teenage sister after she and her boyfriend had sex. His driving and prowling the leafy streets thronged with trick-or-treaters of fictional Haddonville, Illinois (which features palm trees; the film was shot in Southern California), is for no other reason than to satisfy his urge to kill? Still powerful, even when some of those sections switch dramatically from day to night with no rhyme or reason. My favorite Hitchcockian moment in the action comes when the teen women catcall after Michael as he slowly drives past them; he drives down the street, then slows down and stops. And waits. Will he back up the car and come after them? Kill them now or later? This is Carpenter—and the movie—at a peak: scary, witty, visually intelligent, in love with moviemaking and playing masterfully with the audience. Carpenter doesn't appear to be an actor's director, and the script doesn't bother to tell us much more about the victims-to-be other than that they are young and (mostly) female, so it's a good thing that at least one of the actors is given time to show herself as vivid and idiosyncratic.

Apparently, Carpenter wanted to cast Anne Lockhart (daughter of actress June Lockhart) as Laurie Strode, but when she became unavailable (and producer Hill instead saw the publicity value of casting the daughter of *Psycho* star Janet Leigh), nineteen-year-old Jamie Lee Curtis made her movie debut. Deep-voiced, offbeat, gawky, somber-eyed, and sporting a luxurious head of hair, the inexperienced Curtis radiated moody intelligence and grit. Her confrontations with the psychotic are exhilarating and refreshingly transgressive. She can handle him, and it's a beautiful thing. ♟♟♟

THE SILENT PARTNER (1978)

Things get violent when a mild-mannered bank teller and a psychopathic master criminal battle over a stolen fortune.

THE MACGUFFIN: Stolen bank money

When friends ask me to recommend an unsung, deep-cut Hitchcockian movie, *The Silent Partner* often comes to mind. It's a pity that so few have heard of it, let alone seen it, because it is an overlooked gem. Based on a 1969 novel titled *Think of a Number* by Danish author

Anders Boldelsen, it was filmed first for German TV in 1972 by writer-director Rainer Erler (*Sieben Tag*) as *Der Amateur* (*The Amateur*). Curtis Hanson (*The Bedroom Window*, *L.A. Confidential*) adapted it for a second 1978 film version—a Hitchcockian one—directed with a deft, quirky self-assurance and a sure gift for suspense by Daryl Duke (*Payday*). Elliott Gould stars as Miles Cullen, an unassuming collector of rare tropical fish and a Toronto bank employee who observes suspicious behavior in Harry Reikle (Christopher Plummer), who is gigging temporarily as a shopping Santa while casing Miles's bank in preparation for a stickup. Reikle makes the steal from Miles, who proves he's not so unassuming after all: he snakes the lion's share of the cash, stows it in a safe-deposit box, and thinks he's gotten away with it. Except Reikle, a misogynist with a fondness for wearing mascara and false eyelashes, isn't about to let Miles get away with it. Thus begins Reikle playing increasingly bizarre and dangerous *Strangers on a Train*–style cat-and-mouse games with Miles.

Threatening phone calls, gooey with faintly homoerotic undertones ("We're partners, you know that. We're partners and we always have been"). Violent, destructive break-ins at Miles's apartment. Then come a couple of particularly gruesome murders of people close to Miles, who refuses to let go of the stolen money, warning Reikle, "I want you to know one thing: if I ever see you again, I'll kill you." The 106-minute movie is handsomely shot by Oscar winner Billy Williams (*Women in Love*, *On Golden Pond*) and features an arresting score by jazz pianist Oscar Peterson, as well as many allusions not only to Hitchcock but also *Double Indemnity*. Curtis Hanson rushed right in to take over the filming when Daryl Duke quit after producers insisted he film a decapitation scene. Hanson, who wanted to direct the film from the beginning, had no such reservations.

Duke's offbeat casting choices pay off beautifully, with Gould delivering one of his most endearingly quirky and persuasive performances. Susannah York is also good as the office mate with whom Miles toys romantically, and French Canadian actress-singer Celine Lomez (who should have had a thriving film career) is delightfully sexy navigating a tricky role as the sexy femme fatale who must morph from being

Plummer's lover to Gould's accomplice. Plummer is so bizarre and diabolical in this that he is worthy of mention as one of the screen's more memorable villains. In reviewing the film, Roger Ebert described the plot as "worthy of Hitchcock." That's a bit of an overreach, but Elliott Gould apparently became friendly enough with Hitchcock to arrange for him a private screening of *The Silent Partner* that the director is said to have very much enjoyed. It still didn't land Gould the role of the quirky cab driver in *Family Plot*, for which Hitchcock first pursued the too expensive Al Pacino and Robert DeNiro before he gave the role to the marvelous Bruce Dern. ♟♟♟♟

DRESSED TO KILL (1980)

After witnessing the brutal murder of a wife and mother, a sex worker becomes the prime suspect—and a psychopath's target. To unmask the real killer, the victim's son teams up with the prostitute.

THE MACGUFFIN: A wedding ring

It's as impossible to talk about *Dressed to Kill* without talking about Hitchcock's *Psycho* as it is to talk about what movies Brian De Palma would have made if Hitchcock's movies hadn't existed. On its release forty-five years ago, *Dressed to Kill* made a big stir. It was gory, deliberately provocative, shot in hypersaturated colors that match its overheated psychosexual fantasies. Misogynistic and transphobic, some of it plays like a Hitchcock movie reimagined as a puerile soft-core porn. And it starts right from the opening with middle-aged housewife Kate Miller (Angie Dickinson, in one of her best, most touching performances) ignored by her husband as he shaves and she evaluates her body while showering and experiences erotic fantasies that somehow must be punished with brute violence. Later, she and her husband engage in a bout of unfulfilling morning sex while the clock radio yammers away.

Soon, though, we're onto a bravura sequence—the one everyone remembers—set in the Metropolitan Museum of Art, where Kate and an attractive stranger in sunglasses play flirtatious hide-and-seek games from room to room as Ralf D. Bode's camera glides dizzily in tandem with Pino Donaggio's hallucinatory music. Kate momentarily loses her gloves. The stranger has one; the other is the hands of someone else. Then, she realizes she's left her wedding ring and must return to the scene of the tryst to retain it. Being sexually unfulfilled and guilty for feeling that way are topics she and her therapist, Dr. Elliott, talk about often. Of course, this is a De Palma movie, so the stranger turns out to give poor middle-aged Kate venereal disease while the stalker blonde in the black trench coat (simultaneously resembling Janet (*Psycho*) Leigh's daughter Jamie Lee Curtis and Karen Black's disguise in the diamond ransom exchange scene in Hitchcock's *Family Plot*) awaits to slash her to ribbons with a razor while trapping Kate in the confined space of an elevator. Hmmm, Janet Leigh in the shower in *Psycho* much?

Kate gets no loving, vengeful sister like Vera Miles to investigate her death but gets, instead, a high-ticket sex worker (Nancy Allen) who teams with Kate's young son (Keith Gordon) to prove that a patient of Dr. Elliott's is the razor killer. De Palma, ever obsessed with twins and split psyches, plays games with Hitchcock's beloved "doubles" theme (see *Shadow of a Doubt*, *Strangers on a Train*), tarts it up with show-offy, emotionally distancing split screens, exploiting the dual nature of the killer, making sure there are two misplaced gloves, two scenes in a shower, and on an on. In Hitchcock's work, these touches feel thematic and integrated; in the cynical, prankish world of De Palma, they feel shoveled on with a trowel. Give us the De Palma of *Carrie*, *Blow-Out*, or *The Untouchables* any day over the De Palma of *Dressed to Kill*. ♟♟♟

THE FAN (1981)

An aging film star, anxious about making her Broadway musical debut and envious of her ex-husband's relationship with a younger woman, ignores letters from an increasingly unhinged young male superfan.

THE MACGUFFIN: Letters from a deranged superfan

Things didn't go according to plan when producer Robert Stigwood (*Saturday Night Fever*, *Grease*), high on the idea of creating a classy modern Hitchcockian thriller, hitched his wagon to making a film version of Bob Randall's 1977 Edgar Award–winning epistolary novel *The Fan*. To hype the psychological thriller project about an aging movie legend rehearsing to make her Broadway musical star debut while being stalked by a psychotic fan, Stigwood announced that Anne Bancroft, Shirley MacLaine, or Lauren Bacall would star in a screen adaptation by writer Norman Wexler (*Serpico*, *Saturday Night Fever*) for TV and film director Waris Hussein (*The Possession of Joel Delany*). Bacall, fresh from Broadway musical triumphs in *Applause* and *Woman of the Year*, signed on, but then there were considerable production delays, the hiring of two more screenwriters, Hussein's departure over "artistic differences," the hiring of a new first-time feature director, constant rewrites during production, reshoots, a new ending, a financier sued by Stigwood for breach of contract, and, generally, all sorts of chaos. The end result was a decidedly sub-Hitchcock misfire—a mishmash of a lady-in-peril thriller, a backstage musical (with two irresistibly appalling original songs by Marvin Hamlisch and Tim Rice, and even funnier faux Fosse-meets-*Staying-Alive* spangly, go-go-boy production numbers), lame riffs on *All About Eve*, and a slasher horror movie thanks to the mega successful release of *Friday the 13th* during production that persuaded the filmmakers to up the gore ante of *The Fan* before the film's release. Bacall, pretty much playing herself minus the even more legendary bitchiness, is as good as she can be considering the circumstances, and so is James Garner (who called the movie the worst of his career). Michael Biehn is pretty and properly menacing in a role that only reveals the same aspects of his unlikeable character in every scene. The great Maureen Stapleton is caustic, warm, and lived-in playing the equivalent of Thelma Ritter's *All About Eve* role—except Ritter never had to play a scene in which her face gets slashed by a straight razor in a New York subway station. As for the scenes in which Biehn's character slashes a gay chorus boy in a swimming pool and razors a gay pickup before lighting him on fire, they're as homophobic as they are repulsive. The camp elements of *The Fan* are plentiful, but that doesn't quite make it all all-time camp classic. And it is not to be confused with another Hitchcockian misfire called *The Fan*, the 1996 movie that stars Robert De Niro as a volatile baseball obsessive. ♟♟♟

THE SILENCE OF THE LAMBS (1991)

To catch a multiple murderer, an FBI cadet needs help from a jailed cannibalistic serial killer who is a former forensic psychiatrist.

THE MACGUFFIN: Evil incarnate embodied in one man

The connections between Hitchcock's *Psycho* and *The Silence of the Lambs* are many—and they range from the deep to the deeply superficial. Both the 1959 novel *Psycho* by Robert Bloch and the 1998 Thomas Harris novel took some inspiration from real-life Wisconsin mother-obsessed multiple murderer, cannibal, and cross-dresser Ed Gein. (Convicted murderer Doctor Alfredo Ballí Treviño is the real inspiration for Lecter.) Hitchcock encountered such studio resistance to his making *Psycho* that he chose to risk financing the movie himself. Similarly, even before Gene Hackman was associated with *The Silence of the Lambs* (when push came to shove, he decided to neither direct nor act in it, declaring the script "too violent"), *North by Northwest* and *Family Plot* screenwriter Ernest Lehman declined the offer to write the script because he found the Harris novel too disturbing. Director Jonathan Demme, a Hitchcock admirer who previously made the 1979 Hitchcockian homage *Last Embrace*, boarded the project but quickly lost Michelle Pfeiffer as his leading lady because she was not okay with the triumph of evil inherent in the film's conclusion. Unable to envision Jodie Foster in the role of a rookie FBI agent taunted by an erudite, diabolical cannibalistic serial killer, Demme also got turndowns from Geena Davis, Emma Thompson, Ellen Barkin, Meg Ryan, Kim Basinger, and Madeleine Stowe. And when his top choices to play seductive, witty, malicious Hannibal Lecter—Gene Hackman and John Hurt—lost interest, Robert De Niro, Robert Duvall, John Hurt, Jeremy Irons, Jack Nicholson, John Lithgow, and Derek Jacobi watched the role go to Anthony Hopkins.

Five Academy Awards, major critical and financial success, a sequel, two prequels, and two TV series later, the movie—often compared to such so-called elevated horror masterworks as Murnau's *Nosferatu* and Hitchcock's *Psycho*—is the stuff of legend, imitation, and parody.

The main Hitchcock comparisons center on the characters of Lecter as played by Hopkins and Norman Bates as embodied by Anthony Perkins—both highly intelligent, masterfully manipulative, articulate, well-mannered, attractive, dangerous, and improbably sexy. One kills, surgically dismembers, and eats his victims; the other stabs them and disposes of their corpses, especially when they threaten or rile his overly possessive elderly mother. Demme learned well from maestro Hitchcock about the power of tracking shots and the use of silence. But, as when Norman Bates and Marion Crane reveal themselves to each other through dialogue, *Psycho* soars, becoming immensely frightening and, at the same time, deeply sad, the conversations between Lecter and Clarice Starling (who, like Marion, bears the surname of a bird) similarly are among the most brilliant moments in the movie. Both films feature memorable jail cell scenes. Both make superb set pieces out of confined spaces—one in its hair-raising shower murder, the other in Lecter's heart-stopping escape scene. Both are beautifully written and balance strong characterizations with psychological horror. Both films feature transgressive heroines—Clarice by virtue of a profession often dominated by men; the financially struggling Marion who impulsively chooses to steal money from a rich, vulgar predator who boasts about getting richer by lying and cheating. Both movies are first-class thrillers against which others are measured to this day. ♟♟♟♟

SE7EN (1995)

A soon-to-retire veteran homicide detective and his rookie replacement hunt for a brilliant, elusive sadist who targets victims that have committed one of the seven deadly sins.

THE MACGUFFIN: A psychopath obsessed with the seven deadly sins

Hellishly dark and brilliantly realized on almost every possible level, this film was conceived by director David Fincher (*Zodiac*, *Gone Girl*) as a "tiny genre movie, the kind of movie Friedkin might have made after *The Exorcist*." And yet, working from a compelling, psychologically assaultive Andrew Kevin Walker screenplay (endlessly imitated and trivialized since), Fincher created a modern shocker classic, displaying the icy, sardonic worldview, relentlessness, a penchant for a bleak visual style, and level of technical mastery that once positioned him as a potential successor to Hitchcock, Fritz Lang, and, yes, William Friedkin. Such is the high level of intelligence, cinematic know-how, and ability to create dread, suspense, and despair on display that every collaborator seems in tune from the endless rain and gloom, from Darius Khondji's cinematography to Howard Shore's mournfully diabolical musical score. As with most of Fincher's work, the movie is also beautifully cast. Morgan Freeman (masterful) delivers a bone-weary, lived-in performance as the literate, perceptive Lieutenant William Somerset, who has spent decades as a homicide detective on the brutal inner-city streets of a fallen-down world run mad. Having experienced too much of man's infinite capacity for cruelty and violence, he's marking time until his imminent retirement while his youngblood replacement—Brad Pitt's cocky Sergeant David Mills, a newcomer to the city with a young wife (Gwyneth Paltrow, rarely better)—dismisses his senior partner as a burnout. At large is "John Doe," a monster (Kevin Spacey, exceptional) hell-bent on a diabolical, if bizarrely moralistic, mission: to slaughter victims whom he judges guilty of committing one of the seven deadly sins. Victim #1 is an immensely overweight man who apparently explodes from overeating. The word "Gluttony" is right there in the scene; then, a powerful attorney gets found horrifically slaughtered, and at the crime scene is discovered the word "Greed." As the apparently unstoppable John Doe explains, "We see a deadly sin on every street corner, in every home, and we tolerate it. We tolerate it because it's common, it's trivial. We tolerate it morning, noon, and night. Well, not anymore. I'm setting the example. What I've done is going to be puzzled over and studied and followed—forever." (What a masterpiece Fincher might have made of Sondheim's tragicomic Broadway musical about another morals-driven mass murderer, *Sweeney Todd: The Demon Barber of Fleet Street*.) Like Hannibal Lecter, Spacey's hyperintelligent, calculating, patient John Doe runs circles around the flatfoots out to get him. *Se7en* is a modern classic made to a standard that perhaps even Hitchcock

Lawmen Morgan Freeman and Brad Pitt shine a light on a world of pure evil in director David Fincher's *SE7en*.
Hulton Archive/Getty Images

might have envied (if grudgingly). Though it pulls no punches in its many moments of stomach-churning postmurder gore, it is even more insidiously effective in dredging up worse images from viewers' psyches. And the now infamous twist finale is an audacious shocker for the ages. Essential and, once seen, hard to shake. ♟♟♟♟

THE FAN (1996)

As an obsessive knife salesman's personal and professional life unravels, his fixation on a new San Francisco Giants star player leads to violence and mayhem.

THE MACGUFFIN: A fanatic's obsession with a baseball star's losing streak

"You'll love *The Fan*," predicted a well-meaning friend who described it as "like Hitchcock's *Strangers on a Train*, only the psychotic stalker becomes obsessed with a baseball player instead of a tennis player." Well, now that I've seen *The Fan*, I can vouch that it is only vaguely like *Strangers on a Train* because it isn't suspenseful, innovative, shocking, well directed, or even good. In fact, *The Fan*—starring Robert De Niro and Wesley Snipes—is one of the least compelling movies the talented Tony Scott ever directed, right down there with *Beverly Hills Cop II*, *Days of Thunder*, and *Revenge*. DeNiro (who beat out contenders Al Pacino, Brad Pitt, and Wesley Snipes himself or the role) plays foul-mouthed, deeply troubled knife salesman and obsessive San Francisco Giants stan Gil Renard, who goes fully psychotic when his favorite Major League ballplayer Bobby Rayburn, played by Snipes, signs a forty-million-dollar contract and promptly hits a losing streak. The film starts off well with screenwriter Phoef Sutton (writer-producer for *Cheers*), adapting Peter Abrahams's highly praised 1995 novel, playing to De Niro's short-fuse strengths with a banquet of strong scenes that delineate Gil's explosive volatility with his boss (Dan Butler), his clumsy, cringe-inducing phony flirtatiousness toward secretaries, and verbal assaults on uninterested customers. Then there's Gil's rocky relationship with his ex-wife (Patty D'Arbanville), their perpetually frightened young son (Andrew J. Ferchland), and the ex-wife's laid-back new husband (Chris Mulkey), which have led to restraining orders that Gil violates. Once Gil gets fired, the movie goes off the rails. He's such an obvious ticking time bomb, we all know where this is going—especially since we've already seen De Niro lose his marbles in *Taxi Driver*, *This Boy's Life*, *Raging Bull*, *New York, New York*, et al., and most especially if we've seen the 1981 Lauren Bacall psycho thriller also called *The Fan* (see above). There'll be stabbing deaths, a kidnapping of a little boy, an incriminating slice of someone's shoulder kept in a freezer, a baseball player beaten to death with a baseball bat—standard-issue thriller stuff. More inspired (because of its utter goofiness) is a crucial baseball game in which Gil threatens to kill again if Rayburn fails to hit a homer; Tony Scott stages the sequence in Candlestick Park in the pouring rain—merely because he liked the way it looked on film. The impressive performances from the supporting cast includes Ellen Barkin as a wise, spikey radio sportscaster, Benicio Del Toro as a rising baseball star, and John Leguizamo as Snipes's agent; they're so good you wish they were in the better movie, which they, along with De Niro and Snipes, deserve. ♟♟

STOKER (2013)

The death of a teenage girl's father brings the unexpected arrival of her seductive and mysterious "Uncle Charlie," who awakens the teen's suspicions of his ulterior motives toward her and her mother.

THE MACGUFFIN: A neurotic family's fortune

An avowed fan of the work of Hitchcock, the celebrated bloodshed maestro and world-class writer-director Park Chan-wook (*Old Boy*, *Decision to Leave*) made his English-language film debut with this unsettling slow-burn thriller from a script by actor Wentworth Miller (*Prison Break*). *Stoker*, a world apart from the hyperviolent, immaculately filmed vengeance melodramas that put the director on the map, sets different traps and plays different mind games with the audience. Creepy and dread filled, thanks to sinuous camera moves, bizarre, often hyper-tinted images, and a palpable feeling of dis-ease, *Stoker* is so Hitchcockian that it plays like an eroticized companion piece to one of the suspense master's favorite 1940s films, *Shadow of a Doubt*. The artsy, hothouse action (imagine Hitchcock filming something by Henry James) revolves around a neurotic, secretive Connecticut family typified by an aloof mother, Eve Stoker (Nicole Kidman), and her brooding and musically inclined daughter, India, whose beloved father (Dermot Mulroney) dies in a car accident the day India turns eighteen. Seemingly out of nowhere and opportunistically thrusting himself into the Stokers' lives comes charming, devilishly handsome Uncle Charlie (Matthew Goode). Hitchcock fans will (unlike many film critics, apparently) instantly recognize the name of the sophisticated and diabolical "Merry Widow Murderer" (superbly played by Joseph Cotten in Hitchcock's subversive 1943 classic *Shadow of Doubt*), the one who darkens the Norman Rockwell–style existence of his smalltown niece, sister, and brother-in-law in Hitchcock's quietly creepy suspense thriller scripted by Thornton Wilder and Sally Benson. Mia Wasikowska (at her opaque, intelligent best) plays India, and the movie excels so long as Park cants the film's imagery toward her mood and perceptions, especially when they're triggered and aroused by her uncle. In a suspenseful coming-of-age story, we're kept artfully off-balance as to whether some of the film's more baroque touches—such as the spider that India lets crawl up between her legs—are literal, metaphorical, or imagined. Nevertheless, we can't help but notice when the family housekeeper (Phyllis Somerville) vanishes and a worried family member (Jacki Weaver) seems likely to meet a similar fate so long as Uncle Charlie is around to bring the darkness, putting the moves on India's mother and confusing the teen herself with his devilish seductions. It's in the movie's third act, when all the secrets are laid bare, that *Stoker* gets exposed as toothless and not up to much of anything truly twisted at all. What a letdown. ♟♟♟

GONE GIRL (2014)

When a husband in a troubled marriage reports his wife missing on their fifth anniversary, he becomes a prime suspect in her murder.

THE MACGUFFIN: The heroine's diary

When a beautiful blonde wife vanishes on her fifth wedding anniversary, her husband comes under police scrutiny in director David Fincher's scalpel-sharp, immaculately filmed big-screen version of the bestselling page-turner by Gillian Flynn, who also wrote the screenplay. Rolled out on a gurney and spread out for autopsy under Fincher and Flynn's gimlet-eyed and unsparing forensic gaze are an apparently practically perfect couple, writer Nick and his wife Amy Dunne (Ben Affleck and Rosamund Pike); former Manhattanites squeezed out by the 2008 economic crunch, they have relocated to Nick's economically battered boyhood home of Carthage, Missouri, where his mother is dying. On the morning of their anniversary, Amy vanishes; Nick portrays himself as baffled by his wife's disappearance, but evidence bubbles to the surface that their marital relationship was a minefield. And that's where things become an escalating cascade of seriously sick and blood-soaked twists and double crosses that no one—even all these years later—should spoil. Unerringly intelligent, riveting, and mordantly funny, *Gone Girl* may be one of the most ideal matchups of director and literary material since Roman Polanski met *Rosemary's*

Baby or Alfred Hitchcock met *Psycho*. It's not only primo postmodern Hitchcock but also one of the best-cast films in memory.

Exactly as it should have, Pike's brilliant, wry, seductive performance and nouveau Hitchcock blonde presence won the lion's share of the reviews and the award nominations. But there isn't an off performance in a cast that includes Neil Patrick Harris, Tyler Perry, Carrie Coon, Casey Wilson, and Patrick Fugit. Affleck more than rises to the occasion playing Nick and has one of his best moments when he cannot suppress a smug smirk during a public announcement plea for help in finding his wife. Fincher pulls off a stabbing sequence so shockingly and impeccably staged, filmed, edited, and scored (by Trent Reznor and Atticus Finch) that it is an exemplary post-*Psycho* murder scene. The finale is as bleakly funny and ironic as anything Hitchcock or, for that matter, Luis Buñuel might have concocted. The movie leans so hard into a corrosively bleak and jaundiced view of twenty-first-century marriage that it could have been advertised with the tagline, "Don't see it with someone you love." Fincher is—alongside Paul Thomas Anderson and Christopher Nolan—one of our most gifted and temperamentally attuned successors to Hitchcock, so it made sense that in 2015, after the box-office and critical success of *Gone Girl*, he, Affleck, and Gillian Flynn were said to be reuniting on an update of *Strangers on a Train*, Hitchcock's 1951 classic based on Patricia Highsmith's novel. Though, all these years later, nothing seems likely to come of it, we're still waiting anxiously at the station. ♟♟♟♟

7 Gone

Few life events are as devastating or frightening as someone we love vanishing into thin air. Hitchcock exploited such events most powerfully in his two versions of *The Man Who Knew Too Much* (1934, 1956), in which the parents of a young child—drawn inadvertently into international intrigue—suffer when their only child gets kidnapped and taken hostage. Hitchcock returned to lighter, more comic approaches to the primal terror of abduction again with his influential classics *The Lady Vanishes* (1938), *Foreign Correspondent* (1940), and *North by Northwest* (1959).

But it is the 1956 version of *The Man Who Knew Too Much* in which Hitchcock and company most potently dramatized the impact of what pioneering mental health professional Pauline Boss, PhD, described first in the 1970s as "type one ambiguous loss," referring to the specific psychological trauma that occurs when a person goes missing—becomes physically absent but remains strongly psychologically present in the heart and the mind—as a result of kidnapping, war, or natural disaster. Boss's research details how this kind of loss is complicated and exacerbated by "the lack of facts surrounding the loss of a loved one." The people left behind—as portrayed by James Stewart and Doris Day—"deal with disruptive, catastrophic situations and trauma of loss (potentially) without resolution." Played with startling empathy and emotional directness by Day, former singing star and devoted mother "Jo" Conway McKenna undergoes every emotion detailed in Boss's work; unable to grieve without knowing the outcome, she suffers bewilderment, panic, anxiety, anger, sorrow and resolve.

Other filmmakers major and minor have dipped their toes into the same icily terrifying pool as Hitchcock, but few have been as successful at depicting the concept of chaos—whether it's through kidnapping, a case of mistaken identity, an attack on humanity by mother nature— as a force that can not only destroy but can also bring people closer together.

THE MIDNIGHT WARNING (1932)

An oddball detective helps a young woman solve the baffling mystery of how her brother vanished from the fancy hotel at which they were guests.

THE MACGUFFIN: The missing brother

Penned by screenwriters John Thomas Neville and Norman Battle, this old chestnut is the grandaddy of virtually every "lady vanishes" or "gentleman vanishes" movie that followed—including Alfred Hitchcock's *The Lady Vanishes* (1938) and the Terence Fisher and Antony Darnborough–directed *So Long at the Fair* (1950). All, of course, derive from the urban legend of "The Vanishing Hotel Room" (aka "The Vanishing Lady"), about a daughter who allegedly left her mother in their Paris hotel room at the time of an international exposition in Paris. When the daughter returned from her errand, both mother and her entire hotel room had disappeared; no one admitted to the existence of either of them.

The legend inspired a slew of novels and films. *The Midnight Warning* (aka *Eyes of Mystery*) opens with a touch that anticipates David Lynch—a detective's bizarre discovery of a human ear bone in the fireplace of a fancy hotel room. Soon after, a sniper from a building across the way fires a shot into the hotel room from which a young man recently vanished without a trace and to which a famed, unorthodox detective has been asked by the young man's blonde sister, Enid Van Buren (Claudia Dell), to investigate. We may think we're off to the races… until the detective, Thorwaldt Cornish (played by William "Stage" Boyd, arrested on gambling and liquor charges in 1931, and adding "Stage" to differentiate himself from William "Hopalong Cassidy" Boyd), enters the scene and stops the action cold. Boyd poses statically while blathering to his old buddy and fellow Dr. Steve Walcott (Hooper Atchley) about things we care nothing about, such as his one-of-a-kind high-intensity binoculars that aid his spying on criminals and reading lips from great distances.

This long, talky expository scene violates a basic Hitchcock rule of moviemaking: show, don't tell. But if you *must* tell, make certain to put in front of the camera remarkable personalities saying fascinating things. Hitchcock himself does that even late in his career with the long, long and talky opening expositional scene between guilt-stricken elderly matriarch Julia Rainbird (Cathleen Nesbitt) and her phony spiritualist Blanche Tyler (Barbara Harris) in *Family Plot*, but both are interesting screen presences; *The Midnight Warning* has only Boyd and Atchley directed flatly by quickie cliffhanger serial expert Spencer Gordon Bennett (*Secret Service in Darkest Africa*, an inspiration for the *Indiana Jones* movies). Just as Woolcott is about to shed light on moving along the plot—what happened to the brother of Enid Van Buren?—he keels over, and the hotel staff members, nudging and eyeing each other significantly, move like molasses while attending to him. The doctor chalks it up to "a little rush of blood to the head, probably vertigo." If *only*. No, someone took a pot shot at him from across the street, and finally the game is afoot, with the detective and doctor interviewing scads of people as they try to solve the mystery in ways far less delightful and entertaining than in *The Lady Vanishes* or *So Long at the Fair*. There is, at least, an amusing and chilling scene in which the gaslighted heroine gets lured to—and locked inside—a mortuary where the cadavers suddenly seem to be awfully chatty. The whole movie is just too talky, ineptly acted, and sluggish—at only sixty-three minutes—but even for Hitchcockian completists, this one is strictly a museum piece—or, more charitably, a warm-up for *The Lady Vanishes*. ♟♟

SO LONG AT THE FAIR (1950)

When a young tourist awakens in her hotel room the morning after she and her brother arrived to attend the Paris Exposition of 1889, she is startled to learn that her brother has vanished from his room. The entire hotel staff denies he was ever there at all.

THE MACGUFFIN: The vanishing brother

Twelve years after the release of Hitchcock's *The Lady Vanishes* came this intriguing (and very similar) Terence Fisher and Antony Darnborough–directed British thriller scripted by novelist-playwright-screenwriter Hugh Mills (*Personal Property*) from a 1947 Anthony Thorne novel. Intrigue surrounds British siblings Vicky and Johnny Barton (Jean Simmons and David Tomlinson), who check into their luxurious Paris hotel to enjoy the Exposition of 1889. After an evening at a café and taking in the show at the Moulin Rouge, Johnny complains of fatigue and purportedly heads to his room, only to vanish into thin air—along with his entire hotel room, Number 19. His sister, baffled, not a French speaker, and increasingly unnerved by the hotel staff's insistence that she checked in alone (her brother forgot to sign the register), refuses to back down. Vicky, especially as portrayed by the gifted and ethereally beautiful young Simmons, becomes a highly sympathetic figure, especially when the directors juxtapose her panic and resolve against the frenzy and gaiety of the world's most beautiful and romantic city during the unveiling of the Eiffel Tower.

As Vicky's fears and panic intensify while she searches for Johnny—rebuffed by the French police and the British consulate, who refuse to credit her concerns that her brother might have been kidnapped or even worse—the film becomes atmospheric, paranoid, and sinister as every potential clue pursued by the heroine leads her down blind alleys. Just when Simmons begins doubting her own sanity (in the grand tradition of the heroine of *Gaslight* and its army of imitators), enter Dirk Bogarde as dashing artist and fellow Brit George Hathaway, who not only believes her story but also met her brother and borrowed cab fare from him. Bogarde is charming, chivalrous, and, as ever, slightly inscrutable as he and Simmons go undercover to unwrap the mystery; their screen chemistry becomes one of the film's best assets. There are interesting supporting performances, too, from Honor Blackman as Bogarde's friend and the regal Cathleen Nesbitt (*Family Plot*) as the hotel's shadowy, self-protective owner, Madame Hervé. Those who love this film, and there are many, always cite the hot-air balloon scene (in which a potential witness, a hotel maid who met Johnny, is a balloon passenger) for its style, cleverness, power, and suspense.

Style, cleverness, and suspense are plentiful in *So Long at the Fair*, but its lack of genuine excitement and cheeky wit make it a much lesser film than *The Lady Vanishes*. A 1955 *Alfred Hitchcock Presents* episode, directed by Don Medford and starring Patricia Hitchcock (the director's actress daughter, whom he also cast in *Stage Fright*, *Strangers on a Train*, and *Psycho*), was also based on the nineteenth-century urban legend of "The Vanishing Hotel Room" and covered just about the same territory as *So Long at the Fair*, with a much smaller budget and far less flair. Alfred Hitchcock himself was fond of *So Long at the Fair*; when asked why he never bought the screen rights to Hugh Mills's novel, he facetiously replied, "Well, you see, I've made a few costume pictures and I don't much care for the experience. The problem with costume films is that you can't imagine the characters in them ever going to the bathroom." ♟♟♟♙

DANGEROUS CROSSING (1953)

A newlywed heiress becomes increasingly distraught when her young husband disappears immediately after they embark on their transatlantic honeymoon.

THE MACGUFFIN: The vanishing bridegroom

Although this suspense melodrama isn't about someone disappearing into thin air while aboard a train but about someone disappearing from a transatlantic ocean liner full of people out to gaslight its heroine, it is so like Hitchcock's 1938 classic *The Lady Vanishes* that we may as well call it *The Gentleman Vanishes*. In the overly gabby film, adapted by screenwriter Leo Townsend (*White Feather*) from the famed radio drama *Cabin B-13* by that mordant master of terrifying "locked-room" mysteries John Dickson Carr, it is the lovely Jeanne Crain's (*Leave Her to Heaven*, *A Letter to Three Wives*) turn to play the confused and tormented victim trapped in a nasty conspiracy. As brittle Ruth Bowman, Crain, cast usually as fresh-faced nice girls, seizes the opportunity to do lots and lots of acting pretty much from the moment her handsome husband, John (Carl Betz, *The Donna Reed Show*), carries her over the threshold of their shipboard stateroom, tells her he will meet her soon for a drink, says he's going to deposit (Ruth's) money with the purser, and promptly goes missing. Ruth checks with that purser (there's no "Mr. Bowman" on the passenger list, of course); she appears on the passenger list as "Ruth Stanton," her birth name. When questioned by the ship's grizzled captain (Willis Bouchey, *The Man Who Shot Liberty Valence*), Ruth admits she has no ticket, no passport. What's more, she has no wedding ring, she's married to a man she barely knows, and she can't even remember the name of the backwoods town in which she got hastily married only days before. Is this woman a complete ninny? A stowaway? Working an angle? Unhinged? No one aboard admits to having seen John—not even the moonstruck cabin stewardess Anna (Mary Anderson, still at sea after appearing nine years earlier as a shipwrecked waif in Hitchcock's *Lifeboat*) who literally watches John carry Ruth over the threshold. Meanwhile, Ruth begins receiving paranoia-inducing phone calls from John from somewhere aboard the ship and spending her sleepless nights roaming the atmospherically spooky fogbound decks while draped in mink and plaintively calling, "John… John," as foghorns bellow mournfully.

Luckily, her midnight rambles are being shadowed by the ship's tall, dark, and handsome doctor (Michael Rennie, *The Day the Earth Stood Still*), pretty much the only character in the whole movie who doesn't appear to exist solely as a red herring. *Dangerous Crossing* winds down with a perfectly logical (also abysmally obvious and clichéd) explanation, and although the whole seventy-five-minute film, directed by Joseph M. Newman (*This Island Earth*), is meant to be scary and nerve-wracking, its most unnerving moments are the grimace-like smiles Jeanne Crain switches on, then instantly off when she thinks the cameras of the wonderful Joseph La Shelle (*Laura*) aren't noticing. Only then does she reveal herself (*not* the character she is playing) as a true lady in distress. It's enough to break your heart. ♟♟

BUNNY LAKE IS MISSING (1965)

A young American single mother newly arrived in England grows increasingly frantic when her four-year-old daughter vanishes from school and people keep questioning whether she ever existed.

THE MACGUFFIN: The missing child

Director Otto Preminger (*Laura, Anatomy of a Murder*) attempted to go full Hitchcock with this psychological thriller based on a 1957 novel by Evelyn Piper (aka Marryam Modell) for which he hired and fired numerous screenwriters (Dalton Trumbo, Ira Levin, John Mortimer, Penelope Mortimer, among them) to adapt for years. What he got for all his trouble and tinkering is three-quarters of a weird but interesting movie before it collapses in the home stretch. To portray a New York single mother scouring London for her vanished four-year-old, the notoriously tyrannical and abusive Preminger cast lovely Carol Lynley (*The Cardinal*), the latest of his contract blondes since his 1950s failure to vault to stardom the inexperienced and self-conscious Jean Seberg in *Saint Joan* and *Bonjour, Tristesse*. Lynley (one of many young actresses Hitchcock briefly considered as a casting possibility for *The Birds*) is affecting and sympathetic here as a kind of Alice in the disorienting and despairing wonderland that was swinging sixties London, in which she chases clues to Bunny's disappearance in attempting to solve an all-too-obvious "mystery." Preminger clearly gets a kick out of exploiting the shadows and such locales as a doll hospital and a crazy lady's attic apartment.

The supporting cast members are consigned to playing florid eccentrics worthy of Lewis Carroll. There's Keir Dullea (*2001: A Space Odyssey*) as the heroine's obviously oddball journalist brother, Noël Coward plays the Lakes' creepy lecherous landlord (alternately snuggling a chihuahua and a whip and, off camera, needling his cocky young costar with "Keir Dullea, gone tomorrow"), and Martita Hunt (indelible in David Lean's *Great Expectations*) as a weird older woman who claims she spends her days collecting children's nightmares. Meanwhile, the 1960s pop group The Zombies appears in several scenes to perform such forgettable tunes as "Nothing's Changed" and "Remember You" and stamp the film with hip credentials. Among the creative elements that tip their hat to the master of suspense are a credit sequence designed by Hitchcock colleague Saul Bass (*Vertigo*, *North by Northwest*, and *Psycho*) and

Carol Lynley as a distraught mother can't get anyone to believe that her little girl has vanished on her first day of school in *Bunny Lake Is Missing*, Otto Preminger's journey into Hitchcock land.
Silver Screen Collection/Moviepix/Getty Images

performances by such first-rate scene-stealers as Laurence Olivier (*Rebecca*) as a by-the-books Scotland Yard inspector, Anna Massey (later seen in *Frenzy*) as a schoolteacher, and Lucie Mannheim (*The 39 Steps*) as a brusque German cook. Preminger even tried pulling a Hitchcock by unconvincingly *Psycho*-izing the movie's ending, personally narrating its trailer à la Hitchcock in the famous *Psycho* trailer, and announcing that "No one may be admitted to the theater after the picture has started." As it turned out, there weren't enough paying customers to care one way or the other. *Flightplan* (2005) reworked enough of *Bunny Lake*'s elements to nearly be considered an unofficial remake. ♟♟♟

HONEYMOON WITH A STRANGER (1969)

A frantic honeymooner reports his bride has gone missing but when a priest reunites the couple, the husband rejects the woman as an imposter.

THE MACGUFFIN: A woman with red hair

While *Psycho* was taking the moviegoing world by storm in 1960, the press and public grew more curious than ever about how Hitchcock could possibly top it. In the fall, newspapers reported that the director had put aside plans to film in England his Audrey Hepburn–Laurence Harvey comedy-murder-thriller *No Bail for the Judge* to instead focus on two other projects, one of which would be based on actor-playwright Robert Thomas's darkly comic Paris stage hit (reportedly favored by Alma Reville, who recommended it to hubby Hitchcock) *Piège pour un homme seul* (*Trap for a Lonely Man*), in which a husband reports to the police the disappearance of his new wife while they are honeymooning in the Alps. After the police conclude an unsuccessful search for the woman, a local priest materializes with the missing wife in tow—whom the husband instantly rejects as an imposter, despite considerable evidence suggesting otherwise. Is the husband trying to perpetrate a dark scheme? Is he insane? Is he a victim of gaslighting?

Hitchcock planned to cast international stars in the main roles of this diabolically twisty narrative—a plot in the style of novels by the team Boileau-Narcejac, writers of the source works for *Diabolique* and *Vertigo*. (The press reported Hitchcock was considering such tantalizing casting possibilities as Alain Delon, Jean-Paul Belmondo, Yves Montand, Jeanne Moreau, Romy Schneider, and Anouk Aimée.) What is not known is what tone and approach he planned to take to the material. Would it have been one of his so-called "run for cover" projects—something to do quickly and inexpensively while waiting to find a more tantalizing project to tackle? (See *Dial M for Murder*, which he filmed cleverly while adhering closely to the original material.) Or, since he had frequently been using the term "metaphysical" in recent interviews, did he want to rework and deepen the play to continue his explorations of such recurring themes as doubles, shifting identities, and the ultimate unknowability of even those closest to us? (See *The Wrong Man*, *Vertigo*, *Psycho*, and more.) My money's on the latter.

For various reasons Hitchcock abandoned *Piège pour un homme seul*, along with several other proposed post-*Psycho* projects, but that didn't stop other filmmakers from jumping on the Robert Thomas play's then-ingenious twists and turns. Germany got there first with filmed versions titled *Die Falle* (*The Trap*) in 1960 and 1961; a Dutch version followed in 1969, the same year as the broadcast of an ABC Movie of the Week.

This American movie-of-the-week version, titled *Honeymoon with a Stranger*, reduced the Thomas play to a standard woman-in-jeopardy puzzler featuring *Psycho*'s own Janet Leigh as Sandra Latham, newly married to a wealthy Italian, Ernesto (Joseph Lenzi), who vanishes from their Batres, Spain, villa—permanently. Sandra gets some help from a lovelorn police captain (Rossano Brazzi, effective and sympathetic) who quickly shuts down the investigation when Ernesto returns. Only Sandra swears that Ernesto (Cesare Danova) is not Ernesto, even if the man's sister (Barbara Steele) and lawyer (Eric Braeden) insist that he is. Nothing is what it appears to be; no one can be trusted. So what's lovely, enormously likable beleaguered heroine Leigh to do? Why, underplay her many chances for dramatic outbursts scripted by Henry Slesar (a writing staple of *Alfred Hitchcock Presents*) while sporting what look like leftover Lana Turner wigs and costumes while starring in A-level source material treated like a soapy B movie of the kind produced by Ross Hunter (*Midnight Lace*, *Portrait in Black*), that's what. Leigh gallantly perseveres but she, her costars, and Thomas's play deserve so much better.

The material got recycled all over again in 1976 as the TV movie *One of My Wives Is Missing*, somewhat more faithful to the details, if not the spirit, of the source material and starring James Franciscus, Elizabeth Ashley, and Jack Klugman. Underscoring the Hitchcock connection are supporting turns by Ruth McDevitt (*The Birds*), Milton Selzer (*Marnie*), and a sweet, winking reference to *Dial M for Murder*. This version was adapted by Peter Stone (*Charade* and *The Taking of Pelham One Two Three*), but just as he did on the decorative but disappointing *Arabesque*, he insisted on being billed under his pseudonym Peter Marton. In this version, it is Ashley who walks away with the top acting honors, if only because—unlike the usually reliable Klugman as the local investigator and Franciscus as the worried husband—she doesn't mistake hammy bellowing for good acting. In 1986, it was Mike Farrell, Margot Kidder, and Fred Gwynne's chance at the material in the entertaining *Vanishing Act*, set in the snowy Rockies and scripted by Richard Levinson and William Link. The plot still intrigues, but Hitchcock could have made it uncomfortably funny, touching, disturbing, and haunting—but those are abilities that separate him from all the rest. *Honeymoon with a Stranger* ♟♟, *One of My Wives Is Missing* ♟♟

PICNIC AT HANGING ROCK (1975)

In Australia in 1900, three students and a teacher vanish during a St. Valentine's Day outing. Only one young woman returns, her memory of what happened to her completely wiped.

THE MACGUFFIN: The eerie vanishings

This languid, mystical, poetic horror film that launched the brilliant but too brief career of Australian director Peter Weir (*Gallipoli*, *The*

Year of Living Dangerously, *Witness*, *Dead Poets Society*, *Master and Commander*) is uncommonly mesmerizing. As scripted by Cliff Green from Joan Lindsay's novel, the mystery begins on a dreamlike Valentine's Day in 1900 when a group of straw-hatted, white-lace-and-linen-clad young women and two teachers venture forth to Hanging Rock, an ancient volcanic outcropping not far from their rigid all-female boarding school.

The outing proves to be otherworldly, to say the least. Warned against attempting to climb the rock, a few do so anyway. One girl, troubled by the sight of her three classmates falling asleep in synch and arranged in a strange formation, screams for her life, then flees in a state of panic; another gets found after a few days with her memory of the details of the outing (along with her corset) missing. She reports that a prim, laced-up schoolteacher was seen running without a skirt. The women vanish into thin air. Remnants of torn lace found at the scene only deepen the mystery. Were the young Englishmen and the Australian seen near the site involved? Was the enigmatic leader Miranda (Anne-Louise Lambert) filled with premonitions and called by unseen spirits? Did the young women run riot to defy their sexual repression? The aftermath is just as bizarre, grim, and puzzling.

Magically photographed (by the award-winning Russell Boyd) and graced by unsettling and evocative sound design, the film radiates sensuality, longing, repression, and deep horror. In one astonishing moment, the rock itself appears to call out to the young women and then engulfs them. Haunting, stunning, genre-warping, and unforgettable, *Picnic at Hanging Rock*—even for its uniqueness—shares elements in common with films as diverse as *L'Avventura*, *Vertigo*, *A Passage to India*, and *Midsommar*. But its mood, strangeness, and period also suggest what Hitchcock might have accomplished if he hadn't been thwarted by Hollywood in his lifelong dream to make a film of Sir James Barrie's ghostly *Mary Rose*, about a young wife and mother who vanishes from her husband's sight while on a remote Scottish island, just as she did while visiting that same island with her father when she was a child. Years after Mary Rose disappears from her husband and has faded into memory, she returns, untouched by time, and is broken by meeting her lost baby—now a grown man—aged beyond recognition. Hitchcock spent decades trying to convince a studio chief to back *Mary Rose* as an unusual showcase for various favorite leading ladies over the decades. It was one of the great sorrows and frustrations of his career that no studio boss would take a gamble. Our loss. ♟♟♟♟

FRANTIC (1988)

The wife of an American surgeon vanishes from their hotel room, leading to the doctor getting caught up in a violent race to find a nuclear weapons detonator.

THE MACGUFFIN: A missing wife; a phone number in the wrong suitcase

One solid hour of *Frantic* is elegant, gripping Hitchcockian entertainment. The setup, engineered by director Roman Polanski and his longtime screenwriter collaborator Gérard Brach (*Repulsion*, *Jean de Florette*), is beautifully simple and executed to near perfection. Dr. Richard Walker (Harrison Ford) and his wife of twenty years, Sondra (Betty Buckley), arrive jet-lagged for a medical convention in Paris for the first time since their honeymoon. They barely recognize what Paris has become. It appears that Sondra, though she speaks fluent French and seems sharper, more organized, and faster on her feet than her husband, somehow failed to notice that she picked up the wrong piece of luggage at the airport. In a beautifully staged and choreographed scene, Walker takes a shower while Sondra answers a phone call. She gesticulates and mouths something to him, but he can't hear her above the roar of the shower and neither can we. *Why doesn't she simply come into the bathroom and tell him?* Then, looking past Walker through the clear glass shower stall straight into the hotel room, we see Sondra cross to the left side of the screen and disappear, then a suitcase slides from view. It is bone chilling. The doctor exits the shower. Sondra isn't there.

Having already seductively told his wife that they would be spending most of their hotel time making love, Walker arranges their bed with breakfast and strewn roses. He awakens from a nap. Still no Sondra.

Something's very wrong. Walker, who doesn't speak French, can't catch a break from the hotel staff, the police, and an American embassy employee (John Mahoney, wonderfully smug and indifferent). Walker is the only one who believes his wife is missing—except for the drunk who tells him he saw Sondra getting shoved into a car and being driven away. Breaking into the wrong luggage Sondra got at the airport, Weller locates a clue—a phone number. The tingly, paranoid head of steam built up so far by *Frantic* crashes when Weller starts rubbing shoulders with the city's underbelly of druggies, mercenary informants, and cheap crooks and then joins forces with glamorous street-smart smuggler Michelle (Emmanuelle Seigner), who is owed ten thousand francs for slipping into France the suitcase Sondra took by accident. Rooftop chases, cocaine, amoral psychopaths, and discos and glum cinematography by Witold Sobocínski and an icy Ennio Morricone score lend the film a chill, impersonal eighties vibe. But make no mistake, for all the movie's then-modern trappings, it's all strictly out of Hitchcock's playlist of *The 39 Steps*, *The Lady Vanishes*, and *The*

Harrison Ford, as a doctor whose wife has gone missing, clings to a Paris rooftop with mysterious Emmanuelle Seigneur in Polanski's lady-vanishes thriller *Frantic*.
François Duhamel/Sygma/Getty Images

Man Who Knew Too Much. Frantic doesn't live up to its title. Just when you want the hero's nightmare to get crazier and darker, the movie chickens out. A damn shame, too. Polanski was truly onto something entertainingly frightening with this one. ♟♟♟

THE VANISHING (1988)

Years after his girlfriend disappears, a man starts receiving disturbing letters from her abductor.

THE MACGUFFIN: The missing girlfriend

Dutch writer-director and documentarian George Sluizer brought the world nightmares with his terrifying psychological thriller *The Vanishing*. What's most horrifying about it is its matter-of-factness, its ordinariness, its feeling of plausibility. A young Dutch couple (Johanna ter Steege as the impulsive Saskia, Gene Bervoets as the insular Rex) are road-tripping in France when they run out of gas in the middle of a dark tunnel. They argue heatedly, make up, and stop to refuel at a busy gas station. The woman, plagued by a recurring nightmare, goes into the busy convenience store to buy drinks and, in broad daylight with the place packed with Tour de France tourists, disappears. Bewilderment and panic turn to obsession as Rex spends the next three years trying to get to the bottom of what happened to his girlfriend. The pursuit leads to his becoming inexorably lured into a bizarre cat-and-mouse relationship with another obsessive—Raymond, a chillingly banal, cerebral chemistry professor and doting father of two (Bernard-Pierre Donnadieu) who has not only saved a girl from drowning but also knows every meticulous, fully rehearsed detail of Saskia's disappearance and its aftermath. Entirely avoiding the cheap gore, jump scares, and clichéd Big Moments and lazy tropes audiences have come to expect from thrillers, *The Vanishing* instead creates an overwhelming atmosphere of sustained dread leading to a horrific, almost unbearable finale. No wonder Stanley Kubrick was such a big fan. Based on the novella *The Golden Egg* by Tim Krabbé, who also wrote the screenplay, *The Vanishing* is a stone-cold modern classic. Sluizer adheres to most of the rules of a Hitchcockian movie and avoids most of the traps. (Skip, at all costs, Sluizer's unfortunate, watered-down 1993 Americanized remake starring Jeff Bridges, Sandra Bullock, Kiefer Sutherland, and Nancy Travis.) ♟♟♟♟

FLIGHTPLAN (2005)

The young daughter of a newly widowed woman vanishes while they're on a plane flying from Germany to the United States.

THE MACGUFFIN: The vanishing daughter

What is the best thing one can say about this would-be Hitchcockian misfire starring Jodie Foster as a mom who will do just about *anything* to protect her endangered daughter? Don't dare confuse it with the very Hitchcockian *Panic Room* directed by the sometimes Hitchcockian David Fincher. And certainly don't measure it against the classic *The Lady Vanishes* directed by the maestro himself. The setup will be familiar to anyone who has seen any of the infinitely better aforementioned films. Airplane engineer Kyle Pratt (Foster) is an emotionally shattered new widow flying home from Berlin with her nine-year-old daughter, Julia (Marlene Lawston), to lay her husband's body to rest in Long Island. A few hours into the flight, Kyle awakens. Not only has the daughter vanished, but as Foster escalates from worry to full-blown panic and demands to search every nook and cranny of the double-decker jumbo jet—she helped design it, so she knows the territory—none of the other clichéd characters like the rude stewardess, the too-obliging air marshal (Peter Sarsgaard), the skeptical captain (Sean Bean), or the fellow passengers of entitled American families and their unruly kids will admit to having seen little Julia. Thing is, the girl doesn't even appear on the passenger manifest, and in fact a police report lists Julia as having died with her dad in an accident. No one believes Foster; she spends most of the movie's overlong running time fighting tears, screaming, and vilely confronting Arab passengers with wild accusations (the movie shamefully exploits post-9/11 terrorist paranoia for cheap suspense). The so-called big twist is preposterous, and the Peter A. Dowling–Billy Ray screenplay is riddled with Boeing 747-8-sized plot holes. Some have observed that the perpetrators of *Flightplan* took the outline of what made *The Lady Vanishes* great without bothering to flesh it out with great dialogue, memorable characters, or a true sense of urgency. What they really did was gin up the much lesser *Bunny Lake Is Missing*. Forgettable B-movie nonsense, *Flightplan* never should have been cleared for takeoff. ♟♟

8 A Race of Peeping Toms

In a prescient passage of dialogue John Michael Hayes wrote for the no-nonsense home nurse Stella (played by Thelma Ritter) in Hitchcock's *Rear Window*, the character chides the bored, temporarily immobilized photographer (James Stewart) for wasting his hours spying on his Greenwich Village neighbors: "We've become a race of Peeping Toms. What people ought to do is get outside their own house and look in for a change. Yes, sir. How's that for a bit of homespun philosophy?" Pretty good, we'd say. But isn't voyeurism, our inability to look away, our need to *know*, the key to our wanting to watch movies in the safety and anonymity of a darkened theater or our living rooms? Hitchcock knew this instinctively and exploited it powerfully not only in *Rear Window* but also in such films as *Vertigo*, *Psycho*, and *Marnie*, films in which we are alternately rewarded or punished for watching. Few other directors, apart from Luis Buñuel (*Belle de jour, Viridiana*), Michael Powell (*Peeping Tom*), Francis Ford Coppola (*The Conversation*), Michelangelo Antonioni (*Blow-Up*), and the ever reactive Brian De Palma (*Blow Out, Body Double*), were as willing to hold up a mirror to our fascination with seeing without being seen.

Of course, for moviegoers and television viewers discomfited by the notion of being seen, it is easy to dismiss as facile the entire audiences-as-voyeur concept. They argue that, after all, such directors as Hitchcock, Powell, Buñuel, De Palma, and the like are such consummate artists, telling such visually and thematically compelling films, that it is almost humanly impossible to turn away. Things happen in such movies. The characters and their plights—as well as the attractive actors who play them—draw us in and keep us watching.

Certainly, but what about reality TV and YouTube videos that can rack up millions of viewers who addictively watch everyday, average-looking people doing banal things—playing board games, sitting in restaurants, playing with their pets, dancing, embarrassing their boyfriends or girlfriends with pranks? Or doing absolutely nothing?

We've become a race of Peeping Toms indeed, passive voyeurs who watch instead of *do*. Or who record and post videos; anything for attention, anything for clicks.

BLOW-UP (1966)

A bored London fashion photographer who believes he may have captured an actual murder on camera makes discoveries about the nature of reality and perspective.

THE MACGUFFIN: Stolen photos of a couple in a park

Of all the Hitchcockian movies made to date, *Blow-Up* may just be the most beautiful, endlessly rewatchable, most puzzling, and most influential of all. Not going to lie, I think it's a masterwork. Directed by the technically masterful, inimitable, and at times infuriating Michelangelo Antonioni (*L'Avventura*, *Red Desert*) and an art-house sensation in 1967, *Blow-Up* is foundational, a defining movie of its era and of its director's career, a thriller in which the mystery vanishes into thin air, as do many of the director's characters. Antonioni's first English-language film stars the then-unknown David Hemmings (Antonioni replaced Terence Stamp only weeks before production started) as a disaffected fashion photographer who spends his days in his studio filming (and often screwing) blank-eyed beauties and his nights searching for what he mistakes for deeper meaning by photographing lost and forgotten men in a flophouse. He wanders one day to a windswept park, where he spots a distinguished-looking older man and an enigmatic younger woman (an incandescent, almost Garbo-esque Vanessa Redgrave). Are they about to make love? Are they quarreling? The photographer casually stalks them and grabs some clandestine shots, and as he is about to leave, the wide-eyed woman runs toward him, pleading with him to give her the roll of film. He refuses. She trails him into his studio. They kiss. Share a joint. Listen to music. He gets rid of her, palming her off with a decoy roll of film. In a sequence of astonishing technique and worthy of endless revisits—a long, wordless sequence that surely impressed Hitchcock (who raved about the film and its director to his close associates and pursued Redgrave and Hemmings for a film of his own)—the photographer develops the park photos in his darkroom, blowing them up again and again until they are as pointillistic as the precisely premeditated dots and blobs of a Seurat painting. Is that black smudge a shooter hiding in the bushes? Is Redgrave looking frightened as she stares at something offscreen? Is that shadow her companion spread out dead on the grass? Are these photographs of a murder? A random event? An orchestrated conspiracy? The photographer has a new purpose, a meaning after years of aimless catting around and drifting. The following morning in the park, the body has vanished along with the lady. So, too, have his photographs. We see this isn't just a mystery thriller; it's a movie about the nature of reality, of seeing. The performances of Hemmings, Redgrave, and Sarah Miles could hardly be better. The Herbie Hancock score, the club sequence featuring the Yardbirds performing "Stroll On," a psychedelicized take on "Train Kept A-Rollin'," that 1951 R&B scorcher first associated with Tiny Bradshaw and also Johnny Burnette, the scene featuring the photographer's seduction of the model Veruschka, the final scene of teens in white mime makeup playing tennis without a ball (even though we hear the ball being hit)—they're all potential keys to unlock mysteries that will not yield to facile interpretation. ♟♟♟♟

Fashion photographer David Hemmings can't decide whether Vanessa Redgrave is a femme fatale or a victim in Michelangelo Antonioni's enigmatic *Blow-Up*.
Corbis Historical/Getty Images

THE BEDROOM WINDOW (1987)

A young businessman's affair with his boss's alluring wife leads him to cover for her when she witnesses an attempted sexual assault from his bedroom window. Soon becoming the prime suspect, the hapless hero sets out to unmask a vicious sexual psychopath.

THE MACGUFFIN: The killer no one notices

Deep in the night, young businessman Terry Lambert (Steve Guttenberg, trying to prove he had more than a torso and *Police Academy*–level chops) gets up to visit the bathroom when his sophisticated bedmate, Sylvia (Isabelle Huppert), witnesses a rape attempt from the bedroom window. But there's a catch—Sylvia is the wife of the young businessman's boss, Collin Wentworth (Paul Shenar). She knows that going public will alert her spouse to her indiscretions, but she claims she wants to help and so briefs Terry and gets him to testify. Morbidly curious, he clumsily involves himself in investigating "Joe," the prime suspect (Brad Greenquist), trailing him to bars and his haunts around the city. Conveniently, Terry inevitably ends up in the same places as the suspect, at the same time. Thus, he also becomes a suspect. Sylvia won't stick out her neck to save him. But another girl, Denise (Elizabeth McGovern)—the victim of the sexual assault victim Terry supposedly witnessed—falls for Terry's romantic goofiness and frat-jock good looks. Interesting only in fits and starts but preposterous from start to finish, *The Bedroom Window* (based on the novel *The Witnesses* by Anne Holden) is tired, ersatz Hitchcock. Said talented director Curtis Hanson (screenwriter for *The Silent Partner*, director of *L.A. Confidential*), "I was very aware that I was going into Hitchcock territory. I used it as an opportunity to give a tip of the hat to Hitchcock." Hanson's hat tips (if you want to call them that) include *Sabotage*, *Rear Window*, *The Man Who Knew Too Much*, *Psycho*, and *Frenzy*. We've seen it all before, only done infinitely better. The film is especially nicely cast (by Mary Colquhoun) in its supporting roles, although the charming McGovern sinks her baby teeth into playing a tough moll with varying degrees of success. Huppert, so complex, alluring, and enigmatic in her French films, seems to be reading her lines from Berlitz flashcards. The amiable, ever-eager Guttenberg fares no better. He unveils no previously undiscovered depths; however, as expected, he does unveil at every possible opportunity the architecture of his pectorals. It's not a great movie, but the presence and allure of Huppert classes things up and generates at least some modicum of mystery and fascination. ♟♟

DISTURBIA (2007)

A bored high school kid under house arrest begins to suspect a mysterious neighbor has murdered his wife.

THE MACGUFFIN: The ambiguous neighbor

Ever longed to see *Rear Window*, only with Shia LaBeouf as a mixed-up high schooler under arrest and wearing an electronic ankle tag instead of James Stewart as a famed action photographer sidelined by a plaster cast and a wheelchair in a Greenwich Village hotbox apartment, and David Morse as the lady killer role played by Raymond Burr, and model-actress Sarah Roemer subbing for the ultimate Hitchcock blonde, the stylish Grace Kelly as the hero's magazine-world girlfriend? Welcome to *Disturbia*, an uneasy hybrid of Hitchcock thriller and an updated 'Eighties John Hughes teen comedy apparently made for easily impressed twelve- to twenty-year-olds. LaBeouf is very good as Kale Brecht (a ludicrous name unless it's intended satirically), freshly reeling from the car crash death of his father, having recently punched out his Spanish teacher and now feels so caged that he gets his tech-savvy friend (Aaron Yoo) to trick out the house with surveillance equipment that lets him spy on Ashley, the pretty new girl on the block (Roemer) and, especially, an odd and secretive loner, Mr. Turner (played, scarily and persuasively, by David Morse), whom Kale suspects may be a multiple murderer. The movie—directed by D. J. Caruso (*Eagle Eye*), scripted by Christopher Landon and Carl Ellsworth (*Red Eye*)—gives off some playful Rear Window voyeuristic vibes in its better hushed, creepy moments. But it seldom finds its rhythm—or purpose—until a nice, tense, protracted finale that builds slowly and delivers a big bang. Not a terrible thriller by any means, but not stellar as it deserves to be, either, despite LaBeouf's considerable efforts. The moody Geoff Zanelli orchestral score is always more interesting than the rap/pop/alt-rock soundtrack, which sounds as though it was assembled by a committee, the members of which neither knew nor cared what *Disturbia* was about. ♟♟♟

9 Lady Beware

Based on the evidence, audiences never seem to tire of the woman-in-jeopardy thrillers. From the silent-film era of Wild West serials featuring mustachioed villains tying heroines to railroad tracks, to director D. W. Griffith dangerously sending brave, brilliant Lillian Gish floating on an ice floe toward a raging waterfall for 1920's iconic melodrama *Way Down East*, to contemporary thrillers, women have taken the brunt of danger—to the thrill and delight of mainly female audiences. Nineteenth-century playwright Victorien Sardou—whose plays *La Tosca*, *Fedora*, *Gismonda*, and *Madame Sans-Gêne* became enormously popular late nineteenth-century operas and whose work attracted the greatest nineteenth-century actresses, such as Sarah Bernhardt—declared his formula for audience success: "Torture the women." That is, both the heroines of his plays and the women in the audience. Hitchcock often invoked Sardou's dictum as a fulcrum of why the most effective suspense thrillers follow Sardou's lead. And, among some zealous, often performative Hitchcock critics, that endorsement of Sardou gets trotted out as further "proof" of Hitchcock's reigning status as cinema's go-to raging misogynist.

Alrighty then, but when critics write about classic movies of the past, mustn't it be de rigueur for them to raise their fists and adamantly decry the misogyny of such other women-in-peril classics as the 1933 masterpiece *King Kong*? Or must they cheer when Elisabeth Moss ices her psychotic stalker in 2020's *The Invisible Man*, even though the heroine's role is barely sketched in and the weight of making the character convincing is laid on the shoulders of the spectacularly resourceful Elisabeth Moss? If the only options are complete victim, indomitable heroine in a tank top, or superheroine baptized by fire, is that really progress? Have people not realized that the women in Hitchcock's films may be under duress, but they are also intelligent, intrepid, witty, strong, *and* beautiful, working at such careers as journalist, fashion designer, schoolteacher, novelist, industrial designer, homemaker and mother, spy, executive secretary, and psychoanalyst?

THE SPIRAL STAIRCASE (1946)

In a New England hamlet around the turn of the twentieth century, a young mute woman becomes the target of a psychopath who has been stalking and murdering young women with disabilities.

THE MACGUFFIN: The killer repulsed by disabilities in women

This shadowy, prototypically 1940s Gothic horror melodrama is curiously stagey and, lord, is it talky, but it ticks every box and nails every cliché imaginable with style. A vulnerable but plucky heroine? That's delicate but steel-spined Dorothy McGuire (*The Enchanted Cottage, Gentleman's Agreement*) as a mute domestic at a sprawling but claustrophobic Gothic manse where she toils as a companion to a formidable matriarch (Ethel Barrymore, enjoyably hammy, of course earning an Oscar nomination). There isn't a floorboard, door, gate, window, or shutter in the house that doesn't sigh, slam, or creak right on cue. Every visible element of spookiness is captured in exceptional, brooding chiaroscuro cinematography by Nicholas Musuraca (*Cat People*). The crisp, straight-faced, and creepily effective direction is by Robert Siodmak (*Criss Cross*), who ratchets up the tension as best as he can for eighty-three minutes and forty-nine seconds and knows when to stop pressing his luck and wrap things up. Add in a cast overstuffed with quirky potential suspects and crackpots (George Brent, Elsa Lanchester, Sara Allgood, Kent Smith, Rhys Williams, Rhonda Fleming, and more), a dark and stormy night to end them all, and a villain we only see via close-ups of his angry, bloodshot eyes (director Robert Siodmak himself supplied those eyes). The finale— the heroine trapped alone in that old dark house with the maniacal killer—is the main reason to stick with it through the dull stretches, of which there are mercifully few. Everyone plays their role to the hilt, and the few genuine scares land nicely. Interestingly, producer David O. Selznick originally bought the screen rights to the 1933 source novel *Some Must Watch* by Ethel Lina White (*The Lady Vanishes*) with Ingrid Bergman—and later, Selznick's obsession, Jennifer Jones—in mind to star. Selznick reportedly offered the project to Hitchcock who could muster no more enthusiasm for such musty, painfully obvious material than could Bergman. Selznick unloaded the project to RKO to finance the production of *Duel in the Sun*. *The Spiral Staircase* became a big hit and still has fans today, some of whom insist that it out-Hitchcocks

A small-town maniac who abhors female "imperfection" strikes terror in deaf girl Dorothy McGuire alone in an old dark house with the titular spiral staircase.
LMPC via Getty Images

Hitchcock. To which we say, the hell it does. The material got remade for TV in 1961 starring Elizabeth Montgomery and Lillian Gish, again in 1975 with Jacqueline Bisset, and most recently in 2000 with Nicollette Sheridan. ♟♟♟

SCREAM OF FEAR (1961)

A wheelchair-dependent young woman gets summoned to the home of her wealthy estranged dead father and odd stepmother in the south of France, where she somehow keeps seeing her father. The fragile girl enlists her father's chauffeur's to help discover whether she is being gaslighted or simply losing her mind.

THE MACGUFFIN: An inheritance

Hot on the heels of the international sensation that was *Psycho*, Britain's shrewdest ambulance-chasers Hammer (known best for such hot-blooded, heavy-breathing horror Gothics as *The Curse of the Werewolf*, *Brides of Dracula*, and *The Mummy*) veered off into a parallel, decidedly more Hitchcockian direction with a run of psychological thrillers, including *Paranoiac*, *Hysteria*, and *Nightmare*. Hammer called them "mini-Hitchcocks," and "mini" *Scream of Fear* most certainly is. Crisply directed by former film editor Seth Holt (*The Lavender Hill Mob*, *Saturday Night and Sunday Morning*) and luminously shot by the great Douglas Slocombe (*The Lion in Winter*, *Raiders of the Lost* Ark), the murky, atmospheric, improbable goings-on in Jimmy Sangster's screenplay are thick with elements of *Psycho*, bits and bobs from *Rebecca*, *Suspicion*, and *Vertigo*, as well as huge chunks of such Hitchcockian stuff as *Diabolique* and *Gaslight*. It's an old-time Gothic heroine-in-distress melodrama dressed out in midcentury settings, cars, clothes, and attitudes. No shame in that, though. Fragile Susan Strasberg, a placid, soft-voiced, doe-eyed brunette in the Diane Baker mold, plays an heiress confined to a wheelchair after being paralyzed in a horse-riding accident. Still suffering the aftermath of the suicide of a very close female friend, our beset heroine accepts her wealthy, estranged father's invitation to join him at the French Riviera villa he shares with his second wife (the ever-eerie chilly blonde Ann Todd (of

David Lean's *The Passionate Friends* and Hitchcock's *The Paradine Case*). The US version of the movie only runs eighty-two minutes so, mercifully, weird stuff starts happening not long after Penny's arrival. Creaky shutters, flickering candles, papa's old piano tinkling in the empty music room—that sort of thing. Plus, Penny's stepmom acts too studiously nice to be trusted, and the extended absence of Penny's father—who invited her visit, after all!—gets explained away as he's been "called away on business." No wonder Penny shrieks when she spots papa's corpse propped up in a chair in the summer house with a candle burning at his feet. Is the tragedy-prone Penny losing her marbles, or is she yet another in a long line of female victims of cinematic gaslighting? Also on the premises is Robert, the family's hunky live-in chauffeur (Ronald Lewis of William Castle's *Mr. Sardonicus*), who offers to help Penny get to the bottom of the not-so-mysterious mystery. Also lurking about and dining with Penny's stepmother is a French physician, Dr. Gerrard (the always welcome Christopher Lee, struggling to pull off a convincing Gallic accent), who is mostly around just to warn Penny to stop acting so weird. Things race along predictably until an effectively creepy underwater swimming pool scene meant to recall *Diabolique* and a nice twist ending that won't be especially surprising to fans of *Diabolique* or *Psycho*. The movie was a moneymaker and enjoys a cult following today; a pity that plans for a remake from director J. A. Bayona (*The Orphanage*) never came to fruition. Those looking for few mild rainy-day thrills, some terrific cinematography, and a cheeky twist finale could do worse. ♟♟♟

DARK PURPOSE (1964)

A naïve American assistant to a museum curator falls in love with a moody, insular Italian nobleman whose art collection she and her boss are in Italy to assess. The more she learns about him and his life in a cliffside mansion, the more danger awaits her.

THE MACGUFFIN: A madwoman who roams a mansion

When Hitchcock was casting *Psycho* in 1959, one of many actresses he considered briefly was sunny songbird Shirley

Jones, whose surprisingly earthy dramatic performance in *Elmer Gantry* would go on to beat fellow Best Supporting Actress Oscar nominee Janet Leigh's remarkable performance in *Psycho*. The closest that the perky *Carousel* and *Oklahoma!* thrush ever came to making an actual Hitchcock movie was when she got cast as the stylishly dressed ersatz blonde heroine of this faux Hitchcock romantic suspense gothic in which she plays innocent American Karen Williams, assistant to an imperiously bitchy British museum curator-archivist Raymond Fontaine, played by George Sanders (*Rebecca*, *Foreign Correspondent*), who amusingly barks out nasty Noël Coward witticisms at anyone within earshot. Despite Karen's nearly being mauled by a German shepherd guard dog on arrival at the Amalfi coast manse of mysterious, moody nobleman and world-class art collector Count Paolo Barbarelli (Rosano Brazzi), Karen—faster than you can say "Jane Eyre and Mr. Rochester"—falls under the moody count's broodingly romantic spell. Meanwhile, Paolo's mentally amnesiac nineteen-year-old daughter Cora (Giorgia Moll) roams the mansion's halls, raving and ranting about being Paolo's wife, much to interloper Karen's discomfort. We've all read and/or seen *Rebecca* and *Jane Eyre*, so despite the stunning location filming, 1960s costume designs, suspicious tumbles off cliffs, the odd housekeeper who speaks no English (or *does* she?), and contradictory mutterings about what happened to Cora's dead mother, we're way, way ahead of the plot "revelations" about Count Paolo. Attractive, likeable Miss Jones doesn't rivet our interest as the woman in jeopardy, and the usually more charismatic Brazzi seems distracted. The kindest thing to be said about the work of prolific veteran director George Marshall (assisted by Vittorio Sala), who gave the world the much-better *The Blue Dahlia* and *Destry Rides Again*? He knew enough to keep the competent, diverting Ross Hunter–ish (see *Moment to Moment*) film mercifully short at ninety-seven minutes. Here's a would-be suspense thriller guaranteed to give no one a sleepless night—certainly not Alfred Hitchcock, who, for the record, cast the *right* women in *Psycho*. 👤👤

NIGHTMARE (1964)

A young woman whose institutionalized mother went violently mad fears that her horrifying nightmares are signs that the same fate awaits her.

THE MACGUFFIN: The heroine's nightmares

As one of Hammer Studios' several "mini-Hitchcock" thrillers in imitation of *Psycho* go (*Scream of Fear, Maniac, Paranoiac*, etc.), *Nightmare* is another modest, fitfully effective psychological thriller from superb cinematographer-turned-director Freddie Francis (he shot *Sons and Lovers, The Innocents*), screenwriter Jimmy Sangster, and cameraman John Wilcox (*The Third Man, The Guns of Navarone*). The plot—and scares—turn on a boarding school teenager plagued by night terrors triggered by the trauma of witnessing her father stabbed to death by her mentally unhinged mother—on her eleventh birthday, no less. The role of the troubled, wealthy young heroine at risk is ably enough played by Jennie Linden (*Women in Love*), a last-ditch replacement when Julie Christie quit to instead do *Billy Liar* for director John Schlesinger; two years later, the fantastic Christie won the Best Actress Oscar for the Schlesinger-directed *Darling*. Linden gets no award-worthy moments in *Nightmare*, but the atmospheric and lustrously photographed movie is still fun to watch as our loner Janet heroine (a wink at *Psycho* star Janet Leigh?) gets booted from the snooty school for girls and gets shipped home to her brooding family manse in the company of her sympathetic teacher Mary (Brenda Bruce, indelible as the doomed sex worker in the opening of *Peeping Tom*), where she will be tended to by caretaker Grace (Moira Redmond, John Huston's *Freud*), who has been hired by her guardian Henry (David Knight), with whom she's in love. The scenes set in the house are especially persuasive (and more than slightly sapphic) courtesy of flashbacks indicated by elegantly simple lighting changes, long tracking shots through deeply shadowed hallways, and the depiction of recurring nightmares in which Janet is visited by a sad-eyed wraith (Clytie Jessop, also a ghostly presence in *The Innocents*) with an alabaster cheek slashed by a wicked scar. The balance of the film, which involves driving Janet over the brink of insanity, is a twist on *Psycho*, but instead of an important character vanishing permanently after the movie's first third, a key *Nightmare* player vanishes for the entire last third. Meanwhile, the "surprises" become more predictable, the scenery-chewing becomes bananas, and the borrowings from *Psycho*, *Diabolique*, and *Gaslight*, among others, grow enjoyably shameless. Throughout, though, the direction and cinematography, let alone the unique screen presence of both Bruce and Redmond, keep the melodramatic pot boiling. ♟♟♙

ARABESQUE (1966)

A naïve university professor of ancient hieroglyphics becomes embroiled with a crafty, enigmatic femme fatale in international intrigue that involves foiling an assassination plot.

THE MACGUFFIN: A secret code in hieroglyphics

What have we here? A spy thriller for which Stanley Donen (*Charade*) once again paired two insanely attractive movie stars in a script by Peter (*Charade*) Stone that blends suspense, romance, mystery, violence, chases, and international espionage, with a musical score by Henry (*Charade*) Mancini, a psychedelic Maurice (*Charade*) Binder animated credit sequence, all engineered by Universal Pictures, the studio looking for its next Hitchcock-esque, *Charade*-like hit. Surely, this copy of a copy—titled *Arabesque*—should be another *Charade*, shouldn't it? Well, no. For one, fault the absurdly convoluted plot that makes an assassin's target out of a boring American professor at Oxford (Gregory Peck) because he's an expert in hieroglyphics and every meanie in London wants to get his hands on a code written in hieroglyphics that has been snatched from the clutches of a murdered spy warning of an upcoming catastrophic event.

Speaking of catastrophic events, Universal spent almost a half million dollars ($3.9 million in today's terms) hiring a platoon of writers to "fix" the script by Stone (pseudonym, Pierre Marton) based on a 1961 novel by Alex Gordon, *The Cipher*. But the script remained such a jumble—chunks of it borrowed from *Charade* and Hitchcock's *Blackmail* and *North by Northwest*—that Cary Grant, for whom it was written, refused to do it. Director Donen and his superb cinematographer Christopher Challis (*The Tales of Hoffmann*) overcompensate for the miscasting of Peck (hopeless with witty banter and physical comedy) and the script's deficiencies by focusing on the stunning Mata Hari with whom the hero tangles—Dior-clad Sophia Loren at her most chic but also as ill-equipped for witty banter in English with Peck as she is delightful at it in Italian with Marcello Mastroianni. Donen and Challis's other visual ploy is to shovel on tons of psychedelic 1960s visual gimmicks (prisms, tilted frames, kaleidoscopic color splashes, filming through glass tables). They feel cool until they become annoying and exhausting. Nice try, but *Charade* it isn't. ♟♟♟

WAIT UNTIL DARK (1967)

While her husband is away, a newly blind woman must defend herself against a trio of vicious home invaders searching for a doll in which a cache of heroin is stashed.

THE MACGUFFIN: A doll packed with a cache of pure heroin

If people remember anything about *Wait until Dark* it must be the moment when a home-invading sicko leaps from the shadows at brave, blind, waifish heroine Audrey Hepburn. That one, much-talked-about moment alone helped make the movie a box-office hit and seared people's memories, the way a similar moment thirteen years earlier in *Dial M for Murder* had lifted audiences right of their seats when an unsuspecting Grace Kelly gets out of bed to answer the phone in the dark of night and gets pounced on from behind by a hired strangler. Warner Bros. bought the movie rights to both of playwright Fredrick Knott's Broadway and London stage successes, and both times Hitchcock was their director of choice. Hitchcock wasn't interested in *Wait until Dark*, but the workaday, inconsistent Terence Young (*Dr. No*,

From Russia, with Love) was. The script by Robert and Jane Harrington (1966's *Kaleidoscope*) is gimmicky and talky, but, in the last act, it all comes together in a hair-raisingly satisfying conclusion.

While the husband of a recently blinded woman goes away on business, three diabolical thugs invade her New York apartment and terrorize her to reveal the whereabouts of a toy doll stuffed with uncut heroin. (Spoiler alert: she doesn't know and neither does her husband, played by Efrem Zimbalist Jr., to whom the doll was handed by a now-dead friend.) Increasingly sadistic cat-and-mouse games and a wicked, violent con game play out as Susie must use her wiles to stay alive. In the original stage production, Lee Remick played the starring role to the hilt (Honor Blackman did the show in London). In the movie, the effortlessly chic, appealing Hepburn is everything you'd want the newly blind protagonist to be—winsome but brave, vulnerable but resourceful, angry but heroic. She makes the movie work. It's hard to ignore the sense that Hepburn knows she is working overtime to sell thriller material well below *Charade* level, let alone below Hitchcock standards. But playing noble, suffering Susy Hendrix earned her a fifth Best Actress Oscar nomination. Although Richard Crenna, Jack Weston, and Alan Arkin play the hateful trio with high style, it is Arkin who steals the show as the sly, odd master of disguises, delivering crowd-pleasing villainy in a performance is equal parts Peter Lorre and Peter Sellers.

When *Wait until Dark* opened in movie theaters in late October 1967, Warner Bros. presented it with a good old-fashioned promotional stunt. Borrowing the effect that had unsettled Broadway stage audiences, during the last eight minutes of the action—when the heroine smashes her apartment's lightbulbs one by one to put her relentless final attacker on equal footing with her—movie theater house lights got switched off one by one to match the action onscreen, finally going to as much darkness as the law allowed. The gimmick reportedly added millions to the film's big box-office success. Today, of course, audience members presented with the same kind of showmanship would probably (a) wreak havoc, (b) sue, or (c) both. ♟♟♟♟

Relentless home invader Alan Arkin wouldn't kill sympathetic blind lady Audrey Hepburn, would he? The final scene in the movie had audiences screaming in *Wait until Dark*.

Silver Screen Collection/Moviepix/Getty Images

ROSEMARY'S BABY (1968)

A pregnant Manhattan newlywed suspects that her husband has joined hands with their Satan-worshipping neighbors who have diabolical plans for her baby.

THE MACGUFFIN: Tannis root

In 1941's *Suspicion*, Alfred Hitchcock directed winsome Joan Fontaine as the sheltered new young bride hopelessly in love with devilishly attractive Cary Grant even as she feels increasingly isolated, persecuted, and paranoid while her husband apparently lies, betrays, tries to kill, and finally poisons her for money (at least that's the way Hitchcock considered filming it before his own better judgment—and the studio's cowardice—took over). In 1968's *Rosemary's Baby*, Roman Polanski directed uber-winsome Mia Farrow as the sheltered new young bride hopelessly in love with *literally* devilishly attractive John Cassavetes even as she grows increasingly isolated and paranoid while her husband lies, betrays, drugs, and lets Satan rape and impregnate her in exchange for guaranteeing himself a thriving acting career. Hollywood legend has it that Hitchcock himself turned down the chance to acquire the film rights to Ira Levin's bestseller *Rosemary's Baby* because he doubted movie audiences would buy the premise of witches existing in contemporary Manhattan. If that is true, though, better that the movie got directed and scripted to satiric, sadistic perfection and put over with utter conviction by Roman Polanski. Making his American filmmaking debut, Polanski demonstrates his mastery in creating paranoia and bringing out latent menace in ordinary spaces (a closet, a phone booth, a living room, a basement laundry room). As mordantly funny as it is chilling, this is surely one of the most unnerving films ever devised—director-screenwriter Polanski presents the horrors and grotesquerie in such a matter-of-fact style that it makes them even more plausible.

Polanski is too smart and gifted a moviemaker to cheapen things with an unearned jump scare, and *Rosemary's Baby* ranks alongside *Gaslight* as one of cinema's most harrowing and insidious depictions of gaslighting, especially because Farrow conveys such relatable fragility as everyone—her oily actor husband, her presumptuous neighbors, her doctor—patronizes and treats her like a child. "Don't read books. And don't listen to your friends, either," she's told. Plus, John Cassavetes (Robert Redford was the first choice for the role) projects such entirely convincing narcissism and brutal opportunism that he's chillingly perfect as someone who'd casually bully his wife into eating chalky-tasting (i.e., drugged) chocolate mousse, telling her she's being silly for complaining about it ("There's *always something wrong*," he smirks) while he's setting her up to literally be Satan's bride for a night. Even the pediatrician who isn't part of the coven, Dr. Hill (Charles Grodin), sells out the heroine by treating a justifiably terrified woman as a hysteric. "Just send the poor thing to a hospital!" you may be tempted to shout at the screen—it's all she's asking. Farrow, making her movie debut after getting her start in television, is ideal in a role earlier turned down by more established stars, including Tuesday Weld, Jane Fonda, Faye Dunaway, and Julie Christie; Robert Redford, Warren Beatty, Burt Reynolds, Robert Wagner (the mind reels), and more turned down the husband role. Oscar winner Ruth Gordon, as Rosemary's bulldozer neighbor witch-next-door, is one of the secret weapons in a movie of wall-to-wall perfect scenes and unforgettable highlights. A never-to-be-equalled masterpiece, no matter how many times they keep trying to copy it, sequel-ize it, or prequel-ize it, *Rosemary's Baby* is one of the few Hitchcockian movies that did not need Hitchcock to make it wickedly funny, hip, and superb. ♟♟♟♟

Gaslighted pregnant wife Mia Farrow is no match for satanic husband John Cassevetes in *Rosemary's Baby*.
Michael Ochs/Moviepix/Getty Images

WHAT LIES BENEATH (2000)

A trusting wife begins to suspect that she and her lakeside home are endangered not only by a supernatural presence but also by her mysterious, unhappy doctor husband.

THE MACGUFFIN: The sanity of the heroine

An inconvenient and insistent ghost haunts a fabulous lakefront Vermont home in this slow-burn thriller director Robert Zemeckis chose to make after, of all things, his *Forrest Gump* won six Oscars. One of the owners of that waterfront spread is Michelle Pfeiffer, who plays Claire Spencer—a restless, jittery former cellist left alone too often by her genetic scientist husband (Harrison Ford). In her hubby's absence, Claire starts aiming a pair of binoculars (*Rear Window*–style) on her sexy but troubling next-door neighbors (James Remar, Miranda Otto), a duo as noisy when they're fighting as when they're making love. Things take a darker turn when Claire suspects the man may have killed his wife. Why else would she spy him in a downpour in the dead of night hoisting a (body?) bag into his car if his wife's body weren't in it? Our Claire's apparently seen *Rear Window* just like the rest of us. Harrison Ford plays Pfeiffer's disbelieving husband, Norman Spencer (*Norman*, get it Hitchcockians?), as if he suspects his wife might be going mad, ignoring her when doors open and close on their own, their bathtub fills itself with water, and shrieky violins accompany every appearance of a spectral face in the bathwater or on the lake outside their house. Claire swears she is being bedeviled by the ghost of the "murdered" next-door neighbor crying out for vengeance beyond the grave. But she gets the shock of her life when a séance held by her psychic friend (Diana Scarwid) proves otherwise. If you ask us, the real specter is the ghost of Hitchcock grimly amused by how clumsy Zemeckis and screenwriter Clark Gregg are when lifting from *Rebecca*, *Rear Window*, *Vertigo*, *Psycho*, and more. Pfeiffer is superb (and an impressive Hitchcock blonde at that), but Ford is only about as good as he could be in the kind of role Alfred Hitchcock would have expected Cary Grant to put over. By the finale, the whole thing has collapsed into silliness that makes the well-intentioned *What Lies Beneath* as frustrating as it is disposable. ♟♟♟

10 Woman Trouble

Who doesn't love a great movie villain, especially when that villain happens to be a woman? Sure, it is Hitchcock's self-assured, refined, and elusive blonde heroines who get pursued by the handsome heroes whom they enchant, confuse, and dazzle. It's the blondes who get to drive the classiest foreign cars, who wear the furs, the tailored suits, the jewelry, and the best of haute couture. It's the blondes who get the top billing. Ah, but it's the female villains who wow the audience because they refuse to be demure, to play coy romantic games, or play by the rules. They're unruly, disruptive, impactful. They leave a mark. As Hitchcock insisted, "The more successful the villain, the more successful the film." And true to his word, some of the most unforgettable characters in Hitchcock films are females who bring the badassery along with intelligence, agency, and authority. Theatrical powerhouse Judith Anderson dominates every moment she is on screen in *Rebecca* playing the austere and imposing housekeeper obsessively devoted to her dead mistress and hell-bent on driving to suicide the new Mrs. de Winter; Anderson's performance earned one of the nine Oscar nominations ever given to any Hitchcock films. In 1949's *Under Capricorn*, Margaret Leighton, in a similar scene-stealing role, delights in diabolically terrorizing poor Ingrid Bergman by putting a shrunken head in her bed and keeping her liquored up and dependent.

Before Anderson and Leighton, Cicely Oates brought memorable villainy to Hitchcock's 1934 version of *The Man Who Knew Too Much* as the kidnapping accomplice hiding behind the hypocrisy of a phony religious cult; in Hitchcock's 1956 remake, Brenda de Banzie chillingly plays the analogous role of a duplicitous child snatcher masquerading as a chirpy British tourist on holiday. Equally memorable is Mary Clare in *The Lady Vanishes* as the untrustworthy baroness, an imperious, sneering train traveler clad head to toe in black and whose unblinking stare means no goodwill toward the heroine. And, as the domineering, vicious Nazi mother of weak-willed, self-tortured Nazi Claude Rains in *Notorious*, Austrian actress Leopoldine Konstantin—poisoning her son's mind with lies, poisoning her daughter-in-law's body with arsenic—is a villain for the ages. Perhaps her only rival in cruelty is Mrs. Bates in *Psycho*; though heard but largely unseen, she has traumatized viewers and haunted nightmares for decades. Just imagining how, in the name of love, she damaged her only son from infancy to the time of her death is enough to cause shivers.

Unlike other major directors—from David Lean (*Madeline*) to Otto Preminger (*Angel Face*) and from John Stahl (*Leave Her to Heaven*) to Paul Verhoeven (*Basic Instinct*)—Alfred Hitchcock rarely made a film featuring a female villain as the main character. After all, "Rebecca" is only a ghostly presence in the film built around her, and the title character in *Marnie* is as much a victim as a victimizer; the same could be said of Judy Barton and Madeleine Elster, especially because the roles are played so sympathetically by Kim Novak. Arguably, Hitchcock's one villainous heroine is the beautiful and enigmatic Maddalena Anna Paradine—on trial for poisoning her wealthy, blind, much older husband in *The Paradine Case*—who calls herself "a woman—what would you say?—a woman who has seen a great deal of life." But is she, really? In true Hitchcock fashion, the film refuses to resolve that question.

DOUBLE DOOR (1934)

A domineering unmarried multimillionaire dowager will stop at nothing, including murder, tormenting, and abusing her fragile half sister and her newly married brother and his new bride in her father's Gilded Age Manhattan mansion.

THE MACGUFFIN: A valuable heirloom pearl necklace

"The play that made Broadway gasp." That's how the credits describe the source material for this little pre-Code oddity directed by Charles

Vidor (*Gilda*) and adapted for the screen by Jack Cunningham (*The Black Pirate*, *It's a Gift*) and Gladys Lehman (*The Cat Creeps*, *Death Takes a Holiday*) from Elizabeth A. McFadden's 1933 stage success *Double Door*. An unapologetically Gothic melodrama with touches of a full-blown "locked room" horror chiller, *Double Door* offers a banquet of Hitchcockian elements, including a terrifying older madwoman fully capable of psychological and physical violence, a forbidding old dark mansion, a terrorized young bride, well-meaning but ineffectual male characters, a dark family trauma that haunts its successors, a prevailing sense of dread, and more. Yet it predates many of the Hitchcock movies it most resembles—except for his den-of-thieves-in-a-safehouse comedy thriller *Number Seventeen* (1932). Center stage in this proscenium-bound but compelling spiderweb of a movie are two performers from the Broadway production—Anne Revere (Oscar winner for *National Velvet* [1945] as the highly emotional, weak-willed younger half sister Caroline) and Mary Morris, who delivers a barnstorming, spooky, stridently weird performance as the pathologically manipulative, fabulously wealthy, vicious Fifth Avenue spinster Victoria Van Brett. Paramount so wanted the thirty-nine-year-old Morris to repeat her stage role on film—one that rivals formidable women in Hitchcock movies including Mrs. Danvers in *Rebecca*, Madame Sebastian in *Notorious*, Mrs. Bates in *Psycho*, Lydia Brenner in *The Birds*—that the studio postponed filming *Double Door* until Morris completed the last leg of the play's national tour. No wonder. The film immediately introduces Morris as the diabolical antiheroine right in the credits as she glares menacingly into the camera in close-up, floating through a pair of doors accompanied by an organ thundering Bach's "Toccata and Fugue in D Minor." Lon Chaney or Boris Karloff themselves couldn't have asked for a showier entrance. For the next seventy-six minutes, Morris earns the big buildup.

Her Victoria merrily exerts her iron will on everyone, especially the handsome half brother Rip (Kent Taylor, *Death Takes a Holiday*), whom she's psychologically beaten into submission since childhood, and his new bride, Anne (Evelyn Venable, *Death Takes a Holiday*), whom she falsely tries to paint as a two-timing gold-digger having an illicit love affair with a doctor (Colin Tapley). Meanwhile, Victoria mercilessly torments her fragile, whipped puppy of a younger sister (Anne Revere), who sees, hears, and knows too much, so the crazy lady threatens to lock Caroline behind the titular double doors of an airless chamber built originally as the private soundproof sanctuary of their industrialist father, who (very suspiciously) died there. Anne urges her emasculated husband to defy Victoria, leading to a confrontation that lands the new bride smack-dab into that death trap of a hidden chamber. Morris growls and scowls throughout the proceedings, never winking or easing up for a second; it may be a one-note performance, but it's a note that powers the entire movie. So why did *Double Door* mark the film debut and farewell for Mary Morris? Paramount offered her a multiple-film contract, but the actress—who had enjoyed success playing such choice Broadway stage roles as Arkadina in Chekov's *The Seagull* and Abbie in

Broadway's Mary Morris, memorably creepy in *Double Door*, returned to the stage rather than accept Hollywood's plan to make her into "the female Boris Karloff."
LMPC via Getty Images

Eugene O'Neill's *Desire Under the Elms*—liked neither Hollywood nor the studio's plans to cast and promote her as a kind of female Karloff. Save *Double Door* for the next dark and stormy night. ♟♟♟

A WOMAN'S FACE (1941)

A facially disfigured female blackmailer finds attention from two men: a seductive blackmailer who tries conning her into killing an innocent child for the inheritance money, and a married plastic surgeon who complicates her life by restoring her beauty.

THE MACGUFFIN: The woman's soul

MGM gave Greta Garbo first dibs on the starring role in this dark suspense melodrama—made first in Sweden starring Ingrid Bergman in 1938. But Garbo, who possessed one of world's most astonishing faces, declined the role of a beauty whose facial disfigurement in a fire poisons her mind and drives her to a life of crime, self-pity, and self-hatred before her shot at redemption. Hitchcock, on the heels of his acclaimed *Rebecca* and *Foreign Correspondent*, flirted with the idea of directing the film starring the great Margaret Sullavan (*The Shop Around the Corner* star whose talent, vulnerability, distinctive speaking voice, and *Rebecca* screen test impressed him). Those intriguing "what ifs?" never materialized, however.

Instead, George Cukor (*Gaslight*) stepped up to directing the movie and championed as his leading lady glamorous Joan Crawford (*Grand Hotel*, *The Women*); studio boss Louis B. Mayer warned the actress that the role could be a career killer. (By Mayer's logic, wouldn't it have also been for Garbo?) But the star persisted and went on to deliver a go-for-broke performance—she's a proper actress here—that ranks as one of her least affected but most effective turns in her long career. Donald Ogden Stewart (*The Philadelphia* Story) and Elliott Paul (*Rhapsody in Blue*), basing their script on the French play by Francis de Croissant *Il était une fois*, construct the film as a series of flashbacks and courtroom scenes (Anna is on trial in Sweden for kidnapping a child and the murder of her lover [played by Conrad Veidt]);

unfortunately, that structure constantly yanks us out of the flow of what is an already overly busy and contrived suspense thriller. The first half of the narrative, though, is deliciously weird and suggestive, beginning with a scene set in the seedy roadside restaurant run by Anna and her fellow con artists (including Reginald Owen, Connie Gilchrist, and Donald Meek). We're introduced to Anna's suave, satanic lover Torsen (Veidt in a scene-grabbing performance) just after he's hosted a party of friends to a hearty meal at Anna's tavern without having the money to pay for it: to settle the bill, he steals incriminating love letters from married woman Vera (Osa Massen) so that Anna and her gang can blackmail the unfaithful lady for a small fortune. Vera's upright husband, the eminent plastic surgeon Dr. Gustaf Segert (Melvyn Douglas), happens on Anna attempting to blackmail the cheating wife right in their own home. He becomes fascinated by the strange, prickly Anna (he tells her, "Unfortunately for humanity, the light hasn't been invented yet that could look into that interesting heart of yours") and successfully convinces her to let him perform reparative surgery on her. Crawford, now a looker again, becomes far less interesting in this second half of the film, but only because the script shoves her character into clichés and camp as she becomes Miss Joan Crawford of the Movies, entombed in 1940s shoulder pads, falsies, ultra lashes, and posh cinematography by Robert H. Planck (*The Man in the Iron Mask*). Happily, things at least liven up again when Anna's evil suitor Torsen sets up our heroine to play governess to his own angelic little nephew Lars-Erik (Richard Nichols), whom Anna has been assigned to kill so that Torsen can get his hands on the fortune promised to the boy as heir to the estate of his grandfather (Albert Bassermann). Once Anna is torn between duty and her growing love for the little boy, the movie cries out for the perverse complexities of the Hitchcock touch, particularly during two suspense sequences meant to be showpieces—one set on a cable car when Anna struggles with whether to send little Lars-Erik hurling down into an abyss far below, the other aboard a speeding sleigh. Cukor was a consummate craftsman and actor's director supreme, but when it comes to action-suspense, he usually knew enough to leave that stuff to others. Still, he, Crawford, and Veidt made for one hell of a wry and diabolical trio. ♟♟♟

LAURA (1944)

While investigating the murder of a bewitchingly beautiful illustrator and Madison Avenue executive among the victim's high society friends, an obsessed homicide detective finds himself falling in love with a painted portrait of the phantom dead girl.

THE MACGUFFIN: The portrait of Laura

Laura, a murder mystery whodunit set amid a beautiful dead heroine's social set—some of the most perverse, unlikable, and witty suspects in film history—is revered almost despite itself. Like such twisty detective melodramas as *The Maltese Falcon* or *The Big Sleep*, the murky, byzantine plot has never been the element that most absorbs and haunts. Much of the narrative is standard, even talky stuff: a detective's investigation of the possible murder of a successful and gorgeous young Manhattanite for whom nearly everyone fell. But, oh, *what* talk. Says one of Laura's many admirers, "Her youth and beauty, her poise and charm captivated them all." Among "them all" will be a cynical, disaffected detective who, as he interrogates the dead heroine's fancy, backbiting, dodgy Upper East Side friends, becomes fascinated by their affiliations, alliances, and betrayals. ("Are you in love with him?" "Was she in love with you?"). I must have seen it three or four times, but when I do, I never care much about the revelation of the culprit or the motive. Doesn't matter. *Laura* is one for the ages. It features one hell of a twist midway through.

Although its action consists largely of scenes involving people gabbing in rooms, those snaky, self-absorbed characters and the venom they spew is irresistible. The movie is enjoyed best for its atmosphere of swank, camp, and bitchery. Its hands-down scene-stealer is self-enchanted fancy-pants Clifton Webb, ideally cast as an imperious newspaper columnist and Laura's creepily possessive champion (although the notion of physical passion between them is ludicrous). Webb's Waldo Lydecker is the sort of narcissist who coolly addresses the macho detective Mark McPherson (played by Dana Andrews) who enters his swank apartment unannounced as Lydecker soaks in his bathtub typing his latest column, "Haven't you heard of science's newest triumph, the doorbell?" Rising from the tub and asking Andrews, whose mocking gaze flicks up and down, to hand him a towel, Lydecker declares, "Laura considered me the wisest, wittiest, most interesting man she'd ever met. I was in complete accord with her on that point." And then there's brittle Ann Treadwell (brilliantly played by Judith Anderson), who says of her weak, opportunistic kept man, Laura's former fiancé Shelby Carpenter (florid Vincent Price, whose character describes himself as "a natural-born suspect just because I'm not the conventional type"), "He's no good, but he's what I want. I'm not a nice person. Neither is he. He knows I know he's just what he is. He also knows that I don't care. We belong together because we're both weak and can't seem to help it. That's why I know he's capable of murder. He's like me."

Atop those vividly nasty performances under the diamond-hard direction of Otto Preminger is the mesmerizingly romantic score by

In the classic *Laura*, even cynical gumshoe Dana Andrews falls in love with the portrait of society "it" girl heroine (Gene Tierney), missing and possibly dead.
United Archives/Hulton Archive/Getty Images

David Raksin with its haunting theme music that evokes the alluring, ghostly presence of Laura (embodied by the exquisite Gene Tierney) whether she's on screen or off. With that score and that otherworldly portrait of Tierney looming over Laura's living room—and over the entire film—no wonder Dana Andrews's tough guy/chump character falls so hard for a dead girl. Don't we all? Adapted by Jay Dratler, Betty Reinhardt, and Samuel Hoffenstein (*An American Tragedy*; some consider him to be the real screenwriting hero here) from Vera Caspary's novel. Unmissable. ♟♟♟♟

SCARLET STREET (1945)

A lonely, middle-aged, unhappily married man and amateur painter gets victimized by a mercenary young woman he rescues from her abusive boyfriend.

THE MACGUFFIN: A nonexistent fortune

There are movie lovers who prize above all else the tough, hard-bitten crime films and melodramas directed in the 1940s and 1950s by Fritz Lang—*The Woman in the Window, Scarlet Street* and *The Big Heat* among them. These films are often populated by run-of-the-mill hard-luck characters so desperate and ground down by everyday life that they leap at any chance to sink themselves into a darker, dangerous reality through dirty deeds, criminal, carnal, or both. Others prefer Hitchcock's thrillers, mostly populated by wealthy, articulate, well-dressed characters who fall from grace out of the intercession of fate or by making crucial missteps. Both have their pleasures. Take the basic skeletal outline of *Vertigo*, for example: a retired middle-aged detective gets deliberately targeted, duped, and victimized by a much younger, lower-status femme fatale in league with an elegant cad; the detective falls from grace and loses the object of his romantic obsession *and* his sanity, likely forever.

And then there's the setup of *Scarlet Street*: a retired bank cashier gets duped and victimized by a much younger, lowly femme fatale in league with an abusive grifter. And, though the circumstances and specifics are different, the characters have literary and cinematic antecedents in *The Blue Angel*, *Of Human Bondage*, and so many more. While Hitchcock's is the upper-class version of an old trope, Lang's unapologetically dark and tragic *Scarlet Street*—based on Jean Renoir's wonderful, much nastier 1931 film *La Chienne*, based on the work by Georges de La Fouchardiére—is very much like his earlier box-office success starring Edward G. Robinson and Joan Bennett, *The Woman in the Window*. This one is the better, even more lowdown version. In *Scarlet Steet*, the great Robinson—his signature vicious gangster role in *Little Caesar* a distant memory—is a meek, lonely, henpecked husband and longtime bank cashier just given the gold watch by his boss during a retirement party. Christopher Cross is a sensitive soul who finds some relief from his loveless marriage and humdrum existence through painting. Everything changes when, in Greenwich Village on his way home to Brooklyn, he spots young working girl Kitty March (Joan Bennett, better cast and better photographed than in *The Woman in the Window*) getting beaten by Dan Duryea, who plays Johnny, her brassy pimp (or her "boyfriend," if you're a hopeless romantic). The loutish Johnny calls her "Lazy Legs"; he may as well call her "Round Heels." Christopher gallantly rushes to Kitty's rescue, shoves aside Johnny, who runs away when our hero chases down a policeman, and accepts Kitty's offer to take her to the apartment she shares with roommate Millie (Margaret Lindsay, hard as nails and excellent as a lingerie model). Chris invites the cheap, vulgar Kitty for a nightcap at the tavern below; she plays up to him and guesses that he must be an artist. She lies and tells him she is an actress whose play closed that night, pronounces Cézanne as "SEE-zan," and prattles on about "a little picture" she saw in a Fifth Avenue gallery priced at fifty thousand dollars. She's so brassy and mercenary, you can almost imagine her hearing nothing but *ka-ching!* in her brain when she looks at the aging, unprepossessing man sitting across from her. The two agree to have him paint her portrait at the new apartment in which he sets her up; for Chris, so accustomed to surviving only on breadcrumbs of kindness, that's preferable to being confined to paint in the bathroom, as demanded by his shrewish wife, Adele. Right on schedule, poor Chris falls hopelessly in love with the manipulative and seductive mantrap, who, with encouragement from fellow grifter Johnny, milks her sugar daddy for so much money that he's reduced to stealing from his employer and wife. Soon enough, Johnny has Kitty grabbing all the profits and the credit as newly discovered artist "Katherine March," whose paintings get displayed by a fancy art gallery. When, out of desperation, Christopher asks Kitty to marry him, there comes a stunningly brutal and shocking scene that still packs a punch. Such a trio as the needy Christopher, and the sordid and venal Kitty, and loathsome lech Johnny makes *Scarlet Street* into a study in sadomasochism, mutual exploitation, and violence. The characters are damaged goods, yes, but Robinson's heartbreaking performance, the nuanced screenplay by Dudley Nichols (*Bringing up Baby*, *Gunga Din*), and Lang's direction, nasty but humane, make it impossible not to empathize with them. Kitty is coarse and unschooled, but like the far more sympathetic Judy Barton in *Vertigo*, she's just as exploited, frantic to make her life better but without the agency or insight to make that happen. She is as much a victim as a victimizer. As Norman Bates put it, we're all in our private traps. ♟♟♟♟

LEAVE HER TO HEAVEN (1945)

A morbidly possessive woman who marries a successful novelist goes to extremes to eliminate anyone who gets in the way of her obsession with her husband.

THE MACGUFFIN: The heroine's true nature

Director John Stahl's (the 1930s versions of *Magnificent Obsession*, *Imitation of Life*, and *Back Street*) mastery of neurosis and high drama is probably best displayed in this wonderfully gloomy, twisted, and neurotic Gothic classic of mad love, his famous version of the floridly Freudian bestselling psychological thriller by novelist Ben Ames Williams. *Leave Her to Heaven* is so deliciously overheated, played with all the stops out, that it feels like what might have happened if the cool, reserved Hitchcock had thrown caution to the wind and gone wildly, sickly romantic (à la Douglas Sirk) as an early warm-up for *Vertigo*. The screenplay by Jo Swerling (*The Pride of the Yankees*, Hitchcock's *Lifeboat*) certainly lays the groundwork for that with its string of indelible scenes, all given to the transgressive femme fatale heroine Ellen Berendt, as played by the unearthly gorgeous Gene Tierney, the studio's second choice after the stunning but more carnal Rita Hayworth turned down the role. Once seen, though, Tierney is impossible to forget as Ellen in such moments as when she gallops on horseback across a New Mexico mountain scape scattering the ashes of her adored dead father—to the ominous strains of Alfred Newman's magisterial musical score. Or how impassive and inscrutable she is in sunglasses while coolly and monstrously sitting motionless in a dinghy watching as her polio-stricken brother-in-law (Darryl Hickman) drowns without lifting a finger to help him. Or Ellen hurling herself down a flight of stairs to rid herself of the unborn baby that could come between her and her husband. Or Ellen on a

Gene Tierney plays a newlywed so pathologically possessive of her writer husband (Cornel Wilde) that she watches dispassionately as his disabled brother drowns in *Leave Her to Heaven*.
Donaldson Collection/Moviepix/Getty Images

train gazing boldly and unblinkingly at the novelist husband-to-be Richard Harland (Cornel Wilde, looking as thunderstruck by Tierney's beauty as we are), on whom she becomes morbidly obsessed and rushes into marriage. She tells him, "I want to keep your house and wash your clothes and cook your food. I don't want anybody else in this house besides us. Ever." Not only is it bone chilling, but it's also decades before—and smarter, better directed, and scarier than—*Fatal Attraction* and its clones. Ellen is coolly, ruthlessly effective in annihilating everything and everyone Richard holds dear that their marriage goes horribly and swiftly to hell. Says her cold, distant mother of her willful, reckless, pathologically possessive daughter, "There's nothing wrong with Ellen. It's just that she loves too much." Jeanne Crain plays Tierney's antithesis; warm, caring, loving, understanding, and despite Crain's charm and good looks, compared to Tierney's diabolical performance, she's a pallid, insipid bore. On the other hand, Vincent Price as the fiancé Ellen dumps is as colorful and odd as Cornel Wilde is good-looking but tepid. As subversive a film as Hollywood ever filmed in luscious Technicolor, *Leave Her to Heaven* may chill you or leave you cold. For me, this one is an unnerving, despairing stone-cold masterpiece. ♟♟♟♟

THE DARK MIRROR (1946)

A psychiatrist who specializes in the study of twins joins forces with a veteran police detective to solve the stabbing murder of a doctor by a young woman—who happens to be a twin.

THE MACGUFFIN: Which twin has the psychosis?

Hitchcock's *Spellbound* (1945) became an international box-office smash and garnered six Oscar nominations during a glut of detective and mystery thrillers gimmicked up with Freudian psychoanalysis. *The Dark Mirror* is one of the less remembered entries into the genre. It's a standard whodunit—a prominent doctor has been stabbed to death, and witnesses attest to seeing an attractive woman slipping away from the scene of the crime. The twist comes when veteran

Lieutenant Stevenson (venerable scene-stealer Thomas Mitchell) badgers the coolly confident, unflappable suspect Terry Collins (Olivia de Havilland), then meets her identical twin sister, Ruth (that's right, de Havilland again), a hand-wringing nervous type. The twins are fiercely protective of each other and refuse to cooperate, bringing the investigation to a halt. To penetrate the mystery of which sister is the murderer, the policeman asks Dr. Elliott (Lew Ayres) to examine the twins (via Rorschach inkblots, polygraphs, free association tests). The answer does not prove to be cut and dried, especially once the shrink does what all movie shrinks do—falls in love with the nice sister while the envious bad sister gaslights the hell out her psychologically battered sibling. "I'll never leave you, we'll always be together," says de Havilland with that patented coo her fans think of as sincere yet always sounds monstrously artificial and drive-you-up-a-wall passive-aggressive.

Throughout the film, the twisted sisters play head games with the police and the psychiatrists, swapping identities and even switching back and forth their tacky necklaces that spell out "Terry" and "Ruth" until, finally, the truly evil sister (for whom de Havilland rolls out such subtle acting techniques as malicious, rolling side eyes and snarling) is revealed as the crackpot she is. Hitchcock would never have bothered making a feature film with as hoary a gimmick as good/bad twins, but director Robert Siodmak (*Criss Cross*, *The Spiral Staircase*) was no slouch when it came to thrillers. *The Dark Mirror*, photographed by Milton Krasner, opens with a nice Hitchcockian pan across a living room in which our eye is directed to objects lying on the carpet, a cracked wall mirror, and a man's body that lies face down with a knife lodged in his back—smart, economical filmmaking. Although Siodmak was a devotee of chiaroscuro, in this movie the most sinister lighting gets reserved for scenes set in the bedroom in which one jealous sister dominates and infantilizes the other, all in the name of sisterly love, of course. It's chilling what one family member can do to another as real-life sisters de Havilland and Joan Fontaine could have attested about their own fractious relationship. *The Dark*

Mirror is worth a watch, even if it wastes precious time on repetitive conversations between the detective and the shrink. It's those wacky sisters who are clamoring for attention. ♟♟♟

THE LOCKET (1946)

Just as he is about to get married, a bridegroom gets warned by his fiancée's former husband, a psychiatrist, that his wife-to-be is a chronic thief and liar who suffers from serious psychological problems.

THE MACGUFFIN: The locket

The closest thing that Hitchcock ever made to this talky, dark romantic melodrama is *Marnie*, his critically divisive 1964 film about a comely compulsive thief and liar who suffers psychosexual issues resulting from childhood neglect, sexual trauma, and emotional abuse. And it's close, at that, because in the moody, doom-laden *The Locket*, made during the throes of Hollywood's obsession with psychiatry, convoluted flashbacks and even a flashback within a flashback, Laraine Day (better here than for Hitchcock in *Foreign Correspondent*) stars as a vivacious charmer who is secretly a compulsive thief and mantrap emotionally damaged by childhood neglect and emotional trauma. (Previously, Hitchcock colleague and *Shadow of a Doubt* cast member Hume Cronyn optioned the material, wanting to direct his wife, Jessica Tandy, in the key role.)

In the opening scene, our duplicitous heroine, Nancy Monks, presents herself as a charming, radiant bride about to marry into high society via John Willis (Gene Raymond from Hitchcock's *Mr. and Mrs. Smith*). John is clearly smitten, despite his upper-crust relatives questioning why he would marry, of all women, this bewitching "nobody." Like a thunderclap, drama and darkness arrive in the form of suave Dr. Henry Blair (Brian Aherne), who insists on seeing the prospective groom and telling him, in flashback, what he experienced being married to the woman he calls a "hopelessly twisted [creature who] ruined the lives of three men."

At its core, *The Locket* is, like *Marnie*, a case study of a woman compelled to use her appearance and wiles to make her way in a money- and male-dominated world while struggling to repress her obsessions, guilt, and trauma. The deck is stacked against her; in her poor, shadowy background lurks an unjust childhood accusation of theft of an expensive locket given to her by her mother's shrewish employer Mrs. Willis, John's mother (played by Katherine Emery). (Note that the Willis home in *The Locket* is the same set used as the home of Nazi spy Alex Sebastian [Claude Rains] in Hitchcock's *Notorious*; RKO released both films only months apart.) Nancy's verbal and physical beating at the hands of Mrs. Willis, who fires and banishes mother and child on the spot, contributes to her developing emotional issues that eventually result in an innocent man's getting executed for a murder the heroine probably committed during a robbery, another man's suicide, and two other men being pushed to utter ruin.

Cast atypically, Robert Mitchum succeeds by sheer brute-force magnetism as the arrogant but empathetic artist whom the heroine marries first. Aherne, in the loving husband-psychiatrist role, gets saddled with the unenviable task of explaining all those flashbacks to the audience, detailing his former wife's mixed-up psyche; he's better than the script gives him any reason to be. From a Norma Barzman story titled "What Nancy Wanted" and scripted by Sheridan Gibney (a double Oscar winner for the 1936 film *The Story of Louis Pasteur*), the intriguing if overcooked film was directed by John Brahm (*Hangover Square*), filmed impactfully by black-and-white shadow maestro Nicholas Musuraca (*Cat People*, *I Remember Mama*), and scored by Roy Webb (*Notorious*, *Out of the Past*). Rivalrous sisters Olivia de Havilland and Joan Fontaine reputedly vied for the central role played by a never-better Day, who lacks only the otherworldly allure and mystique the role demands. Maybe if Hitchcock himself had made it starring Ingrid Bergman, say, or Gene Tierney (and with a better, more provocative script), *The Locket* might have become something special—beyond its being an intriguing unofficial precursor of *Marnie*. Still, it's worth a look. ♟♟♟

A WOMAN'S VENGEANCE (1948)

Suspicion falls on a rich philanderer when his invalid wife dies under strange circumstances and he promptly marries his much younger girlfriend, stunning an unmarried woman who has been romantically rebuffed by the man, who soon becomes murder suspect.

THE MACGUFFIN: Red currants

From the start of his directing career to his final years, Alfred Hitchcock resonated to the potential for drama inherent in romantic triangles. Think of the continuing theme of love triads in *The Manxman*, *Rich and Strange*, *Rebecca*, *Notorious*, *I Confess*, *Dial M for Murder*, *Vertigo*, *North by Northwest*, *The Birds*, *Marnie*, and *Topaz*. With *A Woman's Vengeance*, writer-director Zoltan Korda (*The Four Feathers*) went one better than Hitchcock by tackling a romantic quadrangle. Aldous Huxley scripted this deeply strange and compelling sleeper, from his 1921 short story "The Giaconda Smile." The film version is "Hitchcockian" through and through. An uncommonly well-acted psychological drama, *A Woman's Vengeance* stars Charles Boyer (*Gaslight*) as rich, cynical, womanizing cad Henry Maurier, who lives unhappily with a shrewish invalid wife, Emily (Rachel Kempson), in their grand country manor, moodily and evocatively shot by Russell Metty (*Touch of Evil*) and made even more atmospheric by its Miklos Rosza musical score.

Meanwhile, our fiftysomething continental Lothario is catting around on the sly with his pregnant eighteen-year-old mistress Doris (Ann Blyth). As if that weren't unsavory enough, he's spent a decade flirtatiously talking art, music, and literature with his and Emily's sensitive, complicated thirty-five-year-old neighbor, Janet Spence (Jessica Tandy of *The Birds*), who is secretly in love with Henry. When Emily dies suddenly (while Henry is out with Doris), Henry accuses Emily's man-hating, religious-zealot nurse (Mildred Natick of *The Trouble with Harry*, handily pocketing every moment of screen time she's given) of speeding along his dead wife's demise by letting her eat red currants. But is Henry himself the killer, or is it one of the women he's wronged?

On the heels of his wife's burial, Henry's callous quickie marriage to Doris unhinges the righteous nurse, unsettles the local doctor (*Rope*'s Sir Cedric Hardwicke, impeccable), and upsets Janet (whose confession of love icy-veined Henry rejects during a terrific scene set during a rip-roaring, symbolic thunderstorm). The rush for an autopsy sets Henry up for a murder trial, with hanging as his likely fate. Had Hitchcock been in the director's chair instead, Korda's cool, intelligent, fascinating film might have made for an infinitely more exciting ninety-six minutes. *A Woman's Vengeance* isn't up to the standards of Hitchcock's best, but it is an uncommonly offbeat, sometimes excitingly bizarre movie worth seeking out. ♟♟♟

ANGEL FACE (1953)

A seemingly sweet but psychopathic mantrap spells doom to those who dare to cross her, especially an ambulance driver whom she ensnares in her malicious plans.

THE MACGUFFIN: An enigmatic woman's motivation

Apart from the first Mrs. de Winter in *Rebecca* and Maddalena Paradine in *The Paradine Case*, Alfred Hitchcock mostly avoided narratives hinged on the machinations of seductive femmes fatales. He might have done far worse than to add heiress Diane Tremayne to his expertly curated gallery of beautiful, willful sirens who always seem to find exactly the right handsome dupe to send to hell in a handbasket. Diane's target is ambitious ambulance driver Frank Jessup, who answers a random (or *is* it?) emergency call to the Tremayne estate, where Diane's stepmother is found near asphyxiation. Was it a suicide attempt, or was someone in the troubled family trying to do her in? On Frank's way out, he is struck by the sight of the disturbingly attractive Diane playing piano soulfully in the music room. The moment she locks eyes on him one can feel the erotic current between them. He's hooked. She's reeled him in. And because Frank is played by sleepy-eyed, insolently sexy Robert Mitchum and Diane is played by petal-lovely, genteel Jean Simmons, subtly revealing her character's sultry, soul-sick allure, we know Mitchum's headed for big trouble.

Diane suddenly starts turning up at diners or the hospital out of which Frank works; soon he's putting off his lovely, prissy Miss Ann of a girlfriend Mary (Mona Freeman), who's pushing up daisies the moment she appears on screen. Like tennis player Guy Haines in *Strangers on a Train*, who doesn't immediately tell the police about his psychopathic stalker Bruno Anthony, Frank seals his doom by making a single bad choice: he takes a chauffeur job with the Tremaynes and moves into their estate. In no time flat, Diane's parents (Barbara O'Neill and Hitchcock film veteran Herbert Marshall) die when their car tumbles backward over a cliff. Suspicion falls on Diane as their only child and sole heir and on Frank for possibly tampering with the car's transmission. Their attorney (Leon Ames) urges them to play to the jury's sympathies by getting married. Frank tries to wriggle out of the idea but caves in. It's too late. He's way past the point of no return, and even today, the climax of the dreamlike, meandering *Angel Face* is dark, shocking, and uncompromising. Of course, the movie was a flop with 1950s audiences, and it remains just as divisive today.

From the sound of it, *Angel Face* is much more fun to watch than it was to make, especially for Simmons; under orders from producer Howard Hughes, whose romantic advances Simmons rejected, the infamously tyrannical director Otto Preminger made things as unpleasant for his star as possible. For instance, when Preminger kept demanding Mitchum hit Simmons harder and harder during a slapping scene, the actor grew so uncomfortable with the pointless sadism of multiple takes that he strode over to Preminger, slugged him, and told his director as he strode off the set, "That's what it felt like." In no other movie are Simmons and Mitchum so powerfully strange and effective as they are in *Angel Face*. There's a fatalistic, lamb-to-the-slaughter passivity in Mitchum's Frank that, contrasting with his bruiser's build and brooding charisma, makes his performance the more intriguing. Simmons is everything the role requires and more—sophisticated, charming, manipulative, blank-eyed, and terrifying. It's Hitchcockian moviemaking at its most bleak and nihilistic. The film's strange, hothouse ambience and unusual performances have worked for me since the first time I saw *Angel Face*, and its power to fascinate only gets stronger and richer with repeated viewings. ♟♟♟♟

WOMAN OF STRAW (1964)

The greedy nephew of a nasty millionaire—learning that he won't inherit his ailing uncle's millions when he dies—conspires with the rich man's sexy nurse to get his hands on the money.

THE MACGUFFIN: The fortune

A major dose of Hitchcock's sense of pace, focus, and know-how might have livened up this expensive-looking, old-fashioned whodunit melodrama that creaks when it should crackle. From the team of producer Michael Relph (*Kind Hearts and Coronets*) and director Basil Dearden (*Dead of Night, Victim, Khartoum*), who adapted Catherine Arley's much grittier novel, *Woman of Straw* got dragged by critics of its day for being too slow and too long and for too often reminding audiences of Hitchcock without being dark, gripping, or, well, *Hitchcockian* enough. Sean Connery (the same year he starred in *Marnie*) plays suave, snakelike Anthony Richmond, nephew of Charles, a hateful, racist, adder-tongued, wheelchair-bound tycoon (Ralph Richardson, stealing the movie) who runs roughshod over everyone in his path, including his black manservant (Johnny Sekka) and his abused dogs. The skirt-chasing wastrel Anthony despises the ailing Charles for many reasons, not the least of which being that he plans on leaving him only a pittance in his will. But Charles's prime victim is Maria Marcello (Gina Lollobrigida), his Italian nurse. Connery, a conniving, brutish piece of work, puts the moves on Maria and suggests that she work her feminine wiles on Charles, get him to marry her, inherit the sick old man's fortune, then share it with Anthony. The idea repulses the highly moral and principled Maria, but she's apparently so turned on by Tony that she gives in.

But instead of the movie hurtling rapidly toward Charles's demise on his yacht off the gorgeous coast of Spain, it instead fritters well over an hour on talky melodrama mostly dramatizing Maria's moral and religious scruples; to signal her turmoil, Lollobrigida knits her brows and wrings her hands like the heroine of a bad 1920s movie. That said, although the movie starts slowly, it picks up speed. Playing cat-and-mouse games, Lollobrigida (dressed by Dior but sporting a cavalcade of dubious wigs) and Connery (also bewigged) are attractive if not especially well matched. But at such a high level of physical appeal as the stars are here, they almost rival the interiors and façade of a fabulous *Downton Abbey*–worthy England manse and the sunny splendors of sixties-era Majorca. The sheer *va-voom* of Connery and Lollobrigida occasionally diverts one from the mustiness of the plot, which ends with perhaps one too many plot twists. Still, *A Woman of Straw* is a fun, if unnecessarily sluggish, watch. ♟♟♟

MOMENT TO MOMENT (1966)

A love affair between the lonely wife of a busy psychiatrist and a young ensign ends explosively. She and her neighbor dispose of the corpse—will the French police expose the heroine as a murderer?

THE MACGUFFIN: The inconvenient corpse

For casual viewers, the biggest mystery of this posh Technicolor old-fashioned romantic suspense melodrama set on the French Riviera is why is the name of veteran director Mervyn LeRoy (*I Am a Fugitive from a Chain Gang*, *Random Harvest*, *The Bad Seed*) on it and not Hitchcock's? More seasoned viewers—especially considering the film's posh trappings, the heroine's dozens of swank costume changes, the glossy, soft-focus photography, rear projection, and soapy dramatics—might ask why Jean Seberg and not Lana Turner or Doris Day is playing the beleaguered heroine in what looks like a Ross Hunter–produced suspense thriller? Promoting the film eons ago on the *Today Show*, perhaps Leroy (whose final movie this was) accidentally gave an oblique answer: "You don't always get what you want." After all, when the hosts asked about working with Seberg, Leroy pivoted the topic to the absence of new young stars "who look like stars" and rhapsodized instead about Julie Christie, whom he called the most exciting actress since the days of Garbo. Funny because the *Moment to Moment* screenplay by Alec Coppel (*Vertigo*) and John Lee Mahin (*Red Dust*, *The Bad Seed*) is so old-school it might have been hanging around since Leroy's years at Warner Bros. and MGM, where he worked with such contemporaries of Garbo's as Joan Crawford, Myrna Loy, and Jean Harlow. For its 1960s glitz and contemporary appreciation of the intriguing, tragic life, and career of Seberg, *Moment to Moment* may play better today than it did back in the day, when it won tepid reviews and struggled at the box office.

Love it not, it drags audiences back to the last gasp of the era of high-style leading ladies nobly suffering for their so-called sins and grappling with such hoary plot complications as amnesia while clad in expensive frocks (Yves Saint Laurent here), fussy wigs, glistening photography by a master cameraman (Harry Stradling), while being enshrined by gorgeous music (Henry Mancini and Johnny Mercer). Despite the film's obvious sets and rear-projection shots, the cast also filmed on locations in Cannes, Nice, and Saint-Paul-de-Vence. What actors are lucky enough to get that royal treatment in our cut-rate era? Universal's executives dreamed of signing Grace Kelly, Audrey Hepburn, or Julie Andrews for the main role; they might have settled for one of their consolation-prize contract players such as Tippi Hedren, Shirley Jones, Rosemary Forsyth, or Diane Baker. But agents for Julie Christie, whom several Universal-based moviemakers (including Hitchcock, Charlton Heston, Clint Eastwood) talked of casting, asked for too much money. So, in the end, Leroy chose Seberg. She's fine when she's being romanced by the hot-tempered seaman played by newcomer Sean Garrison, a stoic John Gavin type who won the role over such young bucks from Universal's stable as Harrison Ford, James Caan, Michael Sarrazin, and Don Galloway. But the movie gets outright stolen by campy, chic Honor Blackman as Seberg's bohemian neighbor pal and by Arthur Hill as Seberg's husband, who inadvertently (or *is* it?) leads a dogged French policeman (Grégoire Aslan) to some inconvenient truths about his wife and her lover. Although Leroy's direction of the high-toned cat-and-mousery is unforgivably lackadaisical, the movie is too deliciously artificial, swoony, and prototypically 1960s to resist. Hitchcock could have had a field day. ♟♟

A half-cocked Hitchcock shot from *Moment to Moment*, director Mervyn Leroy's romantic thriller in which married Jean Seberg's brief indiscretion with young lover (Sean Garrison) leads to an accidental shooting and burial of a body that isn't dead.

Michael Ochs Archives/Moviepix/Getty Images

MISSISSIPPI MERMAID (1969)

A wealthy tobacco plantation owner, who impulsively marries a mysterious woman he only knows through their shared letters, becomes obsessed by the alluring con artist—especially when she drains his bank accounts.

THE MACGUFFIN: The missing bride

On the evidence of his screen versions of *The Bride Wore Black* and *Mississippi Mermaid*, many critics questioned whether Francois

Truffaut was too gentle a soul and too romantic an artist to film the work of hard-edged crime writer Cornell Woolrich, from whose "It Had to Be Murder" Hitchcock made *Rear Window*. Truffaut's cinematic attraction to Woolrich, a veritable prince of darkness, cynicism, and anguish, almost certainly stems from his interview conversations with Hitchcock that led to the 1966 publication of *Hitchcock/Truffaut*. *Mississippi Mermaid*, the stranger, more intriguing, but less successful and less well known of Truffaut's several Hitchcockian exercises, is based on Woolrich's bleak 1947 novel of deceit, obsession, amour fou, and self-destruction *Waltz into Darkness*. From the maker of *The 400 Blows*, *Jules and Jim*, and *Shoot the Piano Player*, this excursion into the floridly Hitchcockian was deemed a box-office disappointment that divided Truffaut fans (me included). But what do you know? Time has been a bit kinder to the film than one might expect—kinder than time may ever be to *Original Sin*, the overripe R-rated 2001 movie starring Antonio Banderas and Angelina Jolie and based on the same Woolrich novel. But back to the saga of *Mississippi Mermaid*. Because the 1969 movie was made by such an avowed Hitchcock acolyte, its credentials are obvious in its echoes of the suspense master's films featuring neurotic, obsessive love affairs and dangerous love objects, including *Suspicion*, *Under Capricorn*, *Vertigo*, and *Marnie*. (Spoiler: Truffaut even got to film a version of the fatalistic plot development Hitchcock discarded in *Suspicion*; Joan Fontaine, the crazy-in-love heroine, might even have accepted death by poisoning from Cary Grant, the man she loves.) Cast against his usual tough-guy type, Jean-Paul Belmondo plays Louis Mahe, a wealthy, unmarried tobacco plantation and cigarette factory owner on the island of Réunion in the Indian Ocean. Louis appears surprisingly willing to accept deception when Julie Roussel, a young woman he met by taking out a personal ad and with whom he has communicated only through letters, arrives to meet him looking nothing like the pretty brunette in the photo sent to him. In fact, she arrives looking like the stunning, blonde Yves-Saint-Laurent–garbed Catherine Deneuve, arguably *the* icy-cool blonde who got away from Hitchcock. Eventually revealing her real name is Marion Vergano, we learn that this is just the beginning of the lies, deception, and reversals she has in store for the dupe she will quickly marry, with whom she will appear blissfully in love but, within days, pretty much clean out his bank accounts and vanish. Devastated and enraged, Louis buys a gun and hunts down his beautiful betrayer while a relentless private detective (the superb Michel Bouquet), hired by Louis and the sister (Nelly Borgeaud) of the real Julie Rousell, hunts down the femme fatale's whereabouts and her sordid and tragic past. Though the balance of the film reveals at least two murders (one of them staged like a scene in *Psycho*) and portrays an edgy pair of lovers who might murder each other at any moment, Truffaut is not especially adept in—nor does he appear especially interested in— the mechanics of mere suspense. Louis and Marion's behaviors may seem illogical, outlandish, appalling, even laughable to those who have never experienced mad passion. But how the director-writer and his two intensely photogenic stars interpret the contradictions of their complex characters—including the heroine's night terrors and sexual dysfunction, and the dark and ambiguous motivations that fuel the central relationship—are the very things that make *Mississippi Mermaid*

Now that's what we call French sangfroid. *Mississippi Mermaid*'s Catherine Deneuve doesn't break a sweat even when she finds a corpse in the entryway.
Corbis Historical/Getty Images

linger in the memory. When it comes to moviemaking, as Hitchcock often said, "Logic is dull." As he or Truffaut might have added, "So are 'normal' relationships." ♟♟♟♟

CARRIE (1976)

A painfully shy and awkward high school social outcast, dominated by her religious extremist mother, wreaks telekinetic havoc on the classmate who abuse and mock her.

THE MACGUFFIN: The heroine's secret powers

People tell me that my respect and emotional response to Hitchcock's work blind me to the genius they see in the work of Brian De Palma. To which I say, "*Obsession, The Fury, Mission to Mars, Casualties of War, The Black Dahlia, Snake Eyes, Domino, Femme Fatale, Raising Cain, Passion*? Genius? Seriously?" But to which I also add, "But *The Untouchables, Scarface, Blow Out, Phantom of the Paradise, Sisters, Mission: Impossible, Body Double*—and best of all, *Carrie*? Yes, more of those, please." Because, to me, what De Palma did with *Carrie* is not only Hitchcockian, it's also a distinctly De Palma triumph, a testament to the many things at which he's best, including technical dazzle, anarchic humor, cruelty, cynicism, florid romanticism, and willingness to embrace both pop culture trash and the lure of vast conspiracy plots. Like Polanski's *Rosemary's Baby*, *Carrie* is one of mainstream cinema's happy miracles, that all too rare circumstance of everything clicking into place. It is ideally cast with then-young, fresh faces (Sissy Spacek, John Travolta, Amy Irving, Nancy Allan, William Katt), all of whom bring exactly what's needed to their underwritten roles. It is a supremely proficient representation of its original source material and a model of terrific suspense moviemaking. Here De Palma got his hands on an ideal source work. (Stephen King's grabby, unpretentious, *short* 1974 debut novel is a beast of efficiency, primal power, and savagery.) The book got turned into a ruthlessly efficient Lawrence D. Cohen screenplay that hits King's high notes and, maybe wisely, loses the lowest ones. Would we have wanted or needed to see Travolta's Cro-Magnon high school stud slitting pigs' throats and deliberately running over dogs with his car, as King has the character do in the novel? But one suspects that budget restrictions, not discretion, kept De Palma from unleashing King's avenging heroine to burn down her entire town, not just her high school, after she's humiliated during a senior prom that begins in soft-focus heaven and ends in raging hell. What makes *Carrie* a much better De Palma film than, say, *Obsession* is how much genuine emotion it evokes in the viewer. Where *Obsession* is supposed to be *about* overwhelming emotion, it is dry, humorless, and emotionally arid, more about swirling *Vertigo*-style camera moves and hallucinatory *Vertigo*-adjacent Bernard Herrmann music than it is about undying passion for a dead lover. And where Cliff Robertson is hopeless in conveying sickly fascination with the past, the otherworldly Sissy Spacek is flat-out phenomenal at letting us in on the pain and rage Carrie suffers because of her adolescent character's otherness and growing sense of power in the face of her sexually repressed, abusive, insane mother (Piper Laurie in a masterclass of a performance). We're 100 percent with her when Carrie blossoms after being named senior prom queen and she's whirled around the dance floor in the arms of the town's best-looking sensitive jock. For those of us who know that the heroine is about to suffer maliciously orchestrated cruelty, De Palma puts us through the wringer as Mario Tosi's camera traces the route of the string attached to the bucket of pig's blood about to rain down on Carrie. We see Carrie, radiant and full of hope, intercut with the glee of those who've engineered the undoing of that hope. If only we could help her, but the movie just keeps right on playing in agonizing slow motion. It pains us to see Carrie's hopes crushed. It's a credit to De Palma's commitment to the material and Sissy Spacek's naked vulnerability that Carrie's vengeance on those smirking small-minded dimwits—and on her Bible-thumping mother for a lifetime of abuse—is as sad as it is cathartic. For once, in *Carrie*, the director's tributes to themes and techniques of Hitchcock movies including *Psycho* (the students go to Bates High School, the powerful shower scenes that occur in both films, the dangerously wacky mother who overcontrols and warps the mind of her only child; there are also bows to *Suspicion* in the plain-girl romanced by the handsome deceiver, to *The Birds* in the camera following the river of spilled gasoline and the smug man who carelessly tosses a match and sparks an inferno, to *Marnie* in the religious-fanatic mother and troubled daughter) make us care rather than feel superior. Yes, De Palma has been as good since *Carrie*, but better? I'm not sure. ♟♟♟♟

STILL OF THE NIGHT (1982)

A Manhattan psychiatrist, obsessed by a mysterious, possibly homicidal blonde, hunts for a psychotic killer whose next victim he may be.

THE MACGUFFIN: A surgical knife

In writer-director Robert Benton's ritzy, silly, would-be romantic thriller *Still of the Night*, pretty much everything is ersatz Hitchcockian—only jazzed up for the tacky, brassy 1980s. Its milieu, lushly shot by Nestor Almendros, is wealthy, Uptown Manhattan (land of classic brownstones, antique dealers, art galleries, museums, and the well-heeled people who inhabit them). Its characters are attractive, articulate, nicely dressed, and chilly. At the center of the film's chromium heart is caring, recently divorced psychiatrist Dr. Sam Rice (an oddly cast Roy Scheider, whose tresses change color alarmingly from one scene to the next because: reshoots), one of whose patients, George Byrum (Josef Sommer)—a married auction house antiquities curator popular with beautiful younger women—has been found with his throat slashed open.

Right on cue, into Dr. Sam's office swans nouveau Hitchcock blonde Brooke Reynolds (Meryl Streep, all furtive glances, twitches, constantly fussing with her hair and, well, just plain *fussing*) with a confession and a request. Brooke was not only Byrum's auction house assistant but also one of his many extramarital flings; though their dalliance was more carnal than emotional, she asks Sam to return to Byrum's widow the Cartier wristwatch he accidentally left with her the night he was murdered. Brooke begins to worry that Byrum's therapy sessions were filled with enough provocative revelations about her (and whether she has murdered at least one man in her past?) that they have already aroused in Sam questions that sound more primal than clinical. Of course, any ethical, real-world psychiatrist should nip this twisted dame's nonsense in the bud, but the script paints doc Sam as caught in an emotional tailspin since his divorce.

But this is a movie—no, *worse*, a movie about *other* movies. And so, like Sean Connery's otherwise hardheaded character who gets turned on by trapping and bedding a blonde whom he knows to be a compulsive thief in *Marnie*, we're meant to buy the emotionally tight Scheider's Dr. Sam as already half in lust with the idea of Brooke even before he meets her. And now that he has laid eyes on her, he gets so obsessed that he starts acting willfully stupidly and self-sabotaging even as he realizes that he is being stalked by a psycho. And here, *Still of the Night* wilts before our eyes, despite its fancy trappings and pedigree; after all, Streep and writer-director Robert Benton made it right after the Oscar-laden *Kramer vs. Kramer*. The tight, macho Scheider isn't a convincing candidate for playing a lovestruck neurotic obsession; meanwhile, the striking, bewigged Streep struggles to create a pitiable, dangerous femme fatale out of a laundry list of script clichés and actory mannerisms. Fatally, the actors generate zero heat together, and so, emotionally detached as they appear to be, we respond the same way. We're left with some nice enough suspense set pieces (set in a hellish Central Park tunnel, a basement laundry room, a high-powered auction) as we watch a promising movie skid off into parody as it dutifully checks off nods to Hitchcock's *Spellbound*, *Vertigo*, *North by Northwest*, *Rear Window*, *The Birds*, and more. Meanwhile we can't help but find ourselves wishing the characters created by Robert Benton and David Newman (*Bonnie and Clyde*) were more complex and wishing even more that the two leading roles were played by actual Hitchcock bluebloods at their career peak. Meanwhile, the outstanding supporting cast includes Sommer as the onerous but persuasive philanderer, Jessica Tandy (*The Birds*) as Scheider's fastidious, frosty, no-nonsense psychiatrist mother, and rumpled everyman Joe Grifos as the dogged police detective on the case. *Still of the Night* is one of the more frustrating Hitchcockian movies because, reportedly, so much good stuff got left on the cutting-room floor. ♟♟♙

BASIC INSTINCT (1992)

A police detective probing a violent murder becomes sexually entangled with the prime suspect—a brilliant, seductive murder-thriller novelist.

THE MACGUFFIN: The ice pick

Back in its day, a censorship furor—and even *more* puritanical hand-wringing—erupted over this notorious R-rated erotic thriller from director Paul Verhoeven (*The 4th Man*) featuring that most deadly and threatening of species: a brilliant, accomplished, filthy rich, gorgeous, sexually liberated heroine who runs circles around any man in her path. And much of that outrage and titillation stem from the scene in which the film's modern-day femme fatale Catherine Tramell (played, in a star-making performance, by Sharon Stone), bestselling author and ice-pick murder suspect, reduces to preadolescent stooges a roomful of cartoonishly macho, misogynistic police interrogators simply by uncrossing her legs. The scene got everyone talking and, in the bargain, contributed to making Stone a star in a role for which Julia Roberts, Demi Moore, Melanie Griffith, Isabelle Adjani, Jodie Foster, Meg Ryan, Emma Thompson, Debra Winger, Kim Basinger, Ellen Barkin, and more were in the running.

The film itself, a deliberately brazen, lurid, explicitly sexed-up version of a 1940s detective thriller, is prime Verhoeven: sardonic, satirical, and laughing up its sleeve about prudish American attitudes toward sex and manhood. What others apparently like in De Palma's work, I see being done better—and much funnier—in Verhoeven's. *Basic Instinct* has Hitchcockian touches all the way through. If somehow Jan de Bont's languorous, hypnotic cinematography of upper-echelon San Francisco does not remind one of *Vertigo*, then Jerry Goldsmith's whirling, melancholy musical ruminations on Bernard Herrmann's certainly should. The film is tense, suspenseful, darkly funny, and riddled with a sense of menace that recalls Hitchcock's. Who is the heroine but a seductive, brainy Berkeley magna cum laude literature and psychology grad, bestselling crime fiction author, world-class bisexual seductress, and head-trip master—a Hitchcock blonde in the

Grace Kelly/Kim Novak mold, only one who is suspiciously handy with an ice pick?

Michael Douglas plays a messed-up, despicable homicide detective with a history of so-called accidental shootings and an emotionally and physically abusive relationship with a terrific woman, Dr. Beth Garner (Jeanne Tripplehorn, excellent), the archetypal earthy, more practical Hitchcock brunette (see Suzanne Pleshette in *The Birds*, Diane Baker in *Marnie*, Barbara Bel Geddes—a sensible ash blonde—*Vertigo*, among others). Aren't Douglas's Nick and Tripplehorn's Beth a dark-mirror version of Scottie and Midge in *Vertigo*? The movie is so obviously Hitchcockian, is it any wonder why during the casting process Michael Douglas reportedly kept holding out for a modern Grace Kelly type—notably, Michelle Pfeiffer—rather than the lesser-known Stone to play the woman he sees as his quarry? (Pfeiffer declined.)

As with most heroes in such gritty crime melodramas as *Out of the Past*, Nick Curran thinks he's in control, way ahead of the game, but he's just another victim, a patsy—duller and more manipulatable than, say, the heroine's homicidal girlfriend (Leilani Sarelle) and her murderous friend Hazel Dobkins (Dorothy Malone, *The Big Sleep*). Sure, the three-million-dollar-making Joe Eszterhas screenplay goes heavy on the sleaze, but the refreshing sexual politics (Douglas has the damsel-in-distress role opposite Stone's predatory heroine), the quality of the performances, and the decadent slickness of it all make *Basic Instinct* a heavy-breathing, entertaining blast that spawned a mini-industry in such would-be sexy neo-noir imitations as Madonna's comically terrible *Body of Evidence* and Bruce Willis's *Color of Night*. ♟♟♟

11 On the Run

If any director successfully exploited the trope of the falsely accused innocent character simultaneously chased by the law and by relentless evildoers (sometimes indistinguishable), it was Hitchcock. Accused of crimes they did not commit, Hitchcock's "wrong man" heroes—in films from *The Lodger* (1927), *The 39 Steps* (1935), *Young and Innocent* (1936), *Foreign Correspondent* (1940), and *Saboteur* (1942) all the way to *Strangers on a Train* (1951), *I Confess* (1953), *To Catch a Thief* (1955), *The Wrong Man* (*1956*), *North by Northwest* (1959), and *Frenzy* (1972)—face similar fates and take similar journeys as they fight to prove their innocence and expose the true culprits, who are actively trying to stop them by any means possible. Meanwhile, these beleaguered characters lose the trust of those closest to them, lose their livelihoods and status, question their own sanity, become fugitives and assassins' targets, let alone rub elbows (or other body parts) with an entirely new class of people. Only sometimes are those people attractive, ambiguously motivated, or out-and-out dangerous blondes.

These films typically involve a frantic pursuit for Hitchcock's most memorable (but, ultimately, utterly disposable) MacGuffins, including a dangerous spy leader with a missing finger, a fancy engraved cigarette lighter, a pre-Columbian statue hiding top-secret microfilm, an incriminating necktie. And for maximum visual impact and for irony, these films also set their most pulse-pounding scenes against such splashy, recognizable public landmarks as Westminster Cathedral, the Statue of Liberty, Mount Rushmore, the United Nations building, and Covent Garden. In these films, Hitchcock was decades ahead of other filmmakers in positing that, for both the innocent and the guilty, the world offers no hiding place, no safe space. The kinds and scale of violence and chaos that once seemed horrific if fanciful in Hitchcock's man/woman-on-the-run movies—whether in the fantastically entertaining spree that is *North by Northwest* or the austere, terrifying, claustrophobic semi-documentary style of *The Wrong Man*—is now the stuff of daily headlines.

Perhaps more than any other genre of Hitchcock movies, these are the films most treacherous but rewarding to emulate, as the best and worst movies in this chapter amply display.

THE CHASE (1946)

A down-on-his-luck war vet gets hired as a chauffeur by a sadistic millionaire and falls in love with his boss's terrified captive wife.

THE MACGUFFIN: A dagger

Here's a strange one—and even more watchable for that strangeness. Certainly, the very oddness of *The Chase*, from a script by Philip Yordan (*Detective Story*, *The Big Combo*), helps account for its cult status. Yordan derived the bare bones of the plot from the novel *The Black Path of Fear* by the prolific, influential Cornell Woolrich (*Rear Window*, *The Bride Wore Black*). But Yordan veered off into some bizarre directions all his own, bless his dark little heart. In its very first moments, the movie—paced in a dreamlike style by director Arthur D. Ripley (*Thunder Road*) and shot and edited accordingly by, respectively, cinematographer Franz Planer (*Criss Cross*, *Letter from an Unknown Woman*) and Edward Mann (*The Birdman of Alcatraz*)—zeroes in on blandly handsome, boyish Robert Cummings (Hitchcock's *Saboteur*, *Dial M for Murder*) as ex-navy man Chuck Scott. Suffering from what we'd now call posttraumatic stress disorder and wearing ill-fitting clothing, he stares hungrily in the window of a downtown Miami greasy spoon watching a grill cook flipping pancakes and bacon slabs. Poor Chuck, starving but stone broke, spots a wallet on the pavement, sees that it is stuffed with cash, and finds the ID, which says it belongs to one Eddie Roman.

After treating himself to breakfast on Eddie Roman's dime, Chuck heads out to his benefactor's menacingly showy home; at the front door, a succession of suspicious eyes peer out through a faintly obscene cherubic peephole while phantom voices give Chuck the third degree about his identity and purpose. Finally ushered inside by Roman's henchman, Gino (Peter Lorre, slimy, menacing, and terrific), Chuck impresses the owner of the wallet as an honest rube, a perfect fall guy. The sadistic tough guy Roman is played by Steve Cochran, (*White Heat*) suave, handsome, dressed to the nines, radiating sexual bravado and menacing machismo. He speaks in a monotone baritone, but he's a hot-wired, violent type who thinks nothing of backhanding his manicurist or the gorgeous, sad-eyed French wife, Lorna (Michèle Morgan, a European acting legend for three decades), he literally keeps captive in his manse. And when he's not abusing women, he's busy eliminating business rivals (Lloyd Corrigan) by having Gino lock them in a world-class wine cellar stocked with priceless bottles of Napoleon Brandy—and an enormous, ravenous attack dog.

It's obvious that racketeer boss Roman has Chuck earmarked for serious insanity when he hires him as his chauffeur. To test Chuck's nerve and loyalty, Roman pulls such insane stunts as jamming his foot on the pedal of a backset gizmo that sends the car careening over one hundred miles an hour straight into the path of an oncoming train. Chuck also gains the trust of the gangster's lonely wife, whom he drives nightly to a secluded dock, where Lorna stares longingly out to over the Atlantic wondering aloud where it leads. To Havana, that's where, and she and Chuck engineer an escape to Cuba that makes the movie light up with weird, hallucinatory imagery and trippy sounds in a nightclub filled with suggestive couplings, danger, and doom, leading to Chuck and Lorna dancing languorously together but ending in her getting stabbed with a dagger. Our hero—Hitchcock's classic wrong man—is now a wanted man on the run in such settings as murky alleys, an antique curio shop, and the apartment of a woman quarantined with the plague. Gino's on hand to stir up trouble, and at the halfway mark in the action, Chuck gets shot and presumably killed (hello Marion Crane in the first half of *Psycho*), and that's when things get even more nightmarish and bizarre. Cummings gives a mostly restrained and engaging performance as the brain-addled war vet, the stunning Morgan brings new shadings to

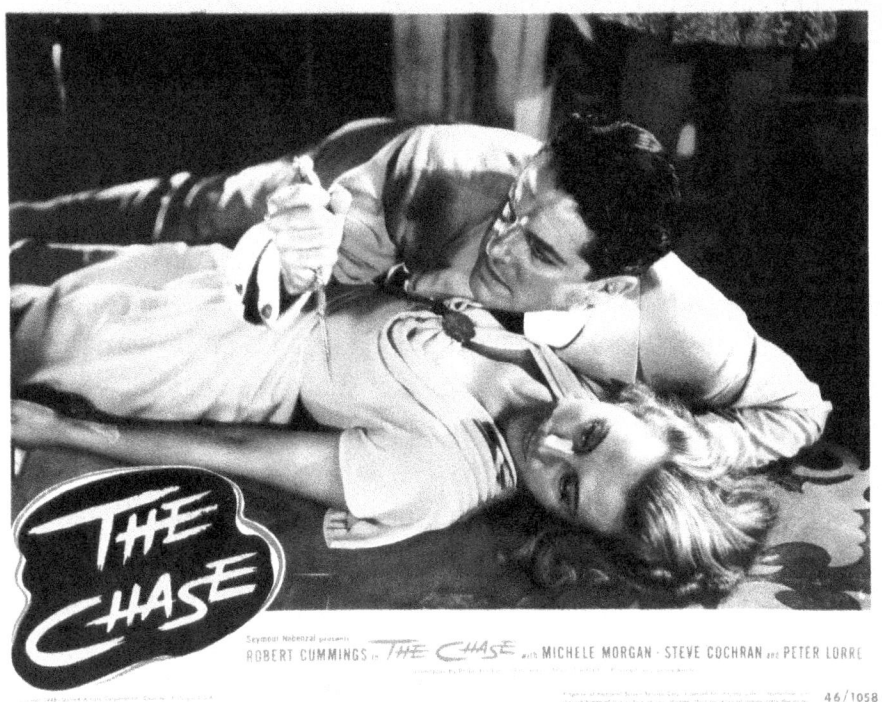

In *The Chase*, one minute Robert Cummings is dancing with unhappily married Michèle Morgan, the next she's been stabbed dead.
LMPC via Getty Images

the classic femme fatale/victim role, and Cochran and Lorre make an especially chilling mobster duo. Running eighty-six minutes, few of them wasted, jam-packed with dreams and hallucinations, a constant sense of disorientation, and *two* endings? Look, we completely understand why many grow impatient with the twists, turns, and it-was-all-a-hallucination gimmicks in *The Chase*. We just don't happen to agree with them. ♟♟♟

ODD MAN OUT (1947)

After being wounded and abandoned in a Belfast robbery gone wrong, an IRA leader searches for escape while British police close in on him.

THE MACGUFFIN: An incriminating gun

It isn't every suspense thriller that begins with an IRA-fueled daytime bank heist that goes terribly wrong, sends its badly wounded central character on the run in the shadows, rain, and snow of Belfast, and ends up becoming a poetic, dreamlike, surreal, and, ultimately, profound and tragic meditation on life, devotion to a cause, religion, and existence. In fact, it is *only Odd Man Out*, a too-little-known masterwork directed by Carol Reed three years before his second postwar masterpiece, *The Third Man*. James Mason gives the film's indelible centerpiece performance playing Johnny McQueen, an IRA leader whose lifeblood is leaking and whose time on earth is running down as he crashes and stumbles through a city short on human kindness. He's doggedly pursued by a policeman (Denis O'Dea), an unrequited love (Kathleen Ryan) who would prefer death to life without him, an elderly priest (W. G. Fay) who bargains for his soul, a sympathetic spinster who does her best to bind his wounds after finding him in the street (Fay Compton), a mercenary rummy ready to sell him out (F. J. McCormick), and a crazed, self-deluded artist who wants to capture his face as he nears death (Robert Newton). Crowding these magnificent performances from start to finish are

Wounded during a botched bank robbery, IRA man James Mason's final odyssey through Belfast becomes a Christ-like parable in Carol Reed's *Odd Man Out*.
Archive Photos/Moviepix/Getty Images

indelible details and moments, infinitely mournful nocturnal images impeccably captured by Robert Krasker (*The Third Man*).

These unforgettable images and moments include a little waif wearing only one roller skate who points the way to Johnny McQueen. The careworn faces of women yanking down their window shades as gunfire rips through the streets. Characters cobwebbed by mist and doom. Snowflakes tumbling through a shattered skylight and down into the entryway of a ruined palatial home. If its makers' ambition and reach sometimes exceeds its weighty Dostoyevskyian aspirations, better a shortfall than a lack of ambition. A stunningly beautiful and powerful film with sustained suspense fully worthy of its intricate screenplay by F. L. Green and R. C. Sherriff. ♟♟♟♟

WOMAN ON THE RUN (1950)

When her estranged husband flees the police after he's the sole witness to the murder of a key trial witness, the embittered wife, helped by a reporter, discovers secrets that make her frantic to save her husband from the killer.

THE MACGUFFIN: A sketch of the real killer

When Hitchcock bought the screen rights to material, he often threw out everything except the central idea, image, or theme that intrigued him in the first place. Watching the little-known gem of a hard-boiled crime thriller *Woman on the Run*, it's difficult to imagine Hitchcock being inspired by its gritty working-class San Francisco milieu, its plot about a failed artist going into hiding after witnessing a murder, or its hard-bitten police and gangster characters. Sure, it's got a classic wrong-man theme, but it is easier to imagine the director becoming intrigued by the script's surprising central theme: the painter's hard-bitten, disappointed wife becomes increasingly frantic to find and save from danger her drifter husband as she slowly discovers his secrets. After all she learns about him, she falls back in love with him, as do the heroines in Hitchcock's *Rich and Strange* and *The Man Who Knew Too Much*. But, when it comes to *Woman on the Run*, other filmmakers got there first, notably, Broadway actor-turned-director-screenwriter Norman Foster (*Journey into Fear*), who adapted an original Sylvia Tate story with fellow former-actor-screenwriter Alan Campbell (*A Star Is Born*, *The Little Foxes*, and twice married to Dorothy Parker, who believed he was gay). Voilà, the sharp-witted, unconventional *Woman on the Run*, filmed by legendarily innovative cinematographer Hal Mohr (*Destry Rides Again*, *A Midsummer Night's Dream*, Hitchcock's photo consultant on *Topaz*) on location in Hitchcock's beloved San Francisco, and featuring one hell of an amusement park finale vying to out-thrill Hitchcock's own in *Strangers on a Train* or Orson Welles's in *The Lady from Shanghai*. Best of all, it showcases a lived-in, world-weary movie-star performance from the wonderful Ann Sheridan, the earthy, wisecracking, husky-voiced glamour-puss who in the late 1930s and early 1940s became an audience favorite for proving more than a match for such screen tough-customer costars as James Cagney, Humphrey Bogart, Bette Davis, and Cary Grant in *They Drive by Night*, *Kings Row*, *The Man Who Came to Dinner*, and *I Was a Male War Bride*. Like many female stars of the era, though, the fifties saw Sheridan getting aged out in favor of younger, more bland confections. At least the modestly budgeted *Woman on the Run*, which Sheridan also produced, provided a role she could sink her teeth into. As Eleanor Johnson, the wife of a man gone missing (*Man on the Run* was the film's original title), she zings a nosy police inspector, played perfectly by Robert Keith (*Written on the Wind*), with such postmortems on her marital relationship as, "It's all past and done with. If you want to snoop into the remains of our marriage, that's up to you." The cynical inspector zings Eleanor back with, "No wonder the world's full of bachelors." Pushy wise-guy reporter Danny Legget, the excellent, chronically undervalued movie tough guy Dennis O'Keefe (*T-Men*, *Raw Deal*), helps Eleanor's search for Frank in dive bars and other hangouts while making unwelcome romantic moves on her; through tiny clues in Frank's paintings and notes left for her, Eleanor realizes exactly where she will find her husband. Before she gets there, though, a few characters will die mysteriously, a trusted character gets revealed as a louse, and it all ends up at an amusement park sequence centered around two hellacious roller-coaster rides that brought the film critic for the *Los Angeles Times* to write, "For a Hitchcock-type thriller…. *Woman on the Run* is really quite a presentable little affair." As long as Ann Sheridan is trading wisecracks with her surly costars, defrosting when she begins to realize the true danger her husband is facing, and emoting like a trouper while strapped into the harrowing Sea Serpent roller-coaster ride filmed at Ocean Park Pier in Santa Monica, the movie is much more than a presentable little affair. And Sheridan is so good that she even manages to hold her own in every moment she plays with a scene-stealing little dog named Rembrandt. That's star power. ♟♟♟♟

THE GAZEBO (1959)

A thriller writer-director decides to murder a blackmailer extorting him for money over scandalous photos of his actress wife as a teenager. But did he murder and bury the wrong man in the foundation of the new gazebo in the backyard of his suburban Connecticut home?

THE MACGUFFIN: The corpse buried under the gazebo

Okay, here's an oddity. *The Gazebo*, based on a hit Broadway play by Alec Coppel (Hitchcock's first screenwriter on *Vertigo*), turns a Hitchcockian black comedy premise (à la *The Trouble with Harry*) on its head and treats it as a knockabout screwball farce. Winning the role played on Broadway by Walter Slezak (*Lifeboat*), Glenn Ford (*Gilda*, *Experiment in Terror*) stars as TV crime show writer Elliott Nash living in the leafy Connecticut suburbs with his Broadway musical comedy star wife, Nell (Debbie Reynolds, game and charming). They've got a horndog assistant district attorney neighbor (Carl Reiner, of whom there is, for once, too much), whose brain Ford regularly picks for technical details on such criminal matters as how to evade the police when you've just happened to have murdered someone. It seems that a blackmailer persists in demanding more money from our hero in exchange for some nudes of the younger, struggling Mrs. Nash. The jittery, bumbling Mr. Nash enacts a plan:

murder the blackmailer and bury the corpse deep in the foundation of their brand-new backyard gazebo. The writer's hare-brained scheme—he even calls *the* Alfred Hitchcock (unseen, unheard) for advice—is as shot through with holes as the lackadaisical screenplay, which requires Ford to mug and throw himself into long, drawn-out bouts of frantic slapstick physical comedy. Try as he might, these gifts are not in Ford's skill set; the strain wears on him—and us. We dream of what fun Cary Grant, William Holden, or even Jack Lemmon might have had with the role, with Hitchcock directing instead of stalwart George Marshall (*Destry Rides Again*, *The Blue Dahlia*) and from a far cleverer and sharper screenplay than what George Wells (*Angels in the Outfield*, *Designing Woman*) has delivered. In *The Gazebo*, the tricky art of blending pitch-black comedy, suspense, satire, and romance eludes Marshall the way it doesn't Stanley Donen with *Charade* or Hitchcock with *The Trouble with Harry*. *The Gazebo* plays like a pleasant but unnecessarily dragged-out episode of *Alfred Hitchcock Presents*. ♟♟

THE RUNNING MAN (1964)

When an insurance company refuses to pay off a lapsed policy after a pilot deliberately crashes his plane, he strikes back by faking his death, assuming another man's identity, and absconding with a fortune in insurance money. He and his wife reunite, but a shy, smitten insurance investigator tails the wife and causes trouble.

THE MACGUFFIN: The insurance money

"A gripping psychological thriller." "The most stylish thriller I have read all year." "I would call [Shelley Smith] the English Patricia Highsmith." It's a wonder that such reviews for British novelist Shelley Smith's delightfully devious 1961 novel *The Ballad of the Running Man* didn't tempt Hitchcock to grab the movie rights. What a movie he could have made of this tale of a cynical pulp novelist who concocts a brilliant plot for his next book—a man takes out a life insurance policy, fakes his own death, collects a fortune in insurance money, and assumes a glamorous new identity with his gorgeous wife. But things get more complicated when the writer convinces his gorgeous would-be-actress wife to carry out the swindle. And that's when things really get interesting. Instead, though, one of Hitchcock's most gifted and prestigious colleagues and rivals, Carol Reed (*Odd Man Out*, *The Third Man*) collaborated with playwright-screenwriter John Mortimer (*The Innocents*, *Bunny Lake Is Missing*) on this movie version, starring Laurence Harvey, Lee Remick, and Alan Bates.

Considering the pedigree of the talent involved, one might have reasonably hoped for a classic. In vain, unfortunately. For one thing, the original novel gets drained of most of its wit, style, plot, locales—and, fatally, its tension. The film opens with plane-crazy pilot Rex Black (Harvey) getting eulogized after a glider accident while his stunning widow Stella (Remick) grieves. Sort of. The service is barely over when sly, sardonic Rex strolls into the house as casually as if he'd been hanging out in the garage. He lays out for Stella how she should collect the insurance payout and meet him in Malaga, Spain; in case we hadn't already figured out the scam, the director and screenwriter subject us to an awkward flashback-within-a-dream sequence in which we learn how Rex is avenging the insurance company's denial of an earlier post-"accident" settlement because the policy had lapsed. With Rex still in the house, in strolls shy British insurance investigator Stephen (Alan Bates), who is immediately smitten by the new widow and tells her how lucky she is to be young and rich, with a whole life ahead of her. This could be a terrific cat-and-mouse scene, but all through it Rex walks around the house—apparently not making a sound? Again, zero tension.

By the time Stella reconnects with Rex in sunny Spain, he's living *la vida loca* as an aimless swinger and kept man, having stolen the passport and copied the platinum-blonde look and suntan of an Australian sheep rancher named Jim Jerome. Stella detests him on sight, but Rex assures her that he's soon going to kill his fake persona, perpetrate another, bigger insurance scam, and devise a whole new identity swap. Back onto the scene comes the insurance man, Stephen, whose presence rattles the larcenous couple in more than one way. Is he there to catch a thief? Or to woo a lover? The last third of the film is almost a travelogue, beautifully filmed by Robert Krasker (*Brief Encounter*, *The Third Man*) and punctuated by Remick's loyalties being torn between two enigmatic men; there is treachery, amusing scenes of Harvey piloting a massive Lincoln through narrow village streets, and a cracking good auto chase that nearly turns fatal. Though Reed gives the thing a professional polish and sheen, he is working with a surprisingly generic script many, many levels below the standards of *The Third Man*, *Odd Man Out*, and *Fallen Idol*. The cast is certainly good to look at, but instead of the icy-cold, self-enchanted Harvey (who was, as usual, much disliked by his costars), imagine, say, peak-period Sean Connery or Steve McQueen in the leading role and the movie might have had more fun, electricity, and sex appeal. A letdown but still worth a look. ♟♟♟

A master director a long way from his Hitchcockian heights.
LMPC via Getty Images

DEAD HEAT ON A MERRY-GO-ROUND (1966)

A persuasive con man—a master of accents and disguises—engineers his early prison parole to plan and pull off a daring heist of the bank at Los Angeles International Airport.

THE MACGUFFIN: The blueprints of the bank

This is one of a slew of comedy caper movies that flooded theaters in the 1960s and 1970s—among them *Dollars* starring Warren Beatty, *Bank Shot* with George C. Scott, *Diamonds* with Robert Shaw—that no one talks about anymore. With good reason. This one, written and directed by Bernard Girard (*The Rebel Set*), is built around a diabolically charming rogue antihero, con-artist supreme, master of accents and disguises, and catnip to beautiful women, Eli Kotch. As played by rugged 1960s screen icon James Coburn (Tony Curtis dropped out when Sidney J. Furie [*The Ipcress File*] did likewise), think of the character as a precursor to Fletch or the real-life con man Leonardo Di Caprio played in *Catch Me If You Can*. In other words, Kotch is the kind of character the young Cary Grant might have played for Hitchcock. (Although a Hitchcock-and-Grant take on *Dead Heat on a Merry-Go-Round*, even during the so-called swinging sixties era of such sexed-up spies as James Bond, Matt Helm, and Derek Flint, surely would have finessed the rampantly smirky, sexist shenanigans in which this movie indulges.)

The film is a breezy, tossed-off lark that takes nothing seriously—meaning it will be anathema to any contemporary contemporary viewer who demands dankness, meaning, or social commentary from their crime movies. It is undeniably sluggishly paced for a heist flick, but the action, such as it is, kicks off with the strictly transactional Kotch seducing a prison psychiatrist (Marian McCargo) solely to win himself an early parole. Once sprung, he beds, robs, and leaves several other perfectly nice women (two of whom are played charmingly by Nina Wayne and a continental Hitchcock-blonde-who-never-was, Camilla Sparv). Between women, he darts around Denver, Boston, and Los Angeles gathering a crime crew and raising the additional eighty-five thousand he needs to buy blueprints to the bank at Los Angeles International Airport, which he intends to rob during the frenzy surrounding the arrival of the premier of the Soviet Union. When the movie calls for it, the lizardy, self-satisfied James Coburn is fun conning marks by donning such guises as a termite inspector, a Swiss shoe clerk, an Aussie police inspector. He may be up to the task of holding the movie together the way he held together his *Our Man Flint* spy capers, but the screenplay does him few favors.

Way too late in the movie, he pulls off the highly complicated bank heist, aided by fellow fraudsters Aldo Ray (*We're No Angels*, *The Marrying Kind*), Michael Strong (*Patton*), and Severn Darden (the original *Planet of the Apes*). The finale puts an ironic twist on the hero's scheming and seducing—and it's a female character who supplies that twist. The film is occasionally amusing but certainly not unforgettable—and neither is the much-talked-about thirty-six-second movie debut of twenty-three-year-old Harrison Ford as a hotel bellboy. To anyone but a Ford stan, it's a nonevent. A few years later, though, with lots more seasoning, Ford might have made a devilishly delightful Eli Kotch. ♟♟♟

JEWEL THIEF (1967)

Tired of being mistaken for a notorious jewel thief, the lookalike gem assessor son of a police commissioner decides to impersonate and expose that thief. Suddenly, the thief poses as the jewel assessor, throwing everything and everyone into confusion.

THE MACGUFFIN: The man with the missing toe

This Bollywood spin on Hitchcock, directed by the legendary Vijay Anand (*Guide*), scripted by Anand and K. A. Narayan, offers lighthearted nods to *To Catch a Thief*, *The 39 Steps*, *North by Northwest*, *The Man Who Knew Too Much*, and *Vertigo*, only with song-and-dance sequences. Sounds like a recipe for disaster but, miracle of miracles, it works like a charm. It's an unpredictable, sexy, delightful visual treat, from its highly stylized Technicolor-like credit sequence (depicting an elegant jewel heist in process) to its riotous heist/musical finale. The plot centers on Vinay (played by debonair Hindi romantic film idol Dev Anand, the director's elder brother and the film's producer). Vinay is cast as a carefree, aimless young flirt who just happens to be an ace diamond assessor and the son of Bombay's police commissioner (Nasir Hussain), who considers him worthless, and an indulgent mother (Pratima Devi), who dotes on him.

Meanwhile, at large is a not-so-average young man, a dashing, brilliant playboy criminal and ladies' man "Prince" Amar (Dev Anand again—surprised?), believed to be responsible for a run of bold, massively lucrative jewel heists that fascinate the public but baffle the frustrated, embarrassed police. The commissioner, newly assigned to the case, has solemnly promised to resign if he does not deliver the thief, dead or alive, on the night of a daring heist of a true prince's priceless crown during a gala party. So the clock is ticking, the noose is tightening. The film's musical soundtrack, costumes, and dialogue encourage us to view Amar as a gentleman master criminal along the lines of Hitchcock's own celluloid version of Arsène Lupin—John Robie of *To Catch a Thief*, played by Cary Grant. The plot hinges on a gimmick: Vijay and Amar look so identical that the former is often mistaken for the latter and vice versa, and both are tired of it. So Vijay agrees to go undercover to help the police catch the thief red-handed—at the same time Amar decides to masquerade as Vijay, throwing into confusion everyone, including both men's bevy of amorous girlfriends and fiancées (played by such popular Hindi actresses as Vyjayanthimala, Anjali Nath, Fariyal, Helen, and Anju Mahendru).

It is a built-in feature of the con game that viewers should be confused right along with the characters when trying to figure out who is who when Amar appears to be posing as Dev and Dev is trying on his Amar identity; the director succeeds in parodying, but also saluting, Hitchcock's career-long fascination with disguises, lookalikes, and doubles. Just when the film threatens to wobble, it shifts into overdrive with an astonishing series of eye-popping music-and-dance sequences by composer S. D. Burman (bits of the *Twilight Zone* theme and James Bond–like music interweave with more authentic Hindi harmonics). What's most ingenious (and Hitchcockian) is how the music and suspense click together—especially during a jewel robbery finale that only a spoilsport would dare to describe exactly. Few films aspire to the sheer brio and infectious sense of fun Hitchcock achieved with such comedic suspense thrillers as *The 39 Steps*, *The Lady Vanishes*, *To Catch a Thief*, and *North by Northwest*. But *Jewel Thief* tries to evoke that spirit.

At its best, the movie is so much fun—and its twist such a stylish one—that one can almost imagine a 1960s-era Hitchcock-directed English-language remake starring, say, the young Sean Connery, Sophia Loren, Claudia Cardinale, and John Williams. Why not? But what about those kaleidoscopic Bollywood musical numbers, especially several that let the characters confess deeper emotions than the dialogue? Aye, there's the rub.

Of course, Hitchcock wove musical numbers, public performances, and entire musical sequences right into the narratives of *Murder!*, both versions of *The Man Who Knew Too Much*, *Young and Innocent*, *Stage Fright*, and *Torn Curtain*, among others. But, after Hitchcock had such a miserable time directing the 1934 Johann Strauss II biographical musical *Waltzes from Vienna* during what he described as a career low point, he never again went near a full musical.

Anyway, *Jewel Thief*—a massive hit in India—proved to be a one of a kind. A disco-ized *Return of the Jewel Thief*, released in 1996, not only missed the gifts of the original's writer-director but also the high style, thrills, and charm of the first movie—and flopped. ♟♟♟♙

ROUGH CUT (1980)

When two sophisticated jewel thieves join forces on a thirty-million-dollar heist of uncut diamonds, love, mistrust, and double crosses threaten to trip them up.

THE MACGUFFIN: A fortune in diamonds

To Catch a Thief, Hitchcock's sun-splashed, playful 1955 romantic comedy/suspense thriller starring Cary Grant as a legendary cat burglar retired to the Riviera and Grace Kelly as a headstrong, thrill-seeking American heiress out to prove "The Cat" is still on the prowl, often gets dismissed as one of the suspense master's most frivolous, disposable light entertainments. If it's such a frothy vol-au-vent, a mere soufflé, then why are its wit, high style, and charm not only so beloved by audiences but also so difficult—if not impossible—to replicate?

Various moviemakers and actors have spent nearly two decades attempting to launch a *To Catch a Thief* remake; in 2022, Paramount announced that screenwriter Eileen Jones (*Highwayman*, *Prodigal Son*) was writing a redo for *Wonder Woman* actress Gal Gadot, who reportedly wanted to play the Cary Grant role. Of course. This despite such previous attempts to emulate Hitchcock's recipe for high-style romance, danger, and suspense as *How to Steal a Million*, *Someone Is Killing the Great Chefs of Europe*, *The Tourist*, *Entrapment*, and—maybe the most try-hard of them all—*Rough Cut*. The latter, based on a dark, intricately detailed 1975 jewel heist novel, *Touch the Lion's Paw* by Derek Lambert, brought together the notorious Broadway producer David Merrick (*Hello, Dolly!*), director Blake Edwards (who'd shown Hitchcockian flair with *Experiment in Terror*), screenwriter Larry Gelbart, and 1970s box-office king Burt Reynolds as star.

Reynolds, eager to stretch beyond what he called such "Levis and cowboy hat" hits as *Smokey and the Bandit* and *Hooper*, announced he wanted to make a "Cary Grant type movie." Hitchcock himself discussed Reynolds to star in what the director described to him as "the suave William Powell–type villain role" in *Family Plot* (opposite Faye Dunaway, Al Pacino, and perhaps Goldie Hawn or Beverly Sills). According to Reynolds, Hitchcock and the studio balked at the stars' salary demands, and the director cast less costly actors. In the end, *Rough Cut* lost Blake Edwards, who disliked the Gelbart script that Reynolds called "brilliant." Four additional screenwriters, four different filmed endings, three directors later—Don Siegel (*Dirty Harry*, *Escape from Alcatraz*) would go on to call making *Rough Cut* "a disaster since day one." Also involved were directors Peter R. Hunt (*On Her Majesty's Secret Service*) and Robert Ellis Miller (*The Heart Is a Lonely Hunter*), the latter of whom filmed Merrick's preferred ending.

When the shooting finally stopped, the movie opened to little critical acclaim or audience approval. All that said, *Rough Cut* is not without its pleasures. Or its Hitchcockian allure, thanks to its large and small nods to *Notorious*, *North by Northwest*, *Marnie*, *Frenzy* and, yes, *To Catch a Thief*. Reynolds plays wealthy, womanizing American diamond thief Jack Rhodes, who while at a swank party catches beautiful Brit Gillian Bromley (Lesley-Anne Down) stealing diamond-encrusted jewelry from her hosts. Jack and Gillian fight their instant physical attraction—swapping insults and bon mots—for instance, she: "Why are you imitating Tony Curtis?" he: "I'm not imitating Tony Curtis, I'm imitating Cary Grant," she: "You're doing Tony Curtis doing Cary Grant. Even Cary Grant doesn't do 'Cary Grant' anymore."

They of course become lovers and, by the last third of the movie, team up to steal thirty million in uncut diamonds. But can they trust each other? Is the heist on the level? Will one betray the other? Take a wild guess. Despite flaccid plotting, whiplash variations in tone from scene to scene, unflattering costumes, and some crude dialogue, Down and Reynolds—photographed by the multi-Oscar-winning Freddie Young (*Lawrence of Arabia*, *Doctor Zhivago*) and underscored by Nelson Riddle's arrangements of Duke Ellington classics—make a glossy couple, and they even manage to generate some screen chemistry. At almost every moment, one can see what the stars and moviemakers are reaching for, but the screenplay keeps cutting them down.

David Niven, smart and crisp as ever in the kind of roguish role that Hitchcock might have given to John Williams (*Dial M for Murder*, *To Catch a Thief*), plays a sly, unhappily married Scotland Yard detective out to arrest our hero as his last official act before retiring. It isn't much of a part, but at least Niven gets to put a spin on some macabre, Hitchcock-esque bits of dialogue about a murderer who dismembers his victims. When something so obiously concocted as a soufflé falls as flat as *Rough Cut*, it's probably best to remember a thing or two. Master chefs the likes of Hitchcock and such sous chefs as *To Catch a Thief* screenwriter John Michael Hayes, cinematographer Robert Burks, and actors Cary Grant, Grace Kelly, John Williams, and Jessie Royce Landis possess once-in-a-lifetime

Jewel thieves played by Burt Reynolds and Lesley-Ann Down seem like they're trying to convince each other—and us—that they are Cary Grant and Grace Kelly in a genuine Hitchcock thriller. But, no, they're only in the troubled *Rough Cut*.
Archive Photos/Moviepix/Getty Images

gifts, unlikely to make a comeback, especially in our cynical, joyless times that could use them so badly. ♟ ♟ ♙

ENTRAPMENT (1999)

After the theft of a forty-million-dollar Rembrandt, a beautiful, ambitious insurance agent pretends to be a thief to entice a legendary thief to join forces with her in stealing a priceless antique—so she can catch and expose him red-handed.

THE MACGUFFIN: A priceless Rembrandt painting and a Chinese mask

This big-budget art heist caper thriller was 1990s Hollywood's modern-day spin on Hitchcock's *To Catch a Thief*. It has an absurd plot—a stunning insurance investigator sets a trap for a legendarily successful, devilishly attractive master thief decades older than she and, of course, gets torn between duty and love when she finds herself attracted to him. The screenplay (engineered by Ron Bass, Michael Hertzberg, and William Broyles Jr.), directed by Jon Amiel (*Sommersby*), plays-up the characters' sexual chemistry, tension, and penchant for snappy dialogue against the backdrop of their pulling off high-risk thefts in glamorous locations—capers that have them hanging upside down from a seventy-story Manhattan skyscraper, scaling the stone walls of a stunning UK castle, and perilously dangling from stings of holiday lights between twin towers in Kuala Lampur, Malaysia—*them* being two gorgeous movie stars of disparate ages but equal animal magnetism (twenty-nine-year-old Catherine Zeta-Jones and sixty-nine-year-old Sean Connery), emulating without duplicating the magic made back when audiences were less freaked out by such pairings as the twenty-six-year-old Grace Kelly and the fifty-one-year-old Cary Grant. *Entrapment* offers a sufficient enough quota of twists, betrayals, and switchbacks to keep viewers guessing; a game supporting cast including Ving Rhames, Will Patton, and Maury Chaykin; and the modern antitheft gimmickry of lasers that require the lithe Zeta-Jones to perform lots of snaky movements while clad in skintight, Emma Peel–style thievery fashions.

If all those elements added up, we should be primed for a breezy, delightful caper film of a high order. Alas, not. It's a passable time waster, but not much more. Look, there's no denying the Hitchcockian fun inherent in casting Connery, who not only chased, trapped, and married a thief in *Marnie* but also became many people's all-time favorite big-screen secret agent. And he's well matched to his leading lady. But if only *Entrapment* had been filmed in the early 1960s, what a scintillating romantic pair he and the as-yet-unborn Zeta-Jones might have made. As dashing and charismatic as Connery may be as silver foxy Robert "Mac" MacDougal, who steals for thrills, his age requires him to constantly fend off and explain away his growing attraction to "Gin" by announcing his strict policy of avoiding personal relationships with his partners in crime.

Throaty-voiced stunner Zeta-Jones as "Gin" Baker is lively, athletic, and strikes sparks with Connery, even risking the potential for an "ick"

Seeing them in the glitzy caper thriller *Entrapment*, Sean Connery and Catherine Zeta-Jones might have been a perfect screen couple—if only Connery had been twenty or more years younger.
Archive Photos/Moviepix /Getty Images

reaction from audiences. (The film made $212 million worldwide but probably wouldn't fly today.) But anyone who's seen *To Catch a Thief* may guess one of the twists almost from the first scene. The supporting players—especially Maury Chaykin as a disturbing but scene-grabbing insurance company head of security—appear to be having lots of fun. Your mileage (and tolerance) may vary. ♟♟♟

THE TOURIST (2010)

A mysterious femme fatale deliberately crosses paths with a brokenhearted college math teacher while on a train, setting him up as a decoy for her thieving lover and marking them both as targets for the police and a mobster.

THE MACGUFFIN: A thief named Alexander Pearce

Anyone who's seen Hitchcock's *To Catch a Thief* or *North by Northwest* (or, for that matter, their Hitchcockian successors *Charade*, *Rough Cut*, *Someone Is Killing the Great Chefs of Europe*, *Entrapment*, et al.) can spot the kind of entertainment the makers of *The Tourist* were trying for—and completely missed. It all must have looked good on paper. Pair two attractive and charismatic movie stars (Charlize Theron and, maybe, Tom Cruise), bet big money that they'll generate sparks and sex appeal under the direction of Lasse Hallström (*My Life as a Dog*, *The Cider House Rules*) in a romantic cat-and-mouse suspense caper set in Paris and Venice (screenplay by *The Usual Suspects* Oscar winner Christopher McQuarrie, based on the 2005 French thriller *Anthony Zimmer*).

So far, so good—until Bharat Nalluri (*The Crow: Salvation*) replaced Hallström, Tom Cruise got announced to star opposite Theron, then Cruise was out and Sam Worthington (of the *Avatar* franchise) in; then, Nalluri was out and Alfonso Cuarón (*Gravity*) was in. When the dust settled, writer-director Florian Henckel von Donnersmarck (known for his starkly dramatic Oscar winner *The Lives of Others*) attracted Angelina Jolie and Johnny Depp, and the rest is, well, one for the history books for all the wrong reasons.

Though the script, rewritten by the first-class von Donnersmarck and Julian Fellowes (*Gosford Park* Oscar winner, *Downton Abbey* creator), sends the absurdly striking Jolie and Depp traipsing around Paris and Venice, dressed to the nines, and throws them into increasingly dangerous circumstances—a flirtatious seduction aboard a train! Breathtaking rooftop pursuits! A boat chase through the Venice canals!—the template was all mapped out decades ago for Jolie and Depp. She's got the Grace Kelly/Audrey Hepburn role, he's got Cary Grant's. Alas, neither rises to the occasion. Jolie plays an ambiguous Brit named Elise who's villainous (unseen) lover, Alexander Pearce, is on the lam after stealing a fortune from mobsters; now she's been asked to find a similar-looking man to set up as a decoy for her boyfriend. Enter Depp as Frank Tupelo, Hitchcock's average man in extraordinary circumstances, a community college math professor traveling solo on a train. The two meet en route to Venice; she's seductive, he's a sad sack who quickly takes the bait, and we're off to the races, what with Frank, standing in for Alexander Pearce, pursued left, right, and center by a tireless Scotland Yard duo (the talented Paul Bettany and Timothy Dalton, both wasted) and the bad guys (Steven Berkoff) Pierce swindled. Rufus Sewell is also in the mix as the shadowy presence known as "The Englishman," but none of these excellent supporting cast actors leave a trace. All that the film is missing is, well, everything a romantic suspense thriller demands between its two main stars. Charm. Sparkle. Heat. Chemistry. Jolie (alluring, utterly opaque) and Depp (all mumbles, weird accent, and completely unfunny) appear to have no connection. Von Donnersmarck ratchets up the tension and springs the plot twists, but just when we ought to be riveted we don't give a damn. Hitchcock, Grant, and Kelly made it all look so effortlessly simply. But, as Leonardo da Vinci said, "Simplicity is the ultimate sophistication." Still, worldwide audiences lapped up *The Tourist*. ♟♟

UNKNOWN (2011)

A brainy American botany professor, newly arrived with his wife for an international conference in Germany, returns to the airport, where he's acccidentally left his briefcase. His taxi cab lunges off a bridge, leaving the professor to awaken from a coma to find that his wife doesn't recognize him and another man with his same memories and experiences stands in his place.

THE MACGUFFIN: The missing briefcase

Reread that synopsis and tell us *that* doesn't sound like a promising start for a Hitchcock thriller movie that might have starred, say, Cary Grant, James Stewart, or even Sean Connery in the prime of their careers. It was that promising premise, adapted by screenwriters Oliver Butcher and Stephen Cornwell from Didier Van Cauwelaert's novel *Out of My Head*, that helped inspire the makers of *Unknown* to spin it into a contemporary *North by Northwest* crossed with *The Lady Vanishes* and the writings of Philip K. Dick. The film even features not one but two contemporary Hitchcock blondes in January Jones (*Mad Men*) as the hero's enigmatic wife and Diane Kruger (Cannes Film Festival

Best Actress 2017 for *In the Fade*) as a resourceful cab driver. In the leading role is Liam Neeson, an actor born too late for such directors as Hitchcock to have cast intelligently.

But in the age of *Bourne Identity*, *Mission: Impossible* movies, and endless spy TV series, audiences now expect insane stunts, car chases, explosions, gunplay, and cutting-edge gadgetry rather than smarts and high style. Even a brainy botanist is now required to fight his Stasi attackers bare-knuckled and stunt drive with the skill of a trained CIA operative. And that's what happens in *Unknown*, its classic 1940s thriller premise buried alive in a routine, bone-crunching conspiracy thriller.

Every so often, though, the good stuff claws its way to the surface with satisfying themes and techniques that feel the most Hitchcockian. Such as when the professorial hero Dr. Martin Harris (Neeson) picks warily through the postcoma debris of his memories and he must force himself to deal with the existential question faced by characters in *Spellbound*, *Strangers on a Train*, *North by Northwest*, *Vertigo*, *Marnie*, and more: Who am I? Who did I used to be? Who mattered most to me? In *Unknown*, the hard-nosed Berlin police and their functionaries won't believe Martin unless he can produce the passport and identity papers from the briefcase he left accidentally on a curb at the airport. Meanwhile, even those he knows and trusts insist that he is not who he thinks he is; besides, there's another Dr. Martin Harris (Aidan Quinn) who not only shares the same memories and anecdotes as our hero but can remember them faster and in just as much (or more) detail.

Credit Spanish director Jaume Collet-Serra (*Orphan*, *Carry-On*) for attempting to make something a tad smarter and more immersive than, say, *Taken*; his surrealistic visual touches that attempt to dunk audiences in the whirlpool of Martin's memories are not only jazzy but also effective. Nice work, too, from Bruno Ganz (*Downfall*) as a Stasi trainee who helps the hero navigate a twist finale that may enthrall, infuriate, or bore you. But, oh, what this movie could have been back in the day. 👥

ENEMIES (2014)

Two men leading completely different lives discover that they are physically identical.

THE MACGUFFIN: An old movie on video

In the hands of first-class director Denis Villeneuve (*Incendies*, the Dune epics), the slow-burn doppelgänger novel *The Double* (the Portuguese title is *O Homem Duplicado*, *The Duplicated Man*) by Nobel Prize–winning Portuguese novelist and literary magician Jose Saramago becomes something anxiety ridden, haunting, and unconventional but half cooked. In the hands of Hitchcock, it might have become a trippy masterpiece. In 1955, Hitchcock himself directed an episode of *Alfred Hitchcock Presents* (one of only seventeen he directed in the series' seven-year run) in which a businessman teeters on the brink of a nervous breakdown when he suspects that a doppelgänger plans to take over his life. Entitled "The Case of Mr. Pelham," the clever, disconcerting episode delivers more queasy laughs and claustrophobic panic than the entire glum but intriguing ninety-five minutes of *Enemies*. Villeneuve's brooding, dreamlike film focuses on Jake Gyllenhaal as an awkward, drab, mopey, logical college history professor who lectures by day to half-empty classrooms of uninterested students and comes home to a beautiful, attentive girlfriend (Mélanie Laurent) with whom he has a bout of perfunctory sex. He casually rents an aggressively stupid video and, in it, sees a background player who looks exactly like a beardless version of himself. Doing some digging, he learns that "Daniel St. Clair" (born Antony) has only several bit parts on his résumé.

More and more curious about this other man who looks and sounds identical to himself—even their handwriting matches, and they both sport matching scars on their torsos—Adam boldly intrudes into Daniel's private life. Daniel is Adam's opposite, dominant rather than recessive, bohemian instead of buttoned-down, impulsive, and sexually vital instead of barely present. Soon, Daniel is expecting a carnal weekend with Adam's girlfriend, although he shares wedding bands with a Hitchcock blonde of his own (nice work by Sarah Gadon). The film, which appears deliberately shot, costumed, and set in a Cronenberg-like world of constant dread in deadening shades of brown, never shows its hand as to whether the doubles are twins, the same person, aspects of one or the other's subconscious—the latter interpretation of which accounts for much of the film's erotic imagery as well as its obsession with women as spiders.

Hitchcock touches are plentiful, and Adam is even given a key stamped "Unica," just as an important wine cellar key reads in *Notorious*. But there's a double meaning going on in *Enemies*. If Adam and Daniel could only combine, they might add up to one, less troubled, more interesting soul. As usual, expect good work from Jake Gyllenhaal in dual roles, but one longs for Villeneuve to unleash the actor's gift for sardonic humor and self-mockery. That might have made for a livelier, more incisive movie. The odd, out-of-nowhere ending is a delight, a laugh-out-loud WTF? puzzlement that makes one reexamine everything one thought one knew. Well done. ♟♟♟

12 Foreign Correspondents

Alfred Hitchcock and his wife traveled extensively throughout Europe—including their thirty-plus stays at Badrutt's Palace Hotel in St. Moritz, Switzerland, where they first honeymooned in December 1926. Despite he and his screenwriters setting his films in such far-flung locales as Switzerland, London, Scotland, Rio de Janeiro, Denmark, and East Berlin, he generally preferred replicating these places on studio backlots and soundstages, where he could exert more control over such potential challenges as weather and crowds. Given his propensity for making films that he called "Slices of cake, not slices of life," it is no wonder that he wanted to more easily bend and shape reality to conform to their creative vision and to make their actors look impossibly "right." Hitchcock's most notable exception was his beloved France.

He resonated with French culture and language and happily traveled there for location work on *To Catch a Thief* (1955) and *Topaz* (1969). During the early-and mid-1960s, Hitchcock (perhaps motivated by his 1962 weeklong series of interviews with French director François Truffaut), immersed himself in private screenings of films from such international giants as Ingmar Bergman, Luis Buñuel, Federico Fellini, and Michelangelo Antonioni. Emerging thunderstruck from one such screening, he reportedly lamented to associates, "I've just seen Antonioni's Blow-Up. These Italian directors are a century ahead of me in terms of technique. What have I been doing all this time?" He not only seriously considered casting stars of some of the most innovative and popular movies of the era, Vanessa Redgrave, David Hemmings, Julie Christie, Catherine Deneuve, Lynn Redgrave, Marcello Mastroianni,

Sophia Loren, Yves Montand among them, but also developed *Kaleidoscope*, a sexually provocative psychological thriller he envisioned shooting on a low budget in New York City, minus major movie stars. He wanted its loose narrative structure to be reminiscent of the freewheeling New Wave style embodied by Truffaut and Goddard yet its imagery to be color-controlled for maximum Antonioni-esque impact. Most importantly, the bolder erotic imagery and tone would announce "the *new* Hitchcock."

Hitchcock's bosses at Universal, in a stunning no-confidence vote, quashed the project.

Would Hitchcock have suffered embarrassment in trying to rebrand himself as hip and edgy—as would such fellow other older directors as William Wyler, Otto Preminger, Charles Chaplin, Stanley Kramer, and more? Or would *Kaleidoscope* have marked a brilliant reinvention for a giant closing in on age seventy? The earliest screenplays are are nowhere near as remarkable, experimental or bold as some have claimed. But, really, we'll never know where Hitchcock and the right screenwriter may have ended up. The irony is that while Hitchcock apparently chased a freer, jazzier, modish "European" directing style—perhaps as much for box-office reasons as artistic ones—many international directors sought to emulate the genres and panache of such "Old Hollywood" giants as Hitchcock himself.

DIABOLIQUE (1955)

The ex-mistress and the sickly wife of the cruel, sadistic head of a boys' school avenge themselves by drowning him in a bathtub. So why does the corpse keep vanishing and reappearing?

THE MACGUFFIN: A life insurance policy

Seventy years on, this French import—a stone-cold shocker in its day—is now so widely imitated, admired and foundational that its thrills and surprises may be too familiar. Still its reputation remains unassailable. Alfred Hitchcock was excited by the film possibilities of the 1952 psychological thriller novel *Celle qui n'était plus* by the writing team Boileau-Narcejac. In it, two people want a third person dead to collect their life insurance money, so they hatch a fiendish plot to drown that inconvenient person in a bathtub. But what happens when the corpse weirdly disappears when the coconspirators aren't looking?

Imagine Hitchcock's frustration on learning that Gallic director-screenwriter Henri-Georges Clouzot (*The Wages of Fear*) beat him to the punch in grabbing the film rights by a matter of hours. Imagine Hitchcock's becoming even more frustrated when Clouzot's 1955 movie version *Les Diaboliques* (released in the United States as *Diabolique*) became an international critical and box-office hit and even got its forty-eight-year-old director hailed as "the French Hitchcock." Not only did Hitchcock immediately buy the film rights to another Boileau-Narcejac novel (he made it into his 1958 masterwork *Vertigo*), but he also jumped on the film rights to *Psycho*, another novel with a grimy setting, workaday characters, a bathtub murder, and an all-time shocker of an ending. That novel birthed another masterpiece. Like Hitchcock, Clouzot bent and shaped the Boileau-Narcejac source material according to his own needs and preoccupations.

Rather than the tale of a traveling salesman and his mistress who hatch a plot to murder the salesman's wife and collect her insurance money, Clouzot and his cowriters flipped the script, hinging *Diabolique* on a revenge murder perpetrated by the icy-cold abused former mistress Nicole (Simone Signoret) and the equally abused, ailing wife (Véra Clouzot) of a despised sadistic tyrant (Paul Meurisse) who runs a seedy boy's boarding school. They lure him to Nicole's apartment, drug and drown him in the bathtub, then dump the corpse in the swimming pool of the boy's school. Except their "perfect crime" goes horribly sideways. The film, shot in grimy black and white on location at a neglected chateau, emits a palpable atmosphere of decay and gloom that seeps into the psyche. Seriously, has there ever been a more disturbing swimming pool in all of cinema than the one in *Diabolique*? And the whole affair, which somehow merges a crime drama with supernatural elements and a bit of all-out horror, also percolates with subtle hints of sexual sadism and lesbianism.

There have been so many subsequent remakes and variations on the theme—including a sledgehammer Sharon Stone–Isabelle Adjani

In the masterful *Diabolique*, French boys' schoolmistresses Simone Signoret and Vera Clouzot, both involved with the same repulsive, cruel man, decide to drown him in a bathtub. Are they guilty as sin? Or was it justifiable homicide? And if their victim is dead, then why does he keep turning up in the least convenient places?
Walter Daran/The Chronicle Collection

remake that could have worked but doesn't—that *Diabolique* is one of those movies you wish you'd seen the first time around when all the surprises had not been spoiled. Signoret is rivetingly butch and icy, Clouzot is febrile and pathetic, and in its bathroom, bedroom and hallway scenes alone, the movie is the stuff of nightmares. *Diabolique* could be one of the few Hitchcockian films that even Hitchcock might have been proud to call one of his own. ♟♟♟♟

PLEIN SOLEIL (1960)

A distraught father sends to Italy his drifter son's friend to bring him back home, but the handsome young sociopathic forger, parasite, and mimic so envies his friend's luxurious lifestyle, girlfriend, and fortune that he goes to violent extremes to claim it as his own.

THE MACGUFFIN: The Greenleaf millions

Because Hitchcock despised film clichés, he loved to cast appealing, stunning-looking performers as dark, complicated, and devious characters who often do their darkest deeds in swank surroundings and sunlight. In his film version of Patricia Highsmith's novel *Mr. Ripley*, director René Clément (*Forbidden Games*), co-adapter Paul Gégauff, and cinematographer Henri Decaë followed suit, conspiring to create one of the sickest but most visually seductive (and most Hitchcockian) suspense films ever made. The sunny pastel vision of 1960s coastal Italy, the beautiful people, fashions, and the music are all part of the movie's elaborate con game. After all, the film, like the novel by Highsmith (who also wrote *Strangers on a Train*), revolves around a young nobody named Tom Ripley, a charming, lying mimic and cunning criminal who learns he is capable of anything if he wants something badly enough.

In Highsmith's novels, Ripley is such an appalling if fascinating sociopathic monster, it is easy to revile him. But when played by the young and astonishingly photogenic Alain Delon—whom Clement and Gégauff brilliantly depict (and Delon plays) as an utter cipher, ignored, mocked, barely noticed—the character is something else again. At this point in his career, Delon was still gauche and unsure enough to play a character just beginning to figure out his effect on others and how much advantage he can take of his physical appeal. Hitchcock pulled off a similar lucky masterstroke by casting the vulnerable, attractive, gangly Anthony Perkins in *Psycho*, a move that assured the audience's sympathy and empathy no matter how shocking his behavior. A similar dynamic is key to *Plein Soleil* (*Purple Noon*) because Highsmith's raw material so often strains credibility.

In the film's opening scenes, the parents of Ripley's wealthy, aimless friend Philippe (the slightly waxen, mature looking Maurice Ronet, whom Clement originally cast as Ripley!) funds Tom's trip to Italy to retrieve his son from his idylls in Rome and return him to San Francisco. Ripley, the ultimate social climber, not only finds himself attracted by Philippe's posh life but also his girlfriend Marge (Marie Laforêt) and, though repressing it, by Philippe himself. Tom begins to talk like Philippe, learns to copy his handwriting, and dresses in his clothes while speaking in Philippe's voice and kissing his reflection in a mirror. Things get wilder when Tom, Philippe and Marge sail together and Philippe, unable to deal with the sexual tension between them, isolates Tom on a rowboat to be rid of him; while Marge and Philippe make love, a violent storm breaks out, the tow rope frays, and Ripley's boat all but capsizes. He gets rescued, vowing revenge. The balance of the film is the best of it all, pure suspense and tension as fate conspires to undo the diabolical plots and schemes Ripley devises to hide his crimes and get away scot-free with his friend's money and Marge, too.

Overall, I prefer this version to Anthony Minghella's excellent 1999 version *The Talented Mr. Ripley* (though Jude Law's Dickie Greenleaf remains the gold standard). But there is no denying Andrew Scott's reptilian, icily mesmerizing performance as *Ripley i*n writer-director Steven Zaillian's gripping 2024 limited series; that eight-episode series boasts a dialogue-free twenty-minute murder sequence that is one of the all-time great Hitchcock suspense sequences not directed by the maestro himself. *Plein Soleil* ♟♟♟½, *The Talented Mr. Ripley* ♟♟♟, *Ripley* ♟♟♟½

In the French classic *Plein Soleil* (*Purple Noon*), heartthrob Alain Delon stars as the talented, sociopathic Tom Ripley, the most lethal, if prettiest, of poisons.
Fotos International/Getty Images

THE BRIDE WORE BLACK (1968)

A suicidal new widow pours her grief into hunting down, toying with, and killing the men who killed her husband.

THE MACGUFFIN: The list of men who killed her husband

François Truffaut, Alfred Hitchcock's longtime admirer, purposefully set out to make a film in the Hitchcock manner. Having recorded fifty audio hours with Hitchcock discussing the director's every film made for an essential 1967 book, Truffaut knew lots of facts about his favorite film director. That knowing facts never substitutes for genius is evident in *The Bride Wore Black*, which stars the fascinating and defiantly inscrutable Jeanne Moreau as Julie Kohler, who becomes a deadly avenger after her new husband gets shot to death on the steps of the church where they've been married just moments earlier. Truffaut's film—from a 1940 Cornell Woolrich novel (he also wrote the source material from which Hitchcock made *Rear Window*)—tries its damnedest to follow in Hitchcock's giant footsteps, but Truffaut's open heart, whimsy, and romanticism lead him away from the heart of the matter. Truffaut is at his lyrical, humanist, authentic best in every moment of *The 400 Blows*, *Jules and Jim*, *Shoot the Piano Player*, *The Soft Skin*, and *Day for Night*. But seeing Truffaut aping Hitchcock in this film, *Mississippi Mermaid* (also based in Woolrich) and *Fahrenheit 451*, is dispiriting because those films feel like the work of a talented imposter trying on a style, form, and visual vocabulary that were invented by someone else, a style that unleashes the inimitable genius in one filmmaker but makes the imitator's work feel cramped, dutiful, and artificial. Where Hitchcock's plotting is riveting and gripping, Truffaut's is looser, attuned to options and possibilities. Hitchcock's visual compositions are tight, immaculate, precisely controlled—always directing the audience's attention to who or what is important. Truffaut's visuals (with the superb cinematographer Raoul Coutard) feel looser, less thought-out, on-the-fly. Where the fates of Hitchcock's characters keep us at the edge of our seats, their destinies compellingly predetermined, Truffaut's characters have wider horizons, mobility, agency. It could be argued that Truffaut's moviemaking style is antithetical to suspense films, and his choosing as the film's composer Bernard Herrmann (whose credit appears eight times on Hitchcock's films) only underlines that disconnect. Happily, *The Bride Wore Black* (which surely helped inspire avowed Hitchcock-trasher Quentin Tarantino's *Kill Bill*, who denied having seen it despite so many similarities) rewards in other ways. Above all, there's the wry, mocking Moreau as the avenging angel dressed only in black or white, crossing out the name of each of the boorish, smug, obnoxious men she rubs out for killing for husband and fearlessly courting high camp when she kills a man with a bow and arrow while bewigged and costumed as the huntress Diana. The great Moreau gets expert support from some of the most compelling French character actors of their day, including Michel Bouquet, Claude Rich, Michel Lonsdale, Charles Denner, Jean-Claude Brialy, and Daniel Boulanger, each more obnoxious and toxic than the last. The movie has its pluses, but Woolrich, as usual, deserved even better. ♟♟♟

Vengeful bride Jeanne Moreau is out to avenge herself on the men who shot her husband just after their wedding. Jean-Claude Brialy and Charles Denner are on her hit list in François Truffaut's film version of Cornell Woolrich's tale filmed as *The Bride Wore Black*.
Photo by Alain Dejean/Sygma via Getty Images

LA FEMME INFIDÈLE (1969)

When a husband hires a private detective to follow his beautiful wife, he uncovers painful secrets that alter their lives forever.

THE MACGUFFIN: A cigarette lighter

Alfred Hitchcock's influence is unmistakable in *La Femme Infidèle* and *Le Boucher*, two of the great 1960s psychological thrillers from Claude Chabrol, yet another director hailed by the press as "the French Hitchcock." In this one, a successful, dull, but loving middle-aged man doubts the whereabouts of his stunning wife, Hélène (Stéphane Audran), during her regular trips from their tasteful, color-coordinated country house to Paris to go shopping, see films, and visit her favorite beauty salon. Discovering that Hélène has a lover, a writer named Victor Pégala (Maurice Ronet), Charles pays a visit to his stylish apartment and, after a disarmingly polite conversation during which he asks for a tour his rival's home, he is moved to tears when he spots on Victor's night table a piercingly personal object of his wife's, a cigarette lighter (a nod to the MacGuffin in *Strangers on a Train*) he'd given her as an anniversary present. Darker emotions overtake him, especially when we see Charles realize that Victor knows more about his beloved wife than he ever will. Chabrol excels in a long, marvelous sequence in which a character struggles to dispose of a dead body (a tip of the hat to *Psycho*), and there's at least one *Vertigo* reference worth noting. But in the hands of a master, these indulgences become wry and playful, not clumsy and distracting window dressing. A subtly but wickedly perverse film, in which writer-director Chabrol dissects crime and savagery among the bourgeoisie with elegant precision, civility, and a complete absence of melodrama, *La Femme Infidèle* is a masterpiece of discretion and sangfroid. Nothing the characters do is predictable, and the film's resolution is moving, humane, and at the same time coolly horrific. The formidable talents of the impassive-looking stage and film legend Bouquet (*Toto le héros*) and Audran are at peak level and, Chabrol is in full command of his unmistakably unique, off-center gifts. Remade in 2002 by director Adrian Lyne from a screenplay by Alvin Sargent and William Broyles Jr. as *Unfaithful*, it feels much less

Hitchcockian but features a stunner of a performance by Diane Lane, who, if only the timing had been right, might have been fascinating under Hitchcock's direction. ♟♟♟♟

LE BOUCHER (1969)

During an outbreak of murders in a tiny French village, a butcher falls in love with an enigmatic schoolteacher.

THE MACGUFFIN: An incriminating cigarette lighter

In my favorite Claude Chabrol–directed thriller—and that's saying something—Helene, a brokenhearted schoolmistress (the impeccable, imposingly chic Stéphane Audran), and Popaul, a butcher haunted by the atrocities he witnessed while in the French Army (Jean Yanne), meet at a wedding in a tiny, picturesque French village. As these two damaged souls tentatively fumble their way toward a relationship, the surrounding woods become a disposal area for the corpses of young women murdered in especially savage ways. *Le Boucher* isn't about surprise but about a slowly spreading miasma of dread and suspense. It's not about *who* did it but about *what* Helene will do with her terrible knowledge. While she and her students are on a lunch break from their field trip to the Lascaux caves, blood drops on the sandwich of one of the students—the blood of the bride we met at the wedding that brought together Helen and Popaul. With Helene's discovery of the victim's body, she also discovers a cigarette lighter, a gift she gave Popaul; she hides it and misinforms the police that there were no clues at the scene of the crime. Later, when she asks Popaul to light her cigarette, Helene breaks out in laughter when the butcher produces a lighter exactly like the one she gave him. It's an example of how the writer-director Chabrol works, constantly subverting expectations and dodging the cheap shocks and easy explanations for which lazy viewers hunger. *Le Boucher* deepens and intensifies in micro-increments, investigating its characters and situations with surprising ambiguity and tension. We keep wondering exactly what Helene knows and exactly what Popaul thinks she knows. We wonder if he's going to kill her, and we speculate that it is his sexual frustration that unleashes uncontrollable violent

In Claude Chabrol's unforgettable *Le Boucher* (*The Butcher*), a rural school headmistress (the impeccable Stéphane Audran) suspects that the local butcher (Jean Yanne) who's been romancing her is a multiple murderer.
Photo by Film Publicity Archive/United Archives via Getty Images

impulses. Finally, Chabrol pulls off one hell of a troubling final twist that feels inevitable and, at the same time, like his response to Hitchcock's *Suspicion* delayed by almost fifty years. ♟♟♟♟

THE 4TH MAN (1984)

A notorious bisexual alcoholic writer, experiencing bizarre premonition dreams, goes off to a seaside village for a speaking engagement and lusts after a younger man but sexually tangles with the young man's girlfriend, a spidery femme fatale.

THE MACGUFFIN: Those scissors!

The sexually charged fever dream of an erotic thriller that launched the international career of Dutch director Paul Verhoeven felt like a coming out party after the more conventional *Soldier of Orange* and *Spetters*.

Gory, carnal, compelling, bristling with mordant humor, and with style to burn, think of *The 4th Man* as a Hitchcock movie high on a cocktail of Viagra and LSD. Even the credits are intense and portentous: a fat spider captures flies while a religious statue looks on impassively. Verhoeven's human fly is Gerard Reve (Jeroen Krabbé, perfection), a louche bisexual and alcoholic writer haunted by dreams foretelling his own death. The spider in human form is hairdresser Christine (Renée Soutendijk, going for broke), a predatory, multiply widowed blonde who compulsively films Gerard during his lecture. Before one can say *Basic Instinct* (*The 4th Man* is its obvious dry run), Gerard and Christine are locked in an erotic S&M-tinged relationship that also encompasses Gerard's lust for a young man (Thom Hoffman) who is also bedding Christine. The entire film, dynamically shot by Jan de Bont, is an intricate, enticing, and sometimes repellent spiderweb woven in the original novel by the real-life Gerard Reve, the screenplay cleverly adapted by Gerard Soeteman and by Verhoeven, who directs with infectious, antic urgency. This one won't be to everyone's taste—what boundary-pushing movie ever *is*? But for others, it is unmissable. ♟♟♟♟

MOTHER (2009)

The brutal murder of a teenage girl forces a crisis in the life of a middle-aged woman who ferociously protects her bullied, mentally challenged twenty-eight-year-old son. Should she fight to prove his innocence, or is the world safer if he's kept locked away?

THE MACGUFFIN: A golf ball with a murder suspect's name on it

Masterful Oscar-winning South Korean director Bong Joon Ho's (*Memories of Murder*, *Parasite*) status as a Hitchcock devotee is abundantly apparent in the sly, subversive ways that he teases out the suspense, horror, and oddball humor from this dark jewel about a mother (Kim Hye-ja, a powerhouse) on a do-or-die mission to prove the innocence of her developmentally challenged twenty-seven-year-old son Do-joon (Weon Bin), who is accused of murder. The police easily extract a full confession from the mentally foggy young man, who sometimes appears to know and understand far more than he lets on. His mother—a boy's best friend—is a formidable force of nature, running a modest village shop dispensing herbs and spices, rushing to pull her easily distracted son to safety when he's about to be hit by a car, hiring a lawyer who turns out to be useless, and attack-dogging the police and others with her barrage of questions no one wants to answer. The more out of her depth she gets, the more compelling and disorienting the film becomes with its whiplash changes of tone. *Mother*, a slow burn, works in wholly unexpected ways. The performances of the two lead actors are so subtly and exquisitely rendered that one is never certain of their motives, intentions, or innocence. A rare psychological thriller worthy of consideration alongside the work of Hitchcock, the underseen *Mother* is flat-out brilliant. ♟♟♟♟

PARASITE (2019)

An impoverished family scrounging out a living in a basement slowly invades the lives of a wealthy family with the intention of staging a hostile takeover.

THE MACGUFFIN: Money.

Brilliant, bold, Oscar-winning moviemaking are the hallmarks of Bong Joon Ho's worldwide hit that is almost two movies in one. The first half of *Parasite* plays like a scathing Luis Buñuel-level social satire; the shocking second half... well, for the sake of surprise, the less said about that the better. We first meet the Kims, a resourceful family of loveable Korean con artists barely eking out a living in a bug-infested semi-underground hovel. Snaking WiFi from a local coffee shop, folding pizza boxes for spare change, they're the unseen collateral damage of our ever increasingly Darwinian world of haves versus have-nots. But it's when the worlds of the rich and poor mesh and collide that *Parasite* goes crazily, inspiringly Hitchcockian. It happens when slick young Kim Ki-woo (Choi Woo-sik), opportunistically renaming himself "Kevin," gets the chance to tutor wealthy Park Da-hye (Jung Ziso) in her odd and awkward family's stunning modern home. She falls hard for him, which fits in nicely with his master plan. This helps Kevin convince his mentee's mother (Park So-dam) to hire an art tutor for the Park family's son. In no time, the whole Kim family has been folded into the idiosyncratic Parks' chic, minimalist home and their private lives. And that's when things go pitch black and bloodily haywire, with the director-screenwriter pulling off so many deeply disruptive and unsettling twists that keep us delighting in the storytelling while rubbing our noses in ugly truths about the widening gulf between those who have and those who don't. Like the best Hitchcock movies, *Parasite* can be savored again and again and still deliver surprises. Bong Joon Ho is one of our finest moviemakers, and though he isn't infallible (looking at you *Mickey One*), his *Parasite* is an all-timer. 👤👤👤👤

DECISION TO LEAVE (2022)

Investigating the mysterious circumstances surrounding a man's death in the mountains, a detective disastrously entangles his fate with the dead man's enigmatic wife, who may or may not be a murderer.

THE MACGUFFIN: The broken watch

Decision to Leave is the latest film in which gifted South Korean director Park Chan-wook (*Joint Security Area*, *The Handmaiden*, *Stoker*) salutes the master of suspense while displaying a degree of stylistic mastery, perversity, and filmmaking brilliance all his own. *Decision to Leave* is heady stuff—mysterious, fatalistic, and intoxicating even if it takes a while to work itself up to the task at hand. Its first hour or so makes one wonder if it will progress beyond the level of a standard thriller about an overworked insomniac cop, Hae-jun (played by Park Hae-il, whom Park Chan-wook describes as "the James Stewart of Korea"), and his stultifying, half-hearted relationship with his wife. Into his life comes Seo-Rae, the mysterious young Chinese immigrant wife (Tang Wei, who is terrific) of a sixty-year-old mountain climber who accidentally falls to his death. It *was* a tragic accident, right? Almost immediately, Hae-Jun's partner sees what Hae-jun cannot or will not—Seo-rae is almost certainly their prime suspect in a maddeningly complex mystery. The director, who cowrote the screenplay, which swirls with echoes of *Vertigo* but goes to strange places of its own, underscores the point by painting Hae-jun as a character who prefers romantic old movies, requires eyedrops for his faulty sight, and is often seen shrouded by dense fog. As Hae-jun tracks the baffling, fascinating Seo-rae's movements, he hurtles straight down the rabbit hole—becoming romantically obsessed, irrational, and blind to the murder (suicide?) case he's charged with solving. The dynamic of Hae-jun's and Seo-rae's chaotic, years-long relationship—forbidden and star-crossed — makes for a ravishingly beautiful movie that wends its way to a tragic, operatic finale. And though it may lack the edge and gut punch of Park's peak work, *Decision to Leave* is an erotic Hitchcockian ode that sings its own romantic and melancholy love song. Park's newest film, the darkly comic *No Other Choice* is based on Donald E. Westlake's novel *The Axe*, in which a longtime paper company employee who, furious at being fired and turned down for any new job for which he applies, levels the playing field by killing off his competition. We're guessing that Hitchcock might have approved. ♟♟♟

Index

Abela, Marisa 58
Abrahams, Peter 180
Adams, Amy 129–31
Adjani, Isabelle 279
Affleck, Ben 182–3
Agee, James 143
Aherne, Brian 235
Albee, Edward 58
Aldrich, Robert 151
Alexander, Erika 97
Alfred Hitchcock Presents 275
All About Eve 39, 96, 108, 175
Allan, Richard 16
Allen, Lewis 86
Allen, Nancy 113–15, 174, 246
Allgood, Sara 3, 208
Ambler, Eric 27, 34
Ames, Leon 239
Amiel, Jon 270
Anand, Dev 265
Anand, Vijay 264
Anderson, Brad 125–6
Anderson, Judith 221, 228
Anderson, Mary 189
Anderson, Michael 23, 109
Anderson, Paul Thomas 98–100, 183
Andrews, Dana 80, 97, 227–9
Andrews, Julie 242
Angel Face 238–9
Antonioni, Michelangelo 201–2, 204, 277
Apartment Zero 119–20
Apollo 13 66
Arabesque 214–15
Arless, Jean 146
Arley, Catherine 240
Aronofsky, Darren 93
Around the World in 80 Days 23, 109
Ashley, Elizabeth 194
Aslan, Grégoire 242
Astaire, Fred 34
Atchley, Hooper 186

Audran, Stéphane 285–7
Ayres, Lew 234

Babatundé, Obba 91
Baby Reindeer 166
Bacall, Lauren 62, 121, 174–5
Baker, Diane 43, 68–9, 155, 175, 210, 242, 251
Balchin, Nigel 107
Bancroft, Anne 174–5
Banderas, Antonio 244
Barkin, Ellen 176
Barnes, George S. 3
Barrymore, Ethel 208
Basic Instinct 4, 222, 250–51
Basinger, Kim 92–3, 176, 250
Bass, Saul 191
Bates, Alan 261
Bates, Kathy 120–21
Battle, Norman 185
Baxter, Anne 108–10
Bayona, J. A. 211
Bazna, Elyesa 39
Bean, Sean 199
Beatty, Warren 219, 263
Bedroom Window, The 204–5
Begley, Ed 9
Belmondo, Jean-Paul 4, 44–6, 244
Ben-Hur 160
Bennet, Spencer Gordon 186
Bennett, Charles 27
Bennett, Haley 129
Bennett, Hywel 163–5
Bennett, Joan 6–7, 33, 230
Benton, Robert 249
Berenger, Tom 73–4
Bergen, Polly 150
Berger, Robert H. 92
Bergman, Ingmar 277
Bergman, Ingrid 1, 4–6, 39, 57, 61, 63, 85, 100, 104, 130, 209, 221, 225, 236

Berkoff, Steven 273
Bernsen, Corbin 74
Bernstein, Elmer 15
Bervoets, Gene 198
Best Years of Our Lives, The 160
Bettany, Paul 273
Betz, Carl 189
Bianchi, Daniela 44
Biehn, Michael 175
Big Country, The 161
Big Heat, The 229
Big Sleep, The 62, 227, 251
Binder, Maurice 24, 214
Birds, The 26, 68, 70, 79, 95, 112, 153, 223, 237, 247, 249, 251
Bisset, Jacqueline 210
Black Bag 57–9, 119
Blackman, Honor 188, 216, 242
Black Swan 93
Blanchett, Cate 58
Blatty, William Peter 79
Bloch, Robert 22, 151, 155, 176
Blow Out 88, 113–15, 174, 201, 246
Blow-Up 113–14, 201, 202–4
Blue Angel, The 230
Bluebeard 6
Blunt, Emily 128–9
Blyth, Ann 237
Bochner, Hart 119–20
Boddey, Martin 23
Bode, Ralf D. 175
Bodelsen, Anders 172
Body Double 116–18, 201, 246
Body Heat 4, 92
Body of Evidence 251
Bogarde, Dirk 110–11, 187–8
Bogart, Humphrey 11, 61, 62, 258
Böhm, Carl (Karlheinz Böhm) 144–6
Boileau-Narcejac 278–9
Bonfire of the Vanities, The 118
Bong Joon Ho 289
Borgeaud, Nelly 245
Bouchey, Willis 189
Boulanger, Daniel 45, 284
Boulting, Roy and John 163
Bouquet, Michel 245, 284, 285
Boyd, Russell 195

Boyd, Stephen 65
Boyd, William "Stage" 186
Boyer, Charles 4, 237
Boyle, Robert F. 149
Brach, Gérard 196
Brackett, Charles 16, 86–8
Braeden, Eric 192–4
Branagh, Kenneth 91
Brando, Marlon 134
Brazzi, Rossano 192–4, 212
Brent, George 208
Breslin, Patricia 146
Brialy, Jean-Claude 284
Bride Wore Black, The 283–4
Broccoli, Cubby 43
Bromfield, John 9
Brontë, Charlotte 2, 3
Brousse, Liliane 154
Brown, Hilyard M. 143
Broyles, William, Jr. 285
Bruce, Brenda 144–6, 213–14
Bruce, Sally Jane 143
Brynner, Yul 134
Buchan, John 27
Buckley, Betty 196
Bujold, Geneviève 89, 90
Bunny Lake is Missing 190–92, 200
Buñuel, Luis 183, 201, 277
Buono, Victor 151–3
Buried 127–8
Burke, Tom 58
Burks, Robert 268
Burman, S. D. 265
Burr, Raymond 206
Burrell, Sheila 154
Butcher, Oliver 273
Butler, Dan 180
Buttolph, David 33

Caan, James 120–21
Cagney, James 258
Caine, Michael 46, 134
Calvert, Phyllis 163–5
Campbell, Alan 258
Cape Fear 149–50
Cardinale, Claudia 266
Carlino, Lewis John 70

Carlson, Richard 30
Caron, Leslie 68
Carpenter, John 169–71
Carrie 246–8
Carroll, Leo G. 42
Carroll, Madeleine 99
Cartwright, Ashley 131–3
Caruso, D. J. 206
Casablanca 4
Casino 81
Caspary, Vera 229
Cassavetes, John 218–19
Castle, William 146–7, 154–6
Cauwelaert, Didier Van 273
Caviezel, Jim 97
Cazenove, Christopher 54–6
Chabrol, Claude 71–3, 285
Challis, Christopher 215
Chapin, Billy 143
Chaplin, Charles 278
Charade 24–6, 215
Chase, Barrie 150
Chase, Chevy 53
Chase, The 253–5
Chase a Crooked Shadow 108–10
Chaykin, Maury 270–71
Choi Woo-sik 289
Christie, Julie 50–52, 219, 277
Christine, Virginia 63
Cilento, Diane 23
Clarkson, Patricia 81
Clément, René 281
Clift, Montgomery 134
Clouzot, Henri-Georges 279
Clouzot, Véra 279–80
Coburn, James 25, 263–4
Cochran, Steve 254
Coffee, Lenore J. 13
Cohen, Larry 124, 131
Cohen, Lawrence D. 246
Collector, The 160–63
Collet-Serra, Jaume 274
Collier, Grace 167
Color of Night 251
Colquhoun, Mary 205
Compton, Fay 256
Connery, Sean 43–4, 54, 59, 61, 240–41, 249, 266, 270–71, 273

Conrad, Joseph 27
Conrad, William 9
Conroy, Will 126
Conversation, The 201
Conway, Tim 53
Coon, Carrie 183
Cooper, Gary 23
Cooper, James Fenimore 27
Copley, Peter 65
Coppel, Alec 241–2, 259
Coppola, Francis Ford 201
Corbett, Glenn 146–7
Cornwell, Stephen 273
Corrigan, Lloyd 254
Cortés, Rodrigo 127
Cortez, Stanley 7, 143
Costigan, James 54
Cotten, Joseph 1, 4, 16, 34–5, 36, 60, 127, 181
Counterfeit Traitor, The 40–41, 66
Coutard, Raoul 283
Coward, Noël 37, 191
Cox, Mitchell 156
Craig, Wendy 110–11, 157–8
Crain, Jeanne 189–90, 233
Crawford, Joan 13, 151–3, 154–6, 225, 242
Cregar, Laird 139–41
Crest, Patricia 156
Crichton, Charles 65
Crisp, Donald 87
Cronenweth, Jordan 92
Cruise, Tom 57, 272
Cukor, George 4–6, 225
Cummings, Robert 253, 255
Cundey, Dean 169–71, 170
Cunningham, Jack 222–5, 223
Curtis, Jamie Lee 115–17, 171, 174
Cushing, Peter 23

Dahlbeck, Eva 40
Dahl, Roald 67
Dalton, Timothy 273
D'Andrea, Tom 61
Dangerous Crossing 188–90
Daniell, Henry 3
Daniels, William H. 42
Danova, Cesare 192–4

D'Arbanville, Patti 180
Darden, Severn 264
Dark Mirror, The 233–5
Dark Passage 61–2
Dark Purpose 211–12
Darnborough, Antony 187
Darnell, Linda 139–41, 140
Darrieux, Danielle 39–40
Daves, Delmer 62
Davion, Alexander 153–4
Davis, Bette 151–3, 158, 258
Davis, Geena 176
Dawson, Anthony 21
Day, Doris 18–19, 20–22, 184, 241
Day, Laraine 235
Day for Night 283
Day-Lewis, Daniel 99
Day of the Jackal 46–7, 66
Dead Again 90–92
Dead Heat on a Merry-Go-Round 263–4
Dead Poets Society 195
Dearden, Basil 240
de Bont, Jan 250
de Broca, Philippe 44–6
Decision to Leave 290–91
de Havilland, Olivia 234
Déjà Vu 96–8
Dell, Claudia 185–6
Delon, Alain 281–2
del Rio, Dolores 35
Del Rio, Rebekah 95
del Toro, Guillermo 87
Demme, Jonathan 25
Deneuve, Catherine 4, 159–60, 244–5, 277
De Niro, Robert 121, 150, 176, 179–80
Denner, Charles 284
Dennis, Mark 8
De Palma, Brian 88–89, 113–15, 116–18, 131, 166–9, 173–4, 201, 246–8, 250
Depp, Johnny 272–3
de Roche, Everett 115–16
Detective Story 161
Devane, William 52
Devi, Pratima 265

Diabolique 210, 211, 214, 278–80
Dial M for Murder 10, 91
DiCaprio, Leonardo 19, 80–81, 263
Dickinson, Angie 173–4
Die Nibelungen 32
Dietrich, Marlene 106
Dillon, Matt 20
Dinelli, Mel 104
Disturbia 205–6
Dix, William 157–8
Dmytryk, Edward 68
Dodsworth 161
Donaggio, Pino 174
Donen, Stanley 67, 214–15, 260
Donnadieu, Bernard-Pierre 198
Donovan, Martin 119
Dorléac, Françoise 44–6
Dorn, Dody 77
Double Door 222–5
Double Indemnity 92, 172
Douglas, Melvyn 226
Douglas, Michael 4, 121, 251
Down, Lesley-Anne 268–9
Dr. Jekyll and Mr. Hyde 61
Dr. Mabuse the Gambler 32
Dratler, Jay 31, 229
Dreier, Hans 9
Dresdel, Sonia 102–4
Dressed to Kill 173–4
Driscoll, Bobby 104–5
Duel 111–13, 115
Duel in the Sun 209
Duke, Daryl 171–3
Dullea, Keir 191
du Maurier, Daphne 2, 3
Dunaway, Faye 48–9, 219
Durning, Charles 166–9
Durant, Jack 35
Duryea, Dan 230
Duvall, Robert 176

Eastwood, Clint 165–6
Ebert, Roger 169
Edwards, Blake 148, 267
Eggar, Samantha 160–63
Ellsworth, Carl 206
Elrich, Max 22
Ely, David 70

INDEX **295**

Emery, Katherine 236
Enemies 275–6
Entrapment 269–71
Erickson, Leif 9, 156
Erler, Rainer 172
Evans, Luke 129
Evans, Robert 50
Experiment in Terror 148
Eye of the Needle 54–6

Fairbanks, Douglas, Jr. 109
Fallen Idol, The 102–4
Family Plot 176
Fan, The (1981) 174–5
Fan, The (1996) 179–80
Fantômas 27
Farnsworth, Richard 121
Farrell, Colin 123–5
Farrell, Mike 194
Farrow, Mia 218–19
Fassbender, Michael 58
Fast, Howard 67
Fatal Attraction 166
Fay, W. G. 256
Fellini, Federico 277
Fellowes, Julian 272
Ferchland, Andrew J. 180
Ferguson, Rebecca 129
Final Analysis 92–3
Fincher, David 121–33, 128, 177, 182, 199
Finlay, Frank 163–5
Finley, William 167
Firth, Colin 119–20
Fisher, Carrie 117
Fisher, Terence 187
5 Fingers 38–40
Fleming, Ian 43
Fleming, Rhonda 208
Fletcher, Lucille 9
Flightplan 192, 199–200
Fly-By-Night 30–31
Flynn, Gillian 182
Follett, Ken 54
Fonda, Jane 219
Fontaine, Joan 2, 13, 99, 120, 217
Ford, Glenn 148, 259
Ford, Harrison 121, 196–7, 220, 264

Ford, John 32
Foreign Affair, A 86
Foreign Correspondent 24, 27, 57, 184, 252
Forrest Gump 220
Forsyth, Frederick 46
Forsyth, Rosemary 242
Foster, Barry 163–5
Foster, Jodie 121–3, 176, 199
Foul Play 52–4
400 Blows, The 244, 283
4th Man, The 250, 287–8
Fowles, John 161
Fox, Edward 46
Fox, James 110–11
Francis, Freddie 213
Franciscus, James 194
Frank, Scott 91
Frankenheimer, John 70
Franklin, Pamela 65
Franklin, Richard 115–16
Frantic 196–8
Franz, Dennis 115
Freeman, David 54
Freeman, Mona 239
Freeman, Morgan 177–9
Frenzy 11, 116, 205, 252, 268
Friedkin, William 178
Friendly Persuasion 161
From Here to Eternity 46
From Russia with Love 43–4
Fugit, Patrick 183
Furneaux, Yvonne 159

Gadon, Sarah 276
Gadot, Gal 267
Gallipoli 194
Ganz, Bruno 274
Garcia, Andy 91
Garner, James 67, 175
Garner, Peggy Ann 3
Garrison, Sean 242, 243
Gaslight 4–6, 18, 110, 140, 210, 214, 218
Gavin, John 21
Gazebo, The 259–60
Gégauff, Paul 281

Gelbart, Larry 267
Gere, Richard 47
Gilchrist, Connie 226
Gilliam, Terry 75
Gilliat, Sidney 28
Gingold, Hermione 23
Girard, Bernard 263
Girl on the Train, The 128–9
Girl Was Young, The 31
Gish, Lillian 141–4, 207, 210
Goff, Ivan 22
Goldberg, Adam 97
Goldman, William 50
Goldsmith, Jerry 250
Gone Girl 182–3
Goode, Matthew 181–2
Goodfellas 81
Gordon, Alex 215
Gordon, Keith 174
Gordon, Mary 31
Gordon, Ruth 219
Gould, Elliott 171–3
Grahame, Gloria 11, 14
Grady, James 47
Grant, Arthur 154
Grant, Cary 1, 13, 24–6, 42–3, 50–3, 67, 107, 120, 138, 215, 217, 220, 258, 260, 263, 265–6, 268, 270, 273
Green, Cliff 195
Green, F. L. 257
Greene, Graham 27, 36, 40, 102
Greenquist, Brad 205
Greenwood, Bruce 97
Gregg, Clark 220
Griffies, Ethel 3
Griffith, D. W. 207
Griffith, Hugh 40
Griffith, Melanie 116–18
Grodin, Charles 219
Grubb, Davis 142
Guffey, Burnett 11, 147
Gunning, Jessica 120
Guttenberg, Steve 204
Gwynne, Fred 194
Gyllenhaal, Jake 275

Hackman, Gene 176
Hale, Barbara 104
Haley, Jackie Earl 81
Haley, Jonathan Nicholas 54–6
Hall, Conrad W. 122
Halloween 169–71
Hallström, Lasse 272
Hamilton, Arthur 70
Hamilton, Linda 117
Hamilton, Patrick 4, 140
Hampden, Walter 39
Hangover Square 139–41
Hanson, Curtis 172, 205
Hardwicke, Cedric 238
Hari, Mata 215
Harlan, Russell 106
Harlow, Jean 242
Harrelson, Woody 125–7
Harrington, Robert and Jane 216
Harris, Barbara 186
Harris, Naomie 58
Harris, Neil Patrick 183
Harris, Richard 134
Harris, Robert H. 68
Harrison, Joan 31
Harrison, Rex 22, 29
Harris, Thomas 176
Hartman, Elizabeth 166
Harvey, Laurence 261
Hathaway, Henry 16, 107
Hawkins, Jack 65
Hawkins, Paula 128
Hawn, Goldie 52–4
Haworth, Ted 70
Hayes, John Michael 107, 201, 268
Hechinger, Fred 130
Hecht, Ben 27
Hedren, Tippi 79, 85, 94–6, 99, 242
Heiress, The 161
Heller, Lukas 152
Hemmings, David 202–3, 277
Henreid, Paul 29
Henrey, Bobby 102–4
Henry, Gregg 116
Henry V 91
Hepburn, Audrey 24–6, 85, 161, 192–3, 215–17, 242

Herrmann, Bernard 3, 24, 89, 108, 149, 169, 284
Hickman, Darryl 232
Hickox, Sidney 62
Higgins, Colin 52
High Noon 46
Highsmith, Patricia 119, 183, 281
Hill, Arthur 242
Hill, Debra 169–71
Hitchcock, Alfred Hitchcock, Alfred ix, 2, 16, 21, 22, 27, 43, 54, 68, 70, 86, 110, 137, 142, 188, 217, 222, 237, 238, 260, 277, 278
Hitchcock, Patricia 188
Hitchcockian, term ix–xii
Hoffenstein, Samuel 229
Hoffman, Dustin 121
Hoffman, Thom 52, 288
Holden, Anne 205
Holden, William 40–41, 134, 260
Holmes, Katie 123–5
Holt, Seth 157–8, 210
Homicidal 146–7
Honeymoon with a Stranger 192–4
Hopkins, Anthony 131–3, 176–7
Household, Geoffrey 32
Houseman, John 3
Howard, Trevor 36
Howe, James Wong 70
How to Steal a Million 267
Hudson, Myra 13
Hudson, Rochelle 156
Hudson, Rock 67, 70–71
Hughes, Dorothy B. 11
Hunt, Martita 191
Hunt, Peter R. 267
Hunter, Ross 20, 194
Huppert, Isabelle 204
Hurt, John 176
Hurt, William 4, 121
Hush ... Hush, Sweet Charlotte 158
Hussain, Nasir 265
Hussein, Waris 174–5
Hussey, Ruth 87–8
Huxley, Aldous 3, 237
Hysteria 210

I Confess 252
In a Lonely Place 11–13
Insomnia 77–8
Intermezzo 4
Invisible Man, The (2020) 207
Irons, Jeremy 176
Irving, Amy 246
Iwao, Junko 93

Jacobi, Derek 90–92, 176
Jane Eyre 2–3
Janney, Allison 129
Jessop, Clytie 213–14
Jewel Thief 264–6
Jezebel 161
Joan of Arc 4
Joanou, Phil 92–3
Jobert, Marlène 72
Johnson, Van 107
Jolie, Angelina 244, 272–3
Jones, Eileen 267
Jones, January 273–4
Jones, Quincy 68
Jones, Shirley 211–12, 242
Joseph, Robert L. 65
Jourdan, Louis 18
Journey into Fear 34–5
Jules and Jim 244, 283
Julie 17–19
Julyan, David 77
Jung Ziso 289

Kael, Pauline 111
Kaleidoscope 146, 278
Kalogridis, Laeta 80
Karas, Anton 36
Karloff, Boris 223–5
Katt, William 246
Keach, Stacy 115–16
Keith, Robert 258
Keller, Marthe 50, 52
Kelly, Grace 16, 19, 85, 99, 206, 215, 242, 268, 270
Kelly, Nancy 31
Kempson, Rachel 237
Kennedy, Arthur 104
Kennedy, George 25, 67

Kerr, Deborah 23
Key Largo 62
Khondji, Darius 122, 178
Kidder, Margot 166–9, 194
Kidman, Nicole 121, 181–2
Kill Bill 284
Kilmer, Val 97
Kim Hye-ja 288
King, Rufus 6
King Kong (1993) 207
Kingsley, Ben 80–81, 126
King, Stephen 120, 246
Kirkbride, Ronald 54
Kiss Before Dying, A 19–20
Kline, Kevin 121
Klugman, Jack 194
Knight, David 213
Knox, Alexander 109
Koepp, David 57, 119, 122
Kohraa (Fog) 109
Kon, Satoshi 93–4
Konstantin, Leopoldine 222
Korda, Alexander 36
Korda, Zoltan 237
Koster, Henry 3
Koteas, Elias 81
Kovács, László 74
Krabbé, Jeroen 288
Kramer, Stanley 278
Krasker, Robert 37, 162, 257, 262
Krasner, Milton R. 108, 234
Krieps, Vicky 99
Kruger, Diane 273–4
Kurnitz, Harry 106

La Chienne 230
Lady from Shanghai, The 258
Lady in the Lake 61
Lady Vanishes, The x, 27–8, 125, 126, 184–6, 189, 197, 200, 209, 221, 273
La Femme Infidèle 285–6
Laforêt, Marie 281
Lambert, Anne-Louise 195
Lancaster, Bruce 9
Lanchester, Elsa 106, 208
Landgut, Inge 136

Landis, Jessie Royce 268
Landon, Christopher 206
Lane, Diane 286
Lang, Charles 15
Lang, Fritz 6–8, 32–3, 129, 135–7, 178, 229
Langan, Glenn 139–41
La Shelle, Joseph 140, 190
Last Embrace 176
Laughton, Charles 106, 141–4
Launder, Frank 28
Laura 97, 227–9
Laurent, Mélanie 275
Laurent, Yves Saint 242
Laurie, Piper 247
L'Avventura 195
Law, Jude 82–3
Lawston, Marlene 199
Lean, David 222
Leave Her to Heaven 231–3
LeBeouf, Shia 205–6
Le Boucher 286–7
le Carré, John 58
Lee, Christopher 211
Lehane, Dennis 79–80
Lehman, Ernest 27, 41–3, 54, 56, 60, 107, 176
Lehman, Gladys 223
Leigh, Janet 146, 174, 192–4, 212
Leighton, Margaret 221
Lenya, Lotte 44
Lenzi, Joseph 192–4
LeRoy, Mervyn 241
Leto, Jared 122
Letter, The 160
Letts, Tracy 129–31
Levine, Ted 81
Levin, Ira 19, 190, 218
Levinson, Richard 194
Lewis, Ronald 211
Lewton, Val 79, 170
Linden, Jennie 213
Lindsay, Joan 195
Lindsay, Margaret 230
Link, William 194
Lithgow, John 115, 176
Little Caesar 230

Little Foxes, The 161
Litvak, Anatole 9
Locked 131–3
Locket, The 235–6
Lockhart, Anne 171
Lockhart, June 171
Lockwood, Margaret 28
Lodger, The: A Story of the London Fog 134, 139–40, 252
Lollobrigida, Gina 240–41
Lom, Herbert 108–10
Lomez, Celine 172
Lonsdale, Michel 284
Loren, Sophia 215, 266, 278
Lorre, Peter 135–7, 254
Lost Weekend, The 86
Love Me or Leave Me 20
Loy, Myrna 242
Lucas, George 45
Lynch, David 94–6
Lynch, John Carroll 81
Lynley, Carol 190–92

M 135–7
MacDonald, Joe 16
MacDonald, John D. 149
MacDonald, Philip 107
MacGuffin, use of x–xii
MacLaine, Shirley 174–5
Magnificent Ambersons, The 7
McGuire, Dorothy 208–9
Mahendru, Anju 265
Mahin, John Lee 242
Mahoney, John 197
Majors, Lee 155
Mallinson, Rory 62
Mallory, Daniel 129
Malone, Dorothy 251
Maltese Falcon, The xi, 227
Mancini, Henry 24, 148, 214–15, 242
Mandell, Daniel 106
Man Hunt 8, 32–3
Mankiewicz, Joseph L. 39
Mann, Edward 253
Mann, Stanley 55, 56
Mannheim, Lucie 192
Manville, Lesley 99

Man Who Knew Too Much, The xi, 1, 20, 27, 50, 52, 107–8, 125, 136, 184, 198, 205, 221, 257, 264, 266
Mara, Kate 125–7
Mara, Rooney 82–3
Marathon Man 50–52
Marlowe, Faye 139–41
Marnie 2, 16, 61, 79, 98, 235, 236, 244, 268, 274
Marquand, Richard 55
Marshal, Alan 138
Marshall, George 212, 260
Marshall, Herbert 22, 239
Marshall, Joan 146
Marsilii, Bill 97
Marta, Jack A. 112
Mason, James 39–40, 43–4, 255–7
Massen, Osa 226
Massey, Anna 144–6, 192
Master and Commander 195
Mastroianni, Marcello 277
Matheson, Richard 112, 113
Matilda Shouted Fire 22
Matsumoto, Rica 93
Matthau, Walter 25, 54, 67
Maugham, Robin 110
Maugham, W. Somerset 27
McAnally, Ray 23
Mcardle, Dorothy 86
McCargo, Marian 263
McCarthy, Kevin 63, 68
McCormick, F. J. 256
McDevitt, Ruth 194
McDowall, Roddy 33
McGovern, Elizabeth 205
McQueen, Steve 134
Mean Streets 81
Medford, Don 188
Meek, Donald 226
Memento 76–7
Men, The 46
Mercer, Johnny 242
Merrick, David 267
Metropolis 32
Meurisse, Paul 279
Midnight Lace 20–22
Midnight Warning, The 185–6

Midsommar 195
Mildred Pierce 155
Miles, Sarah 111, 203
Miles, Vera 16, 99, 146
Milland, Ray 87–8
Miller, David 13
Miller, Robert Ellis 267
Miller, Wentworth 181
Mills, Donna 166
Mills, Hugh 187–8
Mirage 67–9
Misery 120–21
Mission: Impossible 2 56–7
Mississippi Mermaid 4, 243–6, 283
Mitchell, Radha 123
Mitchell, Thomas 234
Mitchum, Robert 141–4, 149–50, 236, 238–9
Mnouchkine, Ariane 45
Mohr, Hal 258
Moll, Giorgia 212
Moment to Moment 241–3
Monroe, Marilyn 15–17
Montand, Yves 278
Montgomery, Elizabeth 210
Montgomery, Robert 137–9
Moore, Dudley 53
Moore, Julianne 129–31
Moore, Roger 46
Moorehead, Agnes 3, 35, 62
Moreau, Jeanne 283
Morgan, Michèle 104, 255
Morricone, Ennio 197
Morris, Mary 223–4
Morse, David 206
Mortimer, Emily 81, 125–7
Mortimer, John 261
Moss, Elisabeth 207
Mother 288–9
Moyzisch, L. C. 39
Mrs. Miniver 161
Mulholland Drive 94–6
Mulkey, Chris 180
Mulroney, Dermot 181–2
Murai, Sadayuki 93
Musuraca, Nicholas 208, 236

Naked Edge, The 22–4
Nanny, The 157–8
Napier, Alan 139–41
Natwick, Mildred 237
Neely, Richard 74
Neeson, Liam 274
Nelligan, Kate 54–6
Nelson, Lori 150
Nesbitt, Cathleen 186, 188
Neville, John Thomas 185
Newman, Alfred 33, 232
Newman, David 249
Newman, Joseph M. 190
Newman, Paul 41, 42
Newton, Robert 256
Newton, Thandiwe 57
Niagara 15–17
Nichols, Dudley 32, 231
Nichols, Richard 226
Nicholson, Jack 46, 176
Nightmare (1956) 62–4
Nightmare (1964) 213–14
Night Must Fall 137–9
Night of the Hunter, The 141–4
Night Train to Munich 28–30, 102
Ninotchka 86
Niven, David 268
No Bail for the Judge 192
Nolan, Christopher 78, 183
Nolan, Jonathan 76
Noriega, Eduardo 125–7
North by Northwest x, 24, 27, 43, 48, 50, 56–7, 79, 116, 176, 184, 249, 252–3, 264, 266, 268, 272–4
Notorious 1, 4, 24, 27, 57, 98
Novak, Kim 222
Number Seventeen 223
Nun's Story, The 46

Oates, Cicely 221
O'Brien, Margaret 3
Obsession 88–90, 247
O'Connor, Una 106
Odd Man Out 102, 255–7
O'Dea, Denis 256
Of Human Bondage 230
O'Keefe, Dennis 34, 258

Oldman, Gary 130
Olivier, Laurence 51–2, 192
O'Neill, Barbara 8, 239
One of My Wives Is Missing 194
Original Sin 244
Osborn, David 109
O'Shea, Oscar 31
Oswald, Gerd 20
Otto, Miranda 220
Our Man in Havana 102
Owen, Reginald 226

Pacino, Al 78, 121, 180
Page, Regé-Jean 58
Paltrow, Gwyneth 177–9
Panic Room 121–3
Pantoliano, Joe 77
Paradine Case, The 222, 238
Paranoiac 153–4, 210
Parasite 111, 289–9
Park Chan-wook 181, 290
Park Hae-il 290–91
Park So-dam 290
Partos, Frank 86
Passage to India, A 195
Patton, Paula 97
Patton, Will 270
Paul, Elliott 225
Pearce, Guy 76–7
Peck, Gregory 1, 60–61, 63, 67–9, 74, 130, 149–50, 214–15
Peeping Tom 144–6, 201
Peoples, David 75
Peoples, Janet 75
Perfect Blue 93–4
Perkins, Anthony 72
Perry, Tyler 183
Petersen, Wolfgang 73–4
Pettet, Joanna 166
Pfeiffer, Michelle 220
Pfister, Wally 77
Phantom Lady 31
Phantom Thread 98–100
Phone Booth 123–5
Piccoli, Michel 72
Picnic at Hanging Rock 194–6
Pidgeon, Walter 32

Piège pour un homme seul (Trap for a Lonely Man) 192–3
Pike, Rosamund 182–3
Pilbeam, Nova 85
Pinter, Harold 110
Piper, Evelyn 158
Pitt, Brad 75, 177–9, 180
Planck, Robert H. 225–6
Play Misty for Me 165–6
Pleasence, Donald 170
Plein Soleil (Purple Noon) 280–82
Plummer, Christopher 171–3
Polanski, Roman 159, 169, 196, 198, 218, 246
Polito, Sol 9
Pollack, Sydney 47–9
Portman, Eric 23
Possessed 155
Postman Always Rings Twice, The 92
Powell, Michael 144–6, 201
Power, Tyrone 106
Powers, Stefanie 148
Preminger, Otto 190, 222, 228, 239, 278
Presle, Micheline 43
Price, Vincent 228
Prize, The 41–3
Promise Her Anything 68
Psycho 21–3, 26, 43, 70, 73, 79, 85, 91, 108, 112, 115–16, 124, 129, 131, 134, 144, 146–9, 151, 154–5, 158–60, 165–6, 169–71, 173–4, 176–7, 183, 188, 191–3, 201, 205, 210–14, 220, 222–3, 245, 247, 254, 279, 281, 285
Pulp Fiction xi

Queen, Ellery 72
Quinn, Aidan 274

Raging Bull 81
Rains, Claude 236
Randall, Bob 175
Randolph, John 70–71
Ransford, Maurice 108
Rappeneau, Jean-Paul 45
Ray, Aldo 264

Ray, Nicholas 11–13
Rayfiel, David 47
Raymond, Gene 235
Readick, Frank 35
Rear Window xi, 11–12, 107–8, 115–16, 130, 145, 167, 201, 205, 220, 244, 249
Rebecca 1, 6, 90, 98, 110, 210, 220–21, 238
Redford, Robert 47–9, 121, 134, 219
Redgrave, Lynn 277
Redgrave, Michael 6, 8, 29
Redgrave, Vanessa 203–4, 277
Redmond, Moira 213
Reed, Carol 28, 36, 255–7, 261
Reed, Oliver 153–4
Reiner, Carl 259
Reiner, Rob 120
Reinhardt, Betty 229
Relph, Michael 240
Remar, James 220
Remick, Lee 148, 216, 261–2
Renard, Gil 180
Rennie, Michael 188–90
Repulsion 159
Requiem for a Dream 93
Resnais, Alain 73
Revere, Anne 7, 224
Reve, Gerard 288
Reynolds, Burt 134, 219, 267–9
Reynolds, Debbie 259
Reynolds, Ryan 127–8
Rhames, Ving 270
Rich, Claude 284
Rich and Strange 1, 125, 257
Richards, Ann 10
Richards, Silvia 6
Richardson, Ralph 104, 240
Richardson, Robert 79
Ripley 282
Ripley, Arthur D. 253
Ritter, Thelma 201
Road Games 115–16
Roberts, Ben 22
Roberts, Eric 92
Robertson, Cliff 89, 90, 247
Robertson, Peggy 99

Robinson, Edward G. 43, 63, 230
Robson, Mark 41–3
Roman Holiday 160
Roman, Lawrence 20
Roman, Ruth 104
Ronet, Maurice 281, 285
Rope 1, 101, 140, 168
Rosemary's Baby 217–19, 246
Ross, Kenneth 46
Ross, Michael Arlen 133
Rossio, Terry 97
Rough Cut 266–9
Ruffalo, Mark 80
Running Man, The 260–62
Russell, Connie 64
Russell, Gail 87, 88
Russell, Kurt 118
Russell, Rosalind 137–9
Russell, Wyatt 130
Rust, Richard 147
Ryan, Kathleen 256
Ryan, Meg 176

Sabotage 27, 205
Saboteur 24, 27, 252
Saint, Eva Marie 67
Salt, Jennifer 166–9
Saltburn 111
Saltzman, Harry 43
Sanders, George 33, 139–41, 212
Sangster, Jimmy 154, 158, 210, 213
Sardou, Victorien 207
Sarelle, Leilani 251
Sargent, Alvin 285
Sarsgaard, Peter 199
Scacchi, Greta 74
Scarlet Street 8, 229–31
Scarwid, Diana 220
Schafer, Natalie 8
Scheider, Roy 52, 248–9
Schlesinger, John 50
Schrader, Paul 89
Schröder, Ernst 40
Schumacher, Joel 124
Schygulla, Hanna 91
Scorsese, Martin 79–81, 87, 150
Scott, Campbell 91

Scott, Dougray 57
Scott, George C. 263
Scott, Janette 153–4
Scott, Tony 96–8, 180
Scream of Fear 210–11
Search, The 46
Seaton, George 41, 67
Seberg, Jean 241–3
Seconds 69–71
Secret Agent 27
Secret Beyond the Door 6–8
Se7en 177–9
Seigner, Emmanuelle 197
Seitz, Hillary 78
Seitz, John 30
Sekka, Johnny 240
Selzer, Milton 194
Selznick, David O. 2, 37, 60, 104, 106, 209–10
Semple, Lorenzo, Jr. 47
Servais, Jean 45
Servant, The 110–11
Sewell, Rufus 273
Seyrig, Delphine 46
Shadow of a Doubt 11, 60
Shane, Maxwell 63
Shattered 73–4
Shearer, Moira 144–6
Shelton, Deborah 116–18
Shenar, Paul 204
Sheridan, Ann 258–9
Sheridan, Nicollette 210
Sherriff, R. C. 257
Sherry, Edna 13
Shoot the Piano Player 244, 283
Shore, Howard 178
Shutter Island 79–81
Side Effects 82–3
Signoret, Simone 279–80
Silence 81
Silence of the Lambs, The 176–7
Silent Partner, The 171–3
Silver, Scott Z. 82
Simmons, Jean 187–88, 238
Sinclair, Charles 109
Siodmak, Robert 30, 31, 139, 170, 208, 234
Sisters 166–9

Skarsgård, Bill 131–3
Skarsgård, Stellan 78
Skinner, Cornelia Otis 87
Slesar, Henry 194
Slezak, Walter 259
Slocombe, Douglas 65, 111, 210
Sluizer, George 198–9
Smith, Dodie 86
Smith, Kent 208
Smith, Robert 13
Smith, Shelley 260
Snipes, Wesley 179–80
Soderbergh, Steven 82
Soeteman, Gerard 288
Soft Skin, The 283
Soldier of Orange 287
Solomon, Bruce 52
So Long at the Fair 185–8
Solt, Andrew 11
Someone Is Killing the Great Chefs of Europe 267
Somerville, Phyllis 182
Sommer, Josef 248
Sorry, Wrong Number 9–10
Sound of Music, The 161
Soutendijk, Renée 288
Spacek, Sissy 246–7
Spacey, Kevin 177–9
Sparv, Camilla 263
Spellbound 1, 6, 23, 24, 91, 233, 249, 274
Spetters 287
Spielberg, Steven 45, 87, 111
Spione 27
Spiral Staircase, The 139, 208–10
Stage Fright 266
Stahl, John 222, 231
Stamp, Terence 134, 160–63, 202
Stanwyck, Barbara 9
Stapleton, Maureen 175
Stars Look Down, The 102
Steege, Johanna ter 198
Steele, Barbara 192–4
Stefano, Joseph 22–4, 60
Sternhagen, Frances 121
Stevenson, Houseley 61
Stevenson, Robert 3, 34–5

Stewart, James 61, 84, 97, 107, 117, 130, 184, 201, 206, 273
Stewart, Kristen 121–3
Stewart, Martha 11
Stewart, Donald Ogden 225
Stewart, Paul 104
Stigwood, Robert 174–5
Still of the Night 248–9
Stoker 181–2
Stone, Andrew L. 18
Stone, Peter 24–5, 67, 194, 214
Stone, Sharon 4, 250, 279
Stowe, Madeleine 75, 176
Stradling, Harry 242
Strait-Jacket 154–6
Strangers on a Train x, 239, 252, 274
Strasberg, Susan 210
Straw Dogs 113
Streep, Meryl 248–9
Strick, Wesley 92
Strong, Michael 264
Substance, The 70
Sudden Fear 13–15
Sullivan, Barry 18
Sunset Boulevard 86, 96, 151
Surtees, Robert 162
Suspicion 18, 24, 98, 210, 244
Sutherland, Donald 55
Sutherland, Kiefer 124
Sutton, John 3
Swank, Hilary 78
Swerling, Jo 232

Takeuchi, Yoshikazu 93
Talented Mr. Ripley, The 282
Tandy, Jessica 237, 249
Tang Wei 290–1
Tapley, Colin 224
Tarantino, Quentin 164, 284
Tatum, Channing 82–3
Tavoularis, Dean 92
Taxi Driver 81
Taylor, Elizabeth 3
Taylor, Kent 223
Taylor, Rod 67
Taylor, Tate 128
Templeton, William 102

Ten Days' Wonder 71–3
Tetzlaff, Ted 104
Tey, Josephine 154
That Man from Rio 44–6
Theroux, Justin 96, 128–9
Third Man, The 28–9, 35–8
Third Secret, The 64–5
39 Steps, The x, 27, 31–3, 48, 50, 55, 57, 59, 197, 252, 264, 266
36 Hours 66–7
Thompson, Emma 91, 176
Thompson, J. Lee 149
Thorne, Anthony 187
Thorpe, Richard 138
Three Days of the Condor 47–9
Thunderball 43
Thurman, Uma 92–3
Tierney, Gene 228, 232–3
To Catch a Thief 25, 252, 266, 268, 269, 272, 277
Todd, Ann 210
Todd, Richard 108–10
To Have and Have Not 62
Tomasini, George 149
Tomlinson, David 187–8
Topaz 27–8, 277
Torn Curtain 27–8, 41, 125, 266
Tourist, The 271–3
Towne, Robert 56, 147
Townsend, Leo 189
Transsiberian 125–7
Travolta, John 113–15, 246
Tripplehorn, Jeanne 251
Truffaut, François 243–4, 283
Turner, Kathleen 4
Turner, Lana 241
12 Monkeys 74–6
23 Paces to Baker Street 107–8
Twisted Nerve 163–5

Ullmann, Liv 54
Under Capricorn 1, 221, 244
Uninvited, The 86–8
Unknown 273–4

Valli, Alida 37
Vanishing, The 198–9

Venable, Evelyn 223
Verhoeven, Paul 222, 250, 287, 288
Vertigo 16, 24, 61, 89, 91, 92, 97, 98, 116, 145, 195, 201, 210, 220, 229, 231, 244, 249, 250, 264, 274
Very Special Favor, A 68
Vidor, Charles 222–3
Villeneuve, Denis 275
Villiers, James 157–8
Viridiana 201
von Donnersmarck, Florian Henckel 272
von Harbou, Thea 135
von Sydow, Max 80–81

Wagner, Robert 19, 219
Wait Until Dark 108, 215–17
Walker, Andrew Kevin 178
Wallace, Irving 41
Walter, Jessica 165–6
Washington, Denzel 96–8
Wasikowska, Mia 181–2
Wasserman, Lew 85
Wasson, Craig 116–18
Watts, Naomi 94–6
Wayne, John 16
Wayne, Nina 263
Weaver, Dennis 111–13
Weaver, Jacki 182
Webb, Clifton 227
Webb, James R. 149–50
Webb, Roy 104, 236
Weir, Peter 194–6
Weld, Tuesday 219
Welles, Orson 3, 16, 34–8, 72–3, 84, 91, 258
Wells, George 260
Westlake, Donald E. 291
Weston, Jack 68
Wexler, Norman 174–5
Whalley-Kilmer, Joanne 74
What Ever Happened to Baby Jane? 151–3, 158
What Lies Beneath 220
Wheeler, Lyle 108

Whitaker, Forest 121–3, 124
White, Ethel Lina
White, Robb 146–7
Whitelaw, Billie 163–5
Whitty, May 137–9
Widmann, Ellen 135–7
Wilcox, John 213
Wilde, Cornel 149, 232–3
Wilder, Billy 86, 151
Wilding, Michael 23
Williams, Billy 172
Williams, Emlyn 137
Williams, John 21, 106, 266, 268
Williams, Michelle 81
Williams, Rhys 208
Williams, Robin 78, 91
Willis, Bruce 47, 75, 251
Wilson, Casey 183
Wilson, Erin Cressida 128
Wilson, Lisle 166–9
Wilson, Michael 39
Window, The 104–5
Winters, Shelley 141–4
Wise, Robert 87
Witness 195
Witness for the Prosecution 105–7
Woman's Face A 225–6
Woman in the Window, The (1944) 8, 229, 230
Woman in the Window, The (2021) 129–31
Woman of Straw 240–41
Woman on the Run 257–9
Woman's Face A 155
Woman's Vengeance A 237–8
Won Bin 288
Woo, John 56
Woodward, Joanne 19
Woolrich, Cornell 244, 253, 283
Worthington, Sam 272
Wrong Man, The 11, 252, 253
Wuthering Heights 160
Wyler, William 160, 278

Yanne, Jean 286–7
Yarovesky, David 133

Yates, Peter 48
Year of Living Dangerously, The 195
Yoakam, Dwight 122
Yoo, Aaron 206
Yordan, Philip 253
Young, Freddie 268
Young, Sean 20
Young, Terence 215
Young and Innocent 252, 266

Zaillian, Steven 282
Zanelli, Geoff 206
Zanuck, Darryl F. 85
Zemeckis, Rebecca 220
Zemeckis, Robert 220
Zeta-Jones, Catherine 82–3, 270–71
Zimbalist, Efrem, Jr. 216
Zinnemann, Fred 46–7
Zsigmond, Vilmos 89